UK TAXATION

A SIMPLIFIED GUIDE FOR STUDENTS

WITHDRAWN

FINANCE ACT 2020 EDITION

COVENTRY UNIVERSITY LONDON
University House
109 - 117 Middlesex Street, London. E1 7JF
Tel: 024 7765 1016
www.coventry.ac.uk/london

Published September 2020 by

Spiramus Press Ltd

102 Blandford Street

London

W1U 8AG

www.spiramus.com

Paperback   ISBN 9781913507053

Digital   ISBN 9781913507060

Printed and bound in Great Britain by Grosvenor Group Ltd, UK

PREFACE TO SIXTH EDITION

As I started to plan this new edition, I anticipated that the delayed Budget announcement following the General Election in 2019 would show the Government taking advantage of its new majority in the House of Commons to change tax laws and prepare for Brexit. At that time few anticipated the arrival of Covid-19. The Budget was dramatically different from expectations and introduced many never before seen emergency measures. As these measures are temporary, I have not amended the main body of the text to include these. However, Chapter 1 now includes a summary of the main legislative changes, in this case also summarising the emergency coronavirus measures.

This text is not intended to be used by tax practitioners or as a tax advice guide but is for students of taxation. It is aimed primarily at undergraduate students but, students on professional courses, AAT, ACCA and perhaps ATT, for example, may also find this useful.

I have tried to use an easy to read style with many worked examples and to keep most chapters short.

The text does not attempt to be a comprehensive guide to the entire UK taxation system but concentrates on the key areas that a student may be required to know.

Finally, I would like to thank Richard Kenyon and Qiang Cai for their helpful comments and suggestions.

Mark Hunt
July 2020

IMPORTANT NOTICE TO STUDENTS
This publication is based on tax law up to and including Finance Act 2020.

CONTENTS

TAX RATES AND ALLOWANCES

Income tax

	Normal rate	Dividend rate	Income bands (£)	
			2020/21	**2019/20**
Basic rate	20%	7.5%	1 – 37,500	1 – 37,500
Higher rate	40%	32.5%	37,501 – 150,000	37,501 – 150,000
Additional rate	45%	38.1%	Over 150,000	Over 150,000

Savings income nil rate band:

	2020/21	2019/20
- Basic rate taxpayers	£1,000	£1,000
- Higher rate taxpayers	£500	£500
Dividend nil rate band:	£2,000	£5,000

A starting rate of 0% applies to savings income where it falls within the first £5,000 of taxable income (2020/21 and 2019/20).

Personal allowances

	2020/21	2019/20
Personal allowance	£12,500	£12,500
Income limit	£100,000	£100,000
Marriage Allowance	£1,250	£1,250

Car benefit

CO_2 Emissions	2020/21 Cars registered from 6 April 2020	2020/21 Older cars
Zero emissions	0%	0%
1g/km to 50g/km:		
Electric range:		
130 miles or more	0%	2%
70 -129 miles	3%	5%
40 -69 miles	6%	8%
30-39 miles	10%	12%
Less than 30 miles	12%	14%
51g/km to 54g/km	13%	15%
55g/km to 59g/km	14%	16%
60g/km to 64 g/km	15%	17%
65g/km to 69 g/km	16%	18%
70g/km to 74 g/km	17%	19%
Each additional 5g/km	+1%	+1%
Diesel supplement (not RDE2)	+4%	+4%
Maximum charge	37%	37%
Car fuel benefit amount	£24,500	£24,500

Authorised mileage rates: cars where employees use their own cars for business purposes (2020/21 (and 2019/20)

	Rate per mile
Annual business mileage up to 10,000 miles	45p
Each additional mile over 10,000 miles	25p

Official rate of interest

2020/21	2.25% (At the time of publication)
2019/20	2.5%

Pension contribution limits

	2020/21	2019/20
Annual allowance	40,000	40,000
Minimum annual allowance	4,000	10,000
Income limit	240,000	150,000

Pensions lifetime allowance

2020/21	1,073,100
2019/20	1,055,000
2018/19	1,030,000
2017/18	1,000,000
2016/17	1,000,000
2015/16	1,250,000
2014/15	1,250,000
2013/14	1,500,000
2012/13	1,500,000
2011/12	1,800,000
2010/11	1,800,000
2009/10	1,750,000
2008/09	1,650,000
2007/08	1,600,000

National insurance contributions 2020/21

Class 1 Employees	£1 to £6,240 per year	-
	£6,240 - £9,500 per year	0%
	£9,500 - £50,000 per year	12%
	Over £50,000 per year	2%
Class 1 Employers	£1 to £8,788 per year	-
	Over £8,788 per year	13.8%
Class 1A	Employers only	13.8%
Class 2	Weekly rate	£3.05
	Small profits threshold	£6,475
Class 4	£1 to £9,500	-
	£9,500 to £50,000	9%
	Over £50,000	2%

Capital gains tax

	2020/21		2019/20	
Annual exemption	£12,300		£12,000	
	Normal rates	Residential property rates	Normal rates	Residential property rates
Standard rate	10%	18%	10%	18%
Higher rate	20%	28%	20%	28%

Business asset
disposal relief
- Lifetime limit   £1,000,000   £10,000,000
                                                         Reduced to £1,000,000 from
                                                              11 March 2020
- Rate   10%   10%

Corporation tax
Corporation tax rates are fixed for financial years:
Financial year 2020   19%
Financial year 2019   19%
Financial year 2018   19%
Profit threshold   £1,500,000

Capital allowances
Plant and machinery
Main pool WDA   18%
Special rate pool WDA   From April 2019   6% (Previously 8%)
Motor Cars
New cars with CO_2 emissions up to 50 grams per km   100%
CO_2 emissions between 51 and 110 grams per km   18%
CO_2 emissions over 110 grams per km   From April 2019   6%
                                            Previously   8%

Annual investment allowance
Rate of allowance   100%
Expenditure limit   From 1 January 2021   £200,000
                       Previously   £1,000,000
Structures and buildings allowance
From April 2020   3%
Previously from 29 October 2018   2%

TAX RATES AND ALLOWANCES

Value added tax

Standard rate   20%

Reduced rate   5%

	2020/21	**2019/20**
Registration limit	£85,000	£85,000
Deregistration limit	£83,000	£83,000

Inheritance tax

	Death rate	Lifetime rate
£0 - £325,000 (Nil rate band)	0%	0%
Over £325,000	40%	20%

In addition, a further nil rate band of up to £175,000 may be available on death in relation to a residence.

CHAPTER 1

Introduction

This textbook can be used either on its own or in conjunction with other texts. It is, however, completely self-contained, including at the front of the book all the various allowances, tax rates etc. that a student may need.

I hope that you find this book to be written in a user-friendly manner. It includes numerous examples throughout the text designed to illustrate particular points and then provides further examples for you to try in Appendix 2. Appendix 3 includes over 100 True or False questions for you to dip into at any time to test your understanding.

I have tried to avoid complex jargon and wherever possible straightforward English is used and I have suggested an approach to studying tax in Appendix 1.

This book also assumes absolutely no prior knowledge about UK taxation whatsoever.

This book covers the five main UK taxes; income tax (paid by individuals), capital gains tax (paid by individuals), corporation tax (paid by companies), value added tax (levied on consumers by businesses) and inheritance tax (normally payable on the death of an individual). National Insurance Contributions are also included.

Although primarily aimed at students studying at undergraduate level, these are the taxes which typically form the core of the syllabus for most of the UK's professional examinations in taxation such as those of the ACCA, AAT and possibly ATT, although no specific professional syllabus has been followed.

In general, each of the chapters should be read through in the order that they are arranged as later chapters often assume knowledge from earlier chapters. Having said this, the Value Added Tax and Inheritance Tax chapters could be studied at any point, as they are both very different from the other taxes studied.

Finally, this book is for students. It is not for tax advisers – this text does not attempt to be a comprehensive tax guide to use for tax planning.

(see also **Appendix 1 – How to study taxation**).

Tax is not a difficult subject to study

Many students believe that tax is difficult. Tax can be a "Marmite" subject for students – some love it, others hate it! I believe that the problem, however, is that many tax textbooks tend to be written in complex language and introduce too many new facts at the same time leaving students confused.

This book tries to avoid this and, as mentioned above, the wording tries to be clear and each new issue is followed by illustrative examples.

Many students believe that learning tax is simply about doing lots and lots of examples. This can be true for some students but to pass any tax examination you need to understand the basic underlying principles. Understanding the basics means that you can cut down the need to simply memorise heaps of facts. This book concentrates on the basics. Understanding the *basic principles* at an earlier stage will pay dividends later.

Tax can be fascinating, enjoyable and can possibly offer the student a rewarding future career.

Tax is dynamic

The UK tax system does not stand still. Each year brings changes introduced by the latest Finance Act and new cases sometimes give surprising outcomes or just seem bizarre (Try an internet search for "Is a Pringle a crisp"!). The question of tax avoidance remains a hot topic in the news.

In studying this text I would suggest that, first, read the brief "Summary" at the end of each chapter; then read the whole of the chapter relatively quickly; then re-read the chapter slowly pausing to try and understand as much as possible, including working through the examples, before moving on to the next part of the chapter.

If understanding any particular part of a chapter proves a little too difficult, move on and come back to it later in your studies. You will be surprised at how often something that you found difficult at one stage of your studies becomes straightforward when you return a bit later.

For ease of understanding, throughout the text, any pence have been dropped from examples. In strictness, most taxes should be calculated to the penny!

So, enjoy the read. Pick up the book when you are in the mood and good luck with your studies! Dip into the true and false questions in Appendix 3 from time to time to check your understanding

One thing is for certain – taxation is not going to disappear!

What's New – Summary of main changes introduced by the Finance Act 2020

Income tax

No changes to the main income tax allowances and rates.

Changes have been introduced to the rates for calculating company car and fuel benefits in kind.

The annual limit for annual investment allowance has decreased to £200,000 from 1 January 2021.

Structures and buildings allowance rate increased to 3%.

The income limits for pensions annual allowance restrictions have increased.

Capital gains tax

Main residence relief is reformed with the deemed final period of ownership reduced from 18 months to nine months.

Lettings relief now only applies to periods where the owner continues to occupy part of the property as their main residence.

The lifetime limit for entrepreneur's relief is reduced to £1million and the relief is renamed Business Asset Disposal relief.

Corporation tax

The proposed reduction in the corporation tax rate has been dropped.

A restriction has been introduced on capital losses brought forward.

National Insurance Contributions

The starting threshold for Class 1 Employees and Class 4 NIC has increased substantially to £9,500.

The employment allowance has increased to £4,000 but now only applies to employers with an annual NIC liability below £100,000.

VAT

No significant changes.

Inheritance tax

The residence nil rate band increases to £175,000.

Emergency Coronavirus Taxation Measures

In response to the coronavirus pandemic, various emergency measures have been introduced by the UK Government to help businesses that have been required to temporally close down. The key taxation measures are detailed below. It is also anticipated that HMRC will take a "reasonable" view to other areas of taxation, such as the tax residence status of an individual that has been required to quarantine in the UK, rather than leave the country as planned.

INTRODUCTION

Job Retention Scheme (JRS)

Most employers with a PAYE scheme can access support under the Job Retention Scheme to continue paying part of their employees' salary instead of laying them off.

The scheme applies where employees have been asked to stop working because of coronavirus, but are kept on the payroll, known as 'furloughed workers'. Under JRS HMRC will pay to employers 80% of each of their employee's wages, up to £2,500 a month, plus the associated Employer National Insurance contributions and pension contributions (up to the level of the minimum automatic enrolment employer pension contribution) on the furlough pay. Employers must claim this and the receipt is taxable on the business, although this will be offset as the payment of the wages will be allowable. The receipt by the employee will continue to be subject to tax and NIC under PAYE as usual. Additional flexibility, allowing employees to partially return to work were introduced from 1 July 2020, with employers only claiming under JRS for the time the individual is not working.

The scheme operates on this basis from 1 March 2020 to 31 July 2020. For August 2020 HMRC will also pay 80% of the wages but employers will pay ER NICs and pension contributions. For September, the scheme will only pay 70% of wages up to a cap of £2,187.50 per employee per month. Employers will pay ER NICs and pension contributions and 10% of wages to make up 80% total up to a cap of £2,500. Finally, for October 2020, the scheme will pay 60% of wages up to a cap of £1,875. Employers will pay ER NICs and pension contributions and 20% of wages to make up 80% total up to a cap of £2,500.

Self-Employment Income Support Scheme (SEISS)

Under SEISS the self-employed (either as an individual or in a partnership), can claim a taxable grant worth 80% of their average trading profits up to a maximum of £2,500 per month, for three months covering the period from April to June 2020.

Individuals are eligible for this scheme if:
- they can confirm that their business has been adversely affected by the coronavirus
- they submitted their Self Assessment tax return for 2018/19 tax year
- traded in 2019/20
- are trading when they apply, or would be except for coronavirus and intend to continue trading in 2020/21 tax year
- their trading profits have been no more than £50,000 for either 2018/19 tax year or as an average of last three financial years
- their trading profits have been more than half of their total income for either 2018/19 tax year or as an average of last three financial years.

The individuals may continue to work and claim under SEISS.

Trading profits do not include dividends paid from a company.

Those eligible under SEISS may claim a second and final grant in August 2020, if they continue to meet the qualifying conditions. However, the grant will only be equal to 70% of their average monthly trading profits, paid out in a single instalment covering three months' worth of profits, and capped at £6,570 in total.

VAT payment deferral

A UK VAT registered business with a VAT payment due between 20 March 2020 and 30 June 2020, has the option to defer payment until 31 March 2021, without incurring interest and surcharge.

Deferral of Self Assessment payments on account

All individuals due to pay a Self Assessment payment on account by 31 July 2020, may defer payment up until January 2021. Again interest or penalties will not be charged during the deferral period.

Further announcements 8 July 2020

Temporary cut to Stamp Duty Land Tax (SDLT)

To help the property market, the Chancellor announced that the nil rate band for SDLT on residential properties in England and Northern Ireland would be extended to £500,000 until 31 March 2021.

Temporary reduction in VAT on certain supplies

The Chancellor also announced that the rate of VAT would be reduced to 5% on certain supplies of food, drink, accommodation and attractions to help to boost the hospitality and tourism sectors from 15 July 2020 to 12 January 2021.

CHAPTER 2

Income Tax: General Principles and Tax Rates

INTRODUCTION

This chapter will introduce various concepts including:

- an introduction to the administration of the UK tax system
- how income is taxed
- the rates of tax which apply
- the categories of income

The following chapters will introduce further aspects of the income tax computation so that by the end of Chapter 4 you should be in a position to calculate an individual's income tax liability. We will then look at the calculation of taxable income and other income tax aspects through to Chapter 12.

HM Revenue and Customs

The UK tax system is managed by HM Revenue and Customs (HMRC). HMRC is responsible for the administration and collection of both direct and indirect taxes in the UK. HMRC has various additional duties including the collection of student loan repayments and enforcement of the National Minimum wage.

HMRC has three strategic objectives:

- to maximise revenues due and bear down on avoidance and evasion;
- to transform tax and payments for their customers; and
- to design and deliver a professional, efficient and engaged organisation.

UK tax law

The UK tax legislation is comprised of several specific taxes acts, for example, the Corporation Tax Act 2010 (referred to as CTA2010), supported by annual Finance Acts. The Finance Acts put into law the announcements made by the Chancellor of the Exchequer in the annual Budget statement to the House of Commons. This text has been updated to include Finance Act 2020 (referred to as FA2020) but older Finance Acts may be referred to in this text where still relevant.

In addition to the statute law, there is a large body of tax case law which can provide binding guidance on the interpretation of tax legislation. All case law originates from a disagreement between HMRC and a taxpayer.

Finally, HMRC provides technical guidance via its website, although it must be considered that this only represents HMRC's view of the law!

Making tax digital

Making Tax Digital is a plan to gradually introduce personalised digital tax accounts for all individuals and businesses and will greatly change the procedures across the UK tax system. The first changes were introduced from April 2019 and will initially only apply to VAT.

Who pays income tax?

Any *individual* who is resident in the UK will pay income tax on their worldwide income (this is explored further in Chapter 11). As we shall see later in the book (Chapter 16) a company does not pay income tax but corporation tax on its profits.

What is income?

Income can include, for example:

- a person's salary/wages;
- a person's trading profits from conducting a business;
- bank interest;
- dividends from companies; and
- rents.

Generally, capital receipts are not subject to income tax.

Exempt income

Some income is specifically exempt from income tax. Common examples of exempt income include:

- Income from an Individual Savings Account (ISA);
- Lottery or gambling winnings;
- Interest on NS&I Savings Certificates; and
- Scholarship awards and educational grants.

What is an income tax liability?

An individual's *income tax liability* is the tax liability on their *taxable income.*

Tax on this taxable income is referred to as *income tax*.

To work out an individual's income tax liability, it is necessary to aggregate all of their income to which they are entitled in a tax year (see below) from all sources (referred to as Total income) and to then make certain deductions from it. Two types of deduction are made:

- a deduction for reliefs; and
- a deduction for a personal allowance

The effect of these calculations is to produce the following definitions:

Net income = total income less reliefs

Taxable income = net income less personal allowance

More will be said about these terms in Chapter 3.

Tax year

An individual's total income for a year is, in fact, the income which arises in the *income tax year*. This is the period 6 April in any year to the following 5 April.

For example, the tax year 2020/21 refers to the period 6 April 2020 to 5 April 2021.

A tax year can also be referred to as a *year of assessment*.

Calculating the income tax liability

Although an individual's income to which they are entitled is aggregated it also needs to be identified as one of three categories:

- Non-savings income
- Savings income
- Dividend income

This categorisation is needed as these different categories are taxed at different rates of income and in a specific order.

Categories of income

Non-Savings income includes:

- rent from letting out a property;
- business profits from the carrying on of a trade;
- income from employment and pensions; and
- any income that does not fall into one of the other categories.

Savings income comprises:

- interest income (e.g. from a bank or building society deposit).

Dividend income comprises:

- dividends from shares.

Order of taxing

- Non-savings income is taxed first
- then Savings income is taxed
- then Dividend income is taxed.

Rates of income tax for the year to 5 April 2021 (2020/21)

		Main rates	*Dividend rates*
Basic rate	£1 – £37,500	20%	7.5%
Higher rate	£37,501 – £150,000	40%	32.5%
Additional rate	£150,000 and over	45%	38.1%

- For *Non-savings income* the first £37,500 of Taxable Income is taxed at the basic rate of 20%; the next £112,500 (i.e. income up to £150,000) is taxed at the higher rate of 40% and everything above £150,000 is taxed at the additional rate of 45%.
- For *Savings income,* which is taxed after Non-savings income (i.e. on top of it), any amount falling in the first £5,000 of Taxable Income is taxed at 0% (referred to as the starting rate for savings). Each £1 of non-savings income reduces the starting rate for savings by £1. Therefore, as is often

the case, if non-savings income exceeds £5,000, this starting rate will not be available.

Then for basic rate taxpayers, the next £1,000 savings income is taxed at 0%, reduced to £500 for higher rate taxpayers (these limits are referred to in the legislation as the savings allowance). Additional rate taxpayers do not receive a savings allowance.

Otherwise, savings income is taxed at the same rates as non-savings income.

- For *Dividend income* which is taxed after both Non-savings and Savings income (i.e. on top of both), the first £2,000 is taxed at 0% (the dividend nil rate). Then any dividend income falling within the basic rate band is taxed at 7.5%, at 32.5% within the higher rate band and 38.1% within the additional rate band.

It should be remembered there is only one set of rate bands. For example, if NSI uses up the full basic rate band, then any SI or DI will be taxed at the higher or additional rates as appropriate.

The 20% rate is referred to as the *basic rate* of income tax.

An individual who is liable to pay income tax at the 40% rate is referred to as a higher rate taxpayer.

An individual who is liable to pay income tax at the 45% rate is referred to as an additional rate taxpayer.

Let us look at how all this works in practice. At this stage reliefs and the personal allowance will be ignored (these items will be looked at in more detail in Chapter 3) and can be assumed to have already been deducted.

First, assume that all of an individual's income is Non-savings income. All calculations in this chapter assume that the figures given are after deducting any available personal allowances and reliefs.

Example 2.1

John has taxable Non-Savings income of £25,000 for 2020/21. He has no other taxable income.

Income tax due:

£25,000 @ 20%		=	£5,000
Therefore total income tax liability		=	£5,000

Example 2.2

Emily has Non-Savings income of £40,000 and no other income for 2020/21.

Income tax due

First	£37,500 @ 20%	=	£7,500
Next	£2,500 @ 40%	=	£1,000
Therefore, total income tax liability		=	£8,500

Example 2.3

Harry has taxable Non-Savings income of £170,000 for 2020/21. He has no other taxable income.

Income tax due

First	£37,500	@ 20%	=	£7,500
Next	£112,500	@ 40%	=	£45,000
Next	£20,000	@ 45%	=	£9,000
Therefore, total income tax liability			=	£61,500

Emily in Example 2.2 is therefore taxed on a part of her income at 20% (i.e. up to £37,500); with only the excess over £37,500 then being taxed at 40%. Harry in Example 2.3 has part of his income taxed in each of the three "tax brackets"

Let us now look at the position if all of the income is Savings income.

Example 2.4

Georgia has taxable Savings income of £25,000 and no other income for 2020/21.

Income tax due

First	Savings starting rate	£5,000	@ 0% =		£0
Next	Savings allowance	£1,000	@ 0% =		£0
Balance		£19,000	@ 20%	=	£3,800
Therefore, total income tax liability				=	£3,800

Example 2.5

Jenny has taxable Savings income of £40,000 for 2020/21 and no other income

Income tax due:

First	Savings starting rate	£5,000	@ 0% =		£0
Next	Savings allowance	£500	@ 0% =		£0
Next	Up to limit of basic rate	£32,000	@ 20%	=	£6,400
Balance		£2,500	@ 40%	=	£1,000
Therefore total income tax liability				=	£7,400

Note that both the savings rate band and savings allowance, although taxed at 0%, use up part of the basic rate band of £37,500. The savings allowance is reduced to £500 as Jenny is a higher rate taxpayer. For an additional rate taxpayer this would be £nil.

Compared to Example 2.2 above Jenny's tax liability is some £1,100 lower (i.e. £8,500 - £7,400). This is explained by the fact that £5,500 of taxable income has been taxed at 0% rather than 20%.

Let us now assume all of the income is dividend income.

Example 2.6

Alfie has taxable Dividend income of £25,000 for 2020/21 and no other income.

First	Dividend allowance	£2,000	@ 0%	=	£0
Balance		£23,000	@ 7.5%	=	£1,725
Therefore, total income tax liability				=	£1,725

Example 2.7

Helen has taxable Dividend income of £40,000 for 2020/21 and no other income.

Income tax due:

First	Dividend allowance	£2,000	@ 0%	=	£0
Next	Balance of basic rate	£35,500	@ 7.5%	=	£2,662
Balance		£2,500	@ 32.5%	=	£812
Therefore, total income tax liability				=	£3,474

In this case, Helen is taxed on a part of her income at 0% up to £2,000 then 7.5% (up to £37,500); the balance is taxed at 32.5%.

Note that the dividend allowance, although taxed at 0%, uses up part of the basic rate band of £37,500.

Finally, we can look at a case where there is a mixture of Non-savings, Savings and Dividend income.

Example 2.8

Alex has the following taxable income for 2020/21:

Non-savings income of	£20,000
Savings income of	£2,500
Dividend income of	£17,500

(Taxable income totals £40,000. Alex is, therefore, a higher rate taxpayer)

Non- savings income:

	£20,000	@ 20%	=	£4,000

Savings income:

Savings starting rate	£500	@ 0%	=	£0
Balance of savings income	£2,000	@ 20%	–	£400

Dividend income:

Dividend allowance	£2,000	@ 0%	=	£0
Balance of basic rate band	£13,000	@ 7.5%	=	£975
Balance of dividend income	£2,500	@ 32.5%	=	£812
Income tax liability				£6,187

This example illustrates that although each category of income is taxed at different rates of income tax and in a specific order, in working out the total income tax liability each category is stacked on top of the other to ascertain what rate of income tax should apply and to how much of that category of income.

Thus, the non-savings income of £20,000 is taxed at 20%. This is so because the amount of non-savings income is not more than £37,500 and therefore the 40% rate does not apply.

With taxable income totalling £40,000, Alex is a higher rate taxpayer. Therefore, the first £500 of savings will be taxed at 0%. However, this amount utilises part of the available basic rate band. None of the savings income falls into the first £5,000 taxable income, so the starting rate for savings is not available. The balance of the savings income, £2,000 falls within the basic rate band.

Therefore, of the £37,500 basic rate band, £22,500 has been used, leaving a balance of £15,000.

INCOME TAX

The first £2,000 of dividend income is taxed at 0%. However, this reduces the available basic rate band, to £13,000. After this has been used, the remaining £2,500 of dividend income falls into the higher rate band and is taxed at 32.5%

SUMMARY

- Non-savings income is taxed at 20%, 40% and 45%
- Savings income is taxed at 0%, 20%, 40% and 45%
- The starting rate for savings will only be available where non-savings income is less than £5,000
- Dividend income is taxed at 0%, 7.5%, 32.5% and 38.1%
- Non-savings income is taxed first; then Savings income; then Dividend income
- There is only one set of rate bands. For example, if NSI uses up the full basic rate band, then any SI or DI will be taxed at the higher or additional rates.
- Each category of income is added to the earlier category of income to ascertain the rates to apply.

APPENDIX

Since 6 April 2019, the Scottish Parliament has used its powers to set income tax rates for individuals resident in Scotland. For 2020/21, for non-savings income, these are as follows:

Starter rate	£1 - 2,085	19%
Basic rate	£2,086 - £12,658	20%
Intermediate rate	£12,659 - £30,930	21%
Higher rate	£30,931 - £150,000	41%
Additional rate	£150,000 and over	46%

However, throughout this text, the tax rates applicable to the remainder of the United Kingdom have been applied.

Although Wales has similar powers, for 2020/21 the tax rates for Welsh taxpayers are the same as applying to England and Northern Ireland residents.

CHAPTER 3

Income Tax Computations

INTRODUCTION

This chapter explains how an individual's income tax liability is calculated for a tax year and introduces tax reliefs and the personal allowance.

TAXABLE INCOME

Chapter 2 identified that:

Net income   **= Total income less reliefs**

Taxable income   **= Net income less personal allowance**

Each of these terms will now be looked at in turn.

Total income

Chapter 2 referred to three different categories of income:

- Non-savings
- Savings
- Dividends

An individual's total income is simply the aggregate of these three categories of income for a particular tax year.

Non-Savings income ("NSI") includes income from the carrying on of a trade (i.e. trading profit), employment income and income received from a property business (e.g. rent).

Savings income comprises interest income typically earned on cash deposits with banks and building societies.

Dividends simply refer to dividend income received from shares (excluding Real Estate Investment Trust (REIT) dividends – these are treated as non-savings income).

Each type of income has its own set of rules which determines both how it is to be taxed (e.g. accruals or receipts basis) and how the appropriate amount to be taxed is to be determined. The rules for each type of income may vary. For example, any profit from a property business is usually determined by offsetting certain expenses paid (e.g. repairs to the property) from the rental income received. On the other hand, dividend income from companies is taxed when paid by the company, without any deductions.

In summary:

Type of income	Basis of assessment
Property income	Normally receipts basis (see Chapter 5)
Trading income	Accruals basis (see Chapter 6)
Interest income	Receipts basis (i.e. when received or credited)

Employment income   Receipts basis

Dividend income   Receipts basis

More will be said later in this book about each of these income categories. It is sufficient, at this stage, to note their existence and the above points.

Reliefs

Having ascertained an individual's total income for a tax year, any available reliefs are then deducted to arrive at net income. By deducting the reliefs from total income in this manner an individual will obtain a reduction in their tax liability.

Reliefs mainly comprise:

- interest payments on qualifying loans; and
- trading losses (see Chapter 8).

Interest on qualifying loan

Not all interest payments qualify for income tax relief and therefore not all interest payments can be deducted in computing net income.

Only interest paid on qualifying loans may be deducted. The following can be qualifying loans:

- loan to purchase shares in an employee-controlled company or invest in a co-operative;
- loan to purchase ordinary shares in a close company. The taxpayer must own at least 5% of the company's ordinary shares or spend the majority of their time working in the company's management;
- loan to purchase an interest in a partnership;
- loan to buy equipment for employment or partnership use; or
- loan to pay inheritance tax.

There is a cap on the maximum income tax reliefs that may be deducted as detailed in Chapter 8.

Example 3.1

Sally has Total Income of £39,000 (assume this income is all non-savings income) for tax year 2020/21.

She pays interest on a qualifying loan (i.e. a relief) of £3,000.

Her net income = total income – reliefs

Net income = £39,000 - £3,000 = £36,000

Personal allowance

Having subtracted any reliefs from total income to obtain net income, it is then necessary to deduct any available personal allowance to find the taxable income.

The personal allowance for an individual is fixed for a tax year and for the 2020/21 tax year it is £12,500. Every individual is entitled to this personal allowance regardless of age, including in the year of birth and death.

If an individual has adjusted net income ("ANI") above £100,000, the personal allowance is reduced by £1 for every £2 ANI above this limit. ANI is calculated as net income less the gross amount of any allowable personal pension contributions and gift aid donations (see Chapter 4).

Example 3.2

For 2020/21, Noah has net income of £105,000 and paid £800 to charity under gift aid. The gift aid must be grossed up to £1,000 (£800 x 100/80). Noah, therefore, has ANI of £104,000.

As this is greater than £100,000, Noah's personal allowance will be reduced by £1 for every £2 ANI above £100,000. The personal allowance of £12,500 will be reduced by £2,000 (1/2 x (ANI less £100,000)) to £10,500. Noah's taxable income will, therefore, be £94,500 (Net income less personal allowance − the gift aid donation does not reduce taxable income).

In addition, the gross personal pension contributions and gift aid donations will extend the rate bands − see Chapter 4.

The personal allowance represents the amount of income to which an individual may be entitled "tax-free" i.e. without being liable to income tax thereon.

It should now be possible to calculate an individual's overall income tax liability for a tax year.

Marriage allowance or transferable personal allowance

An individual can, by election, transfer 10% (rounded up to the nearest £10) of their personal allowance to their spouse or civil partner but only if neither are a higher or additional rate taxpayer.

This relief is given as a 20% "tax reducer" by reducing the individual's tax liability and the transferred personal allowance is not deducted from their income. This election must be made within four years of the end of the tax year of claim.

This claim is useful where one spouse or civil partner is not fully utilising their personal allowances, which, therefore, would otherwise be wasted.

Example 3.3

Peter, has net income of £6,000 for 2020/21. Part of his personal allowance is not being utilised. Peter is married to Pat. Pat has net income for 2020/21 of £27,500 (all non-savings income). Peter can transfer 10% of his personal allowance to Pat. This will reduce Peter's personal allowance to £11,250 and therefore Peter will still be a non-taxpayer.

Pat's income tax liability will be:

```
INCOME TAX
Non-savings income                              £27,500
Less: personal allowance                       (£12,500)
Taxable income                                  £15,000
Income tax
NSI £15,000 @ 20%                                £3,000
Less: marriage allowance £1,250 @ 20%           (£250)
Income tax liability                            £2,750
```

Note

10% of Peter's personal allowance is 1,250 (12,500 x 10%). If Pat was a higher or additional rate taxpayer, Peter would not be able to transfer the marriage allowance.

INCOME TAX COMPUTATION

It should now be possible to calculate an individual's income tax liability for a tax year.

However, before doing so a set of steps is set out below which should be followed whenever working out an individual's income tax liability.

Step 1

Calculate the various amounts of income which are taxable and categorise the individual incomes into one of three categories:

- Non-savings income (i.e. property business income, trading income and employment income)
- Savings income (i.e. interest received)
- Dividend income (i.e. dividends)

Step 2

Add up the amounts under each of these three categories to give three separate sub-totals. The total of the three categories will comprise total income.

Step 3

Deduct from the total for non-savings income under Step 2 the amount of any reliefs.

If total reliefs exceed the total for non-savings income then deduct the surplus from savings income and then any remaining balance from dividend income.

The total of the three categories will comprise net income.

Step 4

Deduct from non-savings income (arrived at under Step 4) the personal allowance to give non-savings taxable income. If net income is less than £100,000, the full personal allowance is available. Otherwise a separate calculation of ANI and available personal allowance will be necessary.

If the personal allowance exceeds the total for non-savings income deduct the surplus from savings income and then any remaining balance from dividend income.

The total of the three categories gives total taxable income.

Step 5

Compute tax liability by applying rates of income tax to each of the three taxable income figures obtained under Step 4. The tax rate bands may be extended by gift aid and personal pension payments (see Chapter 4).

Step 6

Deduct the marriage allowance tax reducer, if applicable, and any other tax reducers to calculate the *income tax liability*.

Step 7

Deduct from the total in Step 6 any income tax which may have been deducted at source from income *received* (e.g. PAYE on salary) to get the *income tax payable*.

In strictness, the deductions under Steps 3 and 4 can be applied to income in any order to give the lowest tax liability, rather than the strict order of NSI, then SI then DI. However, this can require a number of "what if" type calculations. The ACCA Tax-UK examination assumes the set off as per steps 3 and 4 and this text has adopted this convention for simplicity.

Example 3.4

Jas has the following income for tax 2020/21:

Property business profit	£4,000
Trading profit	£15,000
Interest income	£12,000
Employment income (salary as an employee before PAYE)	£25,000
Dividends	£1,000
Interest paid on qualifying loan	£3,500

PAYE of £2,000 has been deducted from Jas' salary.

Calculated Jas' tax liability and tax payable for 2020/21.

Answer

	Non-Savings	Savings	Dividends	Total
	£	£	£	£
Steps 1 and 2				
Property business profit	4,000			4,000
Trading profit	15,000			15,000
Employment income	25,000			25,000
Interest income		12,000		12,000
Dividends			1,000	1,000
Total income	44,000	12,000	1,000	57,000
Step 3				
Less reliefs	(3,500)			(3,500)
Net income	40,500	12,000	1,000	53,500

Step 4

	Non-savings	Savings	Dividend	Total
Less personal allowance	(12,500)	___	___	(12,500)
Taxable income	28,000	12,000	1,000	41,000

Step 5

Tax liability:

Non-Savings income

28,000	@ 20%	5,600

Savings income

500	@ 0%	0
9,000 (37,500-28,000-500)	@ 20%	1,800
37,500		
2,500 (12,000-500-9,000)	@ 40%	1,000
40,000		

Dividend income

1,000	@ 0%	0
41,000		
Income tax liability		8,400

Step 6 – Not applicable

Step 7

Less:	
PAYE deducted	(2,000)
Income tax payable	**£ 6,400**

Notes - *Important*

The above proforma should be applied for all income tax computations.

The total column is very useful. Firstly, it allows for a cross-check to avoid simple addition errors. The Net income total gives you an indicator as to whether the full personal allowance is available or not. Finally, total Taxable income gives an indicator of the highest rate of income tax and can be used to establish the savings income tax rates.

When working out an income tax liability the above layout should be used but do not include the references to the various "Steps" as they have been included for illustration purposes only.

Some important points to note:
- all figures included in a tax computation are *gross;*
- it is necessary to keep three separate columns, one for each category of income;
- deduct the reliefs from the non-savings income column first;
- deduct the personal allowance against the non-savings income column first;
- the personal allowance may be reduced if adjusted net income exceeds £100,000;

- the personal allowance is deducted from net income to give taxable income;
- non-savings income, then savings income and then dividends are taxed in that order; and
- income tax *liability* is different from income tax *payable.*

High income child benefit tax charge

- Although universal child benefit is income tax free, as part of the austerity measures, this stand-alone charge was introduced to claw back up to 100% of the benefit received by a high earner or their partner.
- Introduced by Finance Act 2012, the charge applies where the taxpayer is entitled to child benefit and they or their partner have adjusted net income above £50,000 (the individual must be living with their partner which includes a spouse, civil partner or unmarried partner.
- The charge is calculated as a percentage of the child benefit calculated as (Adjusted net income − 50,000)/100. The resulting percentage is rounded down to the nearest whole number. If ANI is greater than £60,000 the child benefit will be clawed back in full.

Example 3.5

Kate has ANI of £56,520 and received child benefit of £1,820 for 2020/21. What is her High income child benefit tax charge?

Answer

(56,520-50,000)/100 = 65.2 rounded down to 65%

The charge is therefore £1,820 x 65% = £1,183

Notes

The High income child benefit tax charge is added to the income tax liability (at Step 6 of the tax computation as shown above) for the year and collected under self assessment.

High income individuals, with ANI greater than £50,000, may elect not to receive the benefit in which case the charge would not apply.

Income tax liability versus income tax payable

An individual's income tax *liability* is the liability based on aggregate income less certain deductions.

However, where some income has been received after tax at source has been deducted (e.g. PAYE from a salary) in effect this tax deducted represents a partial settlement of the individual's ultimate income tax liability on this income.

This is why any tax deducted from income received must be deducted from the income tax liability calculated (see Step 7), as only the balance is *payable.* It must be remembered that the income tax liability is always calculated on the gross income (i.e. the amount before deduction of tax).

SUMMARY

Reliefs and allowances reduce the income that is taxed for an individual.

The basis of assessment for each category of income is very important (as will be seen later in the book) as is the order that categories of income are taxed.

Each step of the tax computation should be worked through in order.

The proforma layout used to calculate an individual's income tax liability is very important and must be used for all income tax computations.

The income tax liability is before the deduction of any tax deducted at source.

The income tax payable is the income tax liability less any tax deducted at source.

APPENDIX

Blind persons allowance

An individual that is registered blind or severally sight impaired is eligible to claim this additional allowance of £2,500 for 2020/21. Effectively this increases the individual's personal allowance. If the claimant cannot fully utilise the allowance it may be transferred to their spouse or civil partner.

Married couple's allowance

Note that this is not the same as the marriage allowance detailed above.

This is now of limited application and applies to married couples or civil partners where at least one spouse was born before 6 April 1935. The maximum married couple's allowance is £9,075 for 2020/21. This is reduced by £1 for every £2 of adjusted net income above £30,200. A minimum allowance of £3,510 is given. Relief is given at 10% of the allowance as a "tax reducer".

Any unused element of the married couple's allowance on the part of the claimant can be transferred to the spouse or civil partner.

The claim is made by the husband for marriages before 6 December 2017 and the spouse or civil partner with the higher taxable income for marriages or civil partnerships after that date.

CHAPTER 4

Extending the Rate Bands

INTRODUCTION

This chapter will look at the concept of the extended basic and higher rate bands which will apply when an individual makes either charitable donations under gift aid and/or personal pension payments.

What is the extended rate band?

The concept of the extended rate bands refers to how income tax relief is obtained on certain payments made by an individual taxpayer.

Normally, income tax relief for an allowable relief is obtained by deducting the gross payment when working out an individual's Taxable income (remember in Chapter 3 where payments of qualifying interest payments were deducted as reliefs).

The payments to which the extended rate band concept applies are:
- gift aid payments; and
- personal pension contributions.

Gift aid payments are donations to charities where a gift aid declaration has been made.

Personal pension contributions are payments made to provide for a pension; certain employees may make payments under an occupational pension scheme rather than as personal pension payments (see Chapter 12).

Payments made net of basic rate tax

Payments to charity under gift aid or into a personal pension are made net of basic rate income tax (20% for 2020/21).

For example, if a payment of £400 is made under gift aid to a charity, a gross payment of £500 has actually been made as income tax at 20% (i.e. £100) is deducted. The person making the payment only pays £400 and has, therefore, received basic tax relief at source (£500 @ 20% = £100). The charity receiving the payment only receives £400 (i.e. £500 less £100) from the payer and will receive a refund of the £100 tax deducted from HMRC.

To calculate the gross payment from the net, the net amount is multiplied by the fraction 100/80.

Example 4.1

Chloe makes a personal pension contribution of £1,200 and a gift to charity under gift aid of £20. Calculate the gross payments made.

Answer

Personal pension contribution	1,200 x 100/80	= 1,500
Gift aid payment	20 x 100/80	= 25

As a consequence of the tax deducted at source immediate basic rate tax relief has been obtained for the payment.

However, in working out an individual's Net income *no* deduction is made in the actual computation for either the gift aid or Personal Pension payment.

As a consequence, if the taxpayer is a higher rate taxpayer or additional rate taxpayer, additional income tax relief is due.

Extended rate bands

Higher and additional rate tax relief is obtained by extending the basic rate and higher rate bands.

As a result, the level of taxable income at which income tax at the higher rate of tax (i.e. 40%) applies (currently £37,500 for 2020/21) is increased. The increase is equal to the "gross" amount of the Gift aid *or* Personal Pension payments (or the aggregate of both if both payments are made).

The effect of extending the basic rate band is that the 20% rate applies to this extension rather than the 40% rate which would normally apply. The impact is to produce a tax saving of 20% (i.e. 40% minus 20%) on this extra amount or extension.

Example 4.2

During 2020/21 John has taxable non-savings income of £40,000 and makes a payment to charity under gift aid of £1,600 (net). Calculate John's income tax liability.

Answer

The net gift aid payment must be "grossed up". The gross amount is equal to 1,600 x 100/80 =2,000.

The basic rate band is thus extended by £2,000 from £37,500 to £39,500. The 40% rate will now only apply to taxable income above this figure.

	Taxable income £	Tax rate %	Income tax £
First	39,500	20	7,900
(representing the basic rate band plus extension for gross gift aid)			
Next	500	40	200
Total	40,000		8,100

John's tax relief is therefore obtained by deducting income tax at the basic rate (20%) when actually making the payment, amounting to 20% of £2,000 (i.e. £400), and an extra 20% of tax relief is obtained by the saving of 40% minus 20% on the gross payment of £2,000 (i.e. £400) producing total tax relief of £400 + £400 i.e. £800 (£2,000 x 40%).

Example 4.3

Sarah has taxable non-savings income of £33,000, savings income of £5,000 and pays £1,200 to charity under gift aid. Calculate Sarah's tax liability.

Answer

The gross gift aid payment is equal to 1,200 x 100/80 =1,500 (gross)

The basic rate band is thus extended by 1,500 from 37,500 to 39,000. The 40% rate will now only apply to taxable income above this figure.

	Taxable income £	Tax rate %	Income tax £
Non-savings income			
First	33,000	20	6,600
Savings income			
First	1,000	0	0
Next	4,000	20	800
Total	38,000		7,400

Note that by extending the basic rate band Sarah is no longer a higher rate taxpayer and receives the £1,000 savings allowance. Without the basic rate band extension, Sarah would have been a higher rate taxpayer and therefore only £500 savings income would be taxed at 0%.

Both the basic rate and higher rate bands are extended.

Example 4.4

For 2020/21, Sam has taxable non-savings income of £200,000 and pays £2,400 to charity under gift aid. Sam has no other income.

Answer

The gross gift aid payment is equal to 2,400 x 100/80 –3,000 (gross)

The basic rate band is thus extended by 3,000 from 37,500 to 40,500. The 40% rate will also be extended by 3,000 from 150,000 to 153,000.

	Taxable income £	Tax rate %	Income tax £
First	40,500	20	8,100
Next	112,500	40	45,000
	153,000		
Next	47,000	45	21,150
Total	200,000		74,250

Clawback of tax deducted at source

It should be noted that where an individual's total income tax liability is less than the amount which has been deducted from a gift aid payment when it is made, a partial or total clawback of any tax relief given may occur i.e. some or all of the tax deducted when the payment was made may need to be paid to HMRC.

On the other hand, for personal pension payments, no such clawback occurs in such circumstances.

Example 4.5

Trevor's income tax liability for 2020/21 is £500. Trevor made a gift aid payment during the tax year of £2,400 (net).

On making the payment Trevor will have deducted tax at source of 20% x £3,000 = £600 and thus will have received tax relief of £600.

In this case, Trevor's additional income tax liability will be £100 (i.e. £600 - £500).

The gift aid scheme can apply to any charitable donation whether one-off or regular payments (unless covered by the payroll giving scheme).

As already stated, relief at the taxpayer's highest rate of income tax is available by extending the rate bands.

For the charity to be able to recover, from HMRC, the income tax which has been deducted by the donor at source, the donor must be UK resident and must give an appropriate declaration to the charity concerned that the gift is made under the gift aid scheme.

Comprehensive example

The following example brings together all of the elements of an income tax computation explained in Chapter 2 to 4.

Example 4.6

Kim has the following income for 2020/21:
- Business profits £33,000
- Property business profits £20,000
- Dividends £7,500
- Building Society interest £3,750

Kim makes the following payments:
- Interest on qualifying loan of £2,000
- Gift aid payment of £780 (net)

Calculate Kim's income tax liability and his income tax payable for 2020/21.

Answer

	Non Savings	Savings	Dividends	Total
Trading profit	33,000			
Property business profits	20,000			
Building Society interest		3,750		
Dividends			7,500	
Totals	53,000	3,750	7,500	
Less: Interest paid	(2,000)			
Net income	51,000	3,750	7,500	62,250
Less: PA	(12,500)	-	-	(12,500)
Taxable income	38,500	3,750	7,500	49,750

Income tax calculation

The basic and higher rate bands are both extended by £975 (£780 x 100/80)

The basic rate band is therefore increased from £37,500 to £38,475.

The higher rate band limit will be extended to £150,975.

Non savings

£38,475 @ 20%	7,695
£25 @ 40%	10
£38,500	

Savings

£500 @ 0%	0
£3,250 @ 40%	1,300
£3,750	

Dividends

£2,000 @ 0%	0
£5,500 @ 32.5%	1,787
£7,500	
Tax liability	£10,792

SUMMARY

Where an individual makes gift aid donations or personal pension payments neither payment is deducted in working out an individual's taxable income.

Tax relief at the higher and additional rates of tax is obtained by extending the basic and higher rate bands by the gross amount of the gift aid and/or personal pension payment, basic rate income tax relief having been obtained by deducting basic rate income tax at source.

The gross amount is calculated by grossing up the net payment (net x 100/80).

If an individual makes both types of payment then the basic rate band is extended by the aggregate amount of both payments.

Basic rate tax deducted at source when making a gift aid payment may be clawed back if the individual has not suffered sufficient income tax; this is not the case for personal pension payments where any tax relief is retained by the individual.

The comprehensive example above provides a good indication of the various computational elements that make up the calculation of the income tax liability for 2020/21.

Questions for students

See Appendix 2 for practice questions relating to Chapters 1 to 4. Answers are available online.

CHAPTER 5

Income from a property business

INTRODUCTION

This chapter identifies the key issues associated with the taxation of income generated from land and buildings situated in the UK, more correctly referred to as property business profits.

Description

Profits from UK land or property are treated, for tax purposes, as arising from a property business. For each individual, the income and expenses from all properties are combined as one property business. In addition, an individual may have an interest in one or more property business partnerships. For individuals, property business profits are treated as non-savings income.

Whilst property business income primarily consists of rental income it may also consist of the receipt of lease premiums.

A lease premium is a "one-off" lump sum payment which the person renting the property (i.e. the tenant) pays to the person from whom the property is being rented (i.e. the landlord) and may be payable in addition to any rent. It is normally only payable in respect of commercial (offices, warehouses etc.) rather than residential properties.

Other receipts from the use of land, for example, fishing or sporting rights, are assessed as property income. However, commercial farming or running a hotel would be considered as trading.

Basis of assessment and expenses

The profits of a property business are calculated in a similar way as the profits of a trade (see Chapter 6).

The amount assessable is, therefore, the aggregate property income less allowable expenses for the tax year under consideration.

For most individuals, cash basis is now the normal basis of assessment for property business profits.

Cash basis

The cash basis will apply to individuals unless: the cash receipts exceed £150,000 during the year; the property business is carried out by or jointly with a company, LLP or trust; or the individual elects for accruals basis to apply. Under the cash basis rent is taxable when received and allowable expenses allowed when paid.

Accruals or GAAP basis

Where the cash basis does not apply, the accruals basis is used in ascertaining the amount of rental income to be assessed or expenses allowed, for a tax year. Therefore, the actual date of payment or receipt of rent is irrelevant.

Example 5.1

Kulvinder owns a furnished flat which he lets to a tenant for an annual rent of £700 per month payable in advance from 6 April 2020. However, the rent due for January, February and March 2021 was not paid until after 5 April 2021.

Calculate Kulvinder's property business income for 2020/21.

Answer

Kulvinder is assessed on his property business profits on the cash basis.

For tax year 2020/21 he is assessed on 9 months x £700 = £6,300

The three months rent received later in 2021 i.e. in the next tax year (i.e. 2021/22) will be taxed in that year.

If Kulvinder was required to use the accruals basis or had elected to do so, then all of the 12 months rent due during 2020/21 would be assessed for that year.

Real Estate Investment Trusts (REITs)

Dividends received on an investment in a REIT are assessed as property business income on the date of payment.

Expenses

Expenses are also deductible on a cash or accruals basis as appropriate.

Deductible expenses are those allowable under the normal rules for trades/businesses (see Chapter 6) e.g. the expenses are of a revenue nature and must have been wholly and exclusively incurred for the purpose of the property business (and not for private purposes). Typical items include:

- insurance of the property;
- estate agents fees (e.g. for finding tenants and rent collection);
- property maintenance (e.g. redecorating; repairing the roof, broken windows, gardening etc.); and
- bad debts written off (but this could only apply when using accruals basis).

Examples of expenditure which is *not* deductible would include:

- capital expenditure on the property e.g. the initial cost of the property, a kitchen extension, or expenditure on fitting a new and improved roof rather than simply repairing it;
- expenditure incurred repairing a newly acquired property *before* it could be let out e.g. having to solve a major problem of rising damp (in this case the expense is treated as capital expenditure, not revenue expenditure and thus not deductible against rental income);

- general provisions (rather than specific provisions which would be allowable) for bad debts;
- expenditure incurred for private purposes (e.g. landlord lives in a flat above a shop which he rents out. If the whole of a building was redecorated some part of this cost would be disallowed as relating to the landlord's private flat. The percentage of cost allowed would need to be agreed with the tax authorities); and
- depreciation of assets (e.g. furniture in furnished letting).

Example 5.2

Shaista owns an unfurnished house which she lets out regularly. The flat was let out for the whole of the tax year 2020/21. Shaista has no other rental income and therefore the cash basis applies.

Rent of £6,750 was received during the year.

Expenses paid by Shaista during the tax year are as follows:

	£
Buildings insurance	375
Repairs (i.e. painting/decorating and roof repair)	500
Estate agent commissions	1,000
Water rates	250
Council tax	775
Loft conversion	4,250

Calculate Shaista's property business profit assessment for 2020/21.

Answer	£	£
Gross rents		6,750
Less: Expenses:		
Insurance	375	
Repairs	500	
Commissions	1,000	
Water rates	250	
Council tax	775	
		(2,900)
Property business profit		3,850

Notes

1. The loft conversion is capital and therefore not deductible (only revenue expenses are deductible).
2. If the accruals basis applies, any items such as the insurance paid may be required to be spread over the period of the cover.

Other capital expenditure

Under the cash basis, deductions are allowed for certain capital expenditure. Broadly, deductions for expenditure of a capital nature are allowed for some depreciating assets used in the property business except for cars. Depreciating assets are those with an expected useful life of 20 years or less.

No deductions are allowed for capital expenditure on, or assets used in, residential properties – instead, replacement domestic items relief is available (see below).

Under the accruals basis, capital expenditure is not a deductible expense in computing the profits of a property business.

Capital allowances (a form of tax allowed depreciation on capital assets purchased; see Chapter 7) are sometimes available for assets connected with commercial properties and furnished holiday lettings but not residential lettings.

Replacement of domestic items relief

However, in the case of a *residential* property letting capital allowances are not available but a deduction is permitted for the cost of replacing domestic items used in the property. This includes items such as moveable furniture, curtains, carpets, moveable household appliances and kitchenware. Fixtures, for example, baths or fitted wardrobes, do not qualify.

There is no deduction for the original cost of the item but the cost of replacing an item is allowed. The deduction is limited to the cost of replacement with an asset of a similar type and standard. Also, the sale proceeds for the original item reduces the claim.

Example 5.3

Stuart buys a new refrigerator costing £800 for his let furnished property. He trades in the old refrigerator which is given a value of £300 and meets the rest of the cost with £500 of cash. The amount of the deduction for replacement domestic items would be £500 (£800 less £300).

He also buys a new television for £600 to replace an existing one. The new television is much larger and has many more features than the original one. It would have cost £350 to have bought a television of similar quality and standard, therefore his claim is limited to £350.

Finally, Stuart buys a Blu-ray player for the property for £200. There was not previously one of these in the property. Therefore, it is not a replacement and a deduction is not allowed.

Finance costs for residential property (income tax only)

From 6 April 2017, there is a gradually increasing restriction on the amount of income tax relief allowed for interest on loans to buy or improve let residential property. Loans to buy let commercial properties or land are not affected by this.

From 2020/21 onwards, there is no deduction from property business profits for interest paid on loans in connection with let residential property. (For 2019/20, only 25% of the finance costs were allowed as a deduction). The finance costs can be allowed as a tax reducer at the basic rate of tax, 20% (or disallowed proportion of interest for earlier years). The tax reducer is limited to 20% of the lower of the finance costs, the net property business profit (after deducting any losses brought forward) and the non-savings income. Any unrelieved disallowed interest cost can be carried forward to the following year.

Example 5.4

Paula's only income is from her property letting business. Her results for 2020/21 are as follows:

Rents received	£64,400
Allowable expenses	£9,500
Finance costs	£8,800

Her assessable property business profits are therefore

Rental income		64,400
Allowable expenses		(9,500)
Property business profits		54,900

Paula's income tax liability will be

Property business profits		54,900	
Less: Personal allowance		(12,500)	
Taxable income		42,400	
Income tax	37,500	@ 20%	7,500
	4,900	@ 40%	1,960
Less: Tax reducer	£8,800	@ 20%	(1,760) (Finance costs reducer)
Income tax liability			7,700

Notes

The finance costs tax reducer is calculated as 20% of the finance costs.

More than one property

Where more than one property is owned the property business profit is simply the aggregate of the profit or loss arising from each property treated as part of a single property business producing one single profit or loss figure.

This means that any loss which might arise on one property is automatically offset against the profit on any other property.

Example 5.5

Ellie rents out several residential flats. For 2020/21 her income and expenses for each property are as follows:

	Flat 1	Flat 2	Flat 3	Flat 4	Flat 5
Rent received	4,000	7,000	2,500	4,250	1,600
Expenses paid	1,000	1,250	4,000	6,000	4,600

Calculate Ellie's property business profit assessment for 2020/2021.

Answer

	Flat 1	Flat 2	Flat 3	Flat 4	Flat 5
Gross rent	4,000	7,000	2,500	4,250	1,600

Less:

Expenses	1,000	1,250	4,000	6,000	4,600
Profit/loss	3,000	5,750	(1,500)	(1,750)	(3,000)

Assessment = 3,000 + 5,750 + (1,500) + (1,750) + (3,000) = 2,500

Note

The property business profit is simply the total for all the properties - profits and losses are automatically offset.

If an individual is also a member of a property business partnership, any profit share is not aggregated with their own property business.

Premiums received for the grant of a short lease

As indicated earlier, the profits from a property business include not only rental income but also lease premiums (i.e. a lump sum payable by the tenant to landlord normally on commencement of a lease). However, only premiums paid in respect of the grant of short leases (i.e. of 50 years or less) are taxable as income.

For tax purposes, only part of a premium is effectively treated as if it was rental income for the landlord.

Basis of assessment

A premium is assessed in the tax year in which the lease is granted.

Taxable element of a premium

Only a part of the premium is assessable as income.

The income element of the premium is worked out according to the formula:

Amount assessable =

$$\text{Premium} - [2\% \times \text{Premium} \times (\text{duration of lease (in years)} - 1)]$$

Note: premiums for an *assignment* i.e. where entire property interest is sold are treated as a capital receipt.

Example 5.6

Jack received a premium of £10,000 on 1 June 2020 when he let out a property under a 10-year lease. Monthly rent of £500 payable on the first day of each month is also chargeable. All of the monthly rent due had been received by the end of 2020/21.

Calculate Jack's property business income for 2020/21.

Answer

Property business income comprises both the rent and a proportion of the premium.

Taxable element of premium = 10,000 – [2% x 10,000 x (10 – 1)] = 8,200

Rents received = 500 x 11 = 5,500

Property business income = 8,200 + 5,500 = 13,700

---

11 months rent would be received – the first on 1 June 2020 and the last on 1 April 2021 (Under the accruals basis the rent received in advance on 1 April 2020, would fall into the following tax year).

Any allowable expenses could then be deducted to arrive at the assessable property business profits.

Grant of a sub-lease

Where a tenant grants a sub-lease to a sub-tenant any premium paid by the subtenant to the tenant is assessed on the grantor tenant as above.

However, if that tenant had paid a premium on receiving their own lease then a measure of relief from the assessment on the sub-lease premium is available. The relief is:

> Duration of sublease   x Taxable premium for the head lease
> Duration of head lease

Example 5.7

Annie grants a lease to Bev for 40 years on 1 March 2017 with a premium of £16,000 paid by Bev to Annie.

Bev grants a sub-lease to Carl on 1 June 2020 for 10 years with Carl paying Bev a premium of £30,000.

How is Bev taxed for 2020/21?

Answer

Taxable element of Premium received by Bev on sub-lease =
30,000 – [2% x 30,000 x (10 – 1)]   =   24,600

Less:
Allowance for the premium paid by Bev to Annie =
[16,000 – [2% x 16,000 x (40 – 1)]] x 10/40   =   (880)
Premium taxable on Bev for 2020/21   =   23,720

Trading expense deduction

Part of the *receipt* of a lease premium, as indicated above, is taxable as part of the profits from a property business.

However, a deduction is also available to the payer of the premium as a trading expense if the payer is carrying on a trade (see Chapter 6) and the property is used in the trade.

The amount allowable/deductible is equal to the amount assessable on the landlord per the above formula divided by the number of years of the lease. This amount is then deductible for each year for the life of the lease.

Rent-a-room scheme

Gross receipts up to £7,500 for 2020/21 are exempt from income tax if they relate to the letting of furnished accommodation which is a part of a main residence, for example where a lodger rents a room in a house. The receipts can include both rent and other services, such as the provision of meals.

However, up to £7,500 the taxpayer can instead ignore the above exemption and calculate the property income assessment under the normal rules. This would only be helpful if under the normal rules a loss arises.

If gross receipts exceed £7,500 the normal rules apply. However, the taxpayer may elect to be assessed instead on the excess of gross receipts over £7,500 with no expense deductions.

Example 5.8

Matt rents out a room in his house for £6,000 for the tax year 2020/21. His allowable expenses are £1,000.

As the rent is below £7,500 it will be exempt. It would not make sense for Matt to claim to be assessed on £6,000 less £1,000 i.e. £5,000 under the normal rules.

If, however, he let the room for £8,500 with expenses of £2,000, under the normal rules, Matt would be assessed on £8,500 less £2,000 i.e. £6,500. In this case, an election to be taxed on the excess of £8,500 over £7,500 should be made reducing the assessable income to £1,000.

Property allowance

From 6 April 2019, an annual property allowance of £1,000 is introduced. Individuals with gross rental income, excluding Rent-a room scheme lettings, of up to £1,000 in total will be exempt from income tax on this rental income. If gross rental income exceeds £1,000 the individual may elect for partial relief. This means that they will be assessed on their gross rental income less £1,000 instead of gross rental income less allowable expenses.

Furnished holiday lettings

If any individual receives rent from the commercial letting of furnished holiday accommodation in the UK or European Economic Area, these receipts and associated expenses do not form part of their property letting business.

Where an individual lets both furnished holiday lettings and other lettings (i.e. non-holiday lettings) two separate calculations are carried out keeping the furnished holiday letting profits separate from the profits arising from the other properties. This is because the profit from furnished holiday lettings is treated differently for tax purposes (see below).

Accommodation is classed as furnished holiday accommodation if:
- it is available for commercial letting to the public for ≥ 210 days in the tax year, *and* is so let in this period for ≥ 105 days; *and*
- if occupied by the same person for more than 31 days, there is a total of no more than 155 days of such long term occupation.

The taxation consequences of classification as furnished holiday accommodation are as follows:
- income is regarded as earnings for pension purposes (see Chapter 12);
- losses can only be used against future furnished holiday lettings income;

- capital gains tax gift, rollover and business assets disposal relief may apply (see Chapter 15);
- capital allowances may be claimed (see Chapter 7); and
- the restriction on residential property finance costs does not apply.

The points above do not apply to rental income arising from property which does not qualify as income from furnished holiday accommodation.

If a taxpayer owns two or more properties each of which satisfies the 210-day condition but which do not all satisfy the 105-day condition these properties can be regarded as satisfying the 105-day rule if their average number of days let is at least 105 days.

Property business losses

Any loss arising from a property business can only be carried forward to be offset against future profits of the same property business.

In certain circumstances, to the extent that losses are related to capital allowances, a claim to offset against general income may be available (ITA 2007 section 120).

Companies

It may be appropriate to read this section after having studied Chapter 16.

The tax treatment of rents whether received by an individual or company is very similar.

However, there are some differences. For a company in receipt of rental income and/or lease premiums:

1. the accruals basis of assessment will always apply;
2. relief for interest on loans for the purchase or improvement of property is dealt with under the loan relationship rules;
3. the restriction for allowable interest for residential let property does not apply;
4. the basis period for assessment is the *accounting period* of the company, not the *tax year* which applies to an individual;
5. for a company any losses arising from a property business can be claimed against total profits (before qualifying charitable donations) of the same accounting period (see Chapter 19); and/or group relieved (see Chapter 20); any surplus loss then remaining being eligible to be carried forward for offset against future profits of the company.

SUMMARY

- Rental income and a proportion of lease premiums from land and buildings in the UK less expenses are taxed as property business profit
- Rental income is normally taxed on individuals on a cash basis and for companies on an accruals basis

- Part of a lease premium granted for 50 years or less is taxed as income in the tax year of grant of the lease
- Rental income and expenses of more than one property are simply aggregated to produce one property business profit assessment
- Interest payable on loans to acquire or improve let residential property is not allowable when calculating the profits of a property business for an individual. However, the interest will be treated as a tax reducer
- The property allowance can exempt from income tax a property business with receipts of up to £1,000
- Rent-a-room relief can exempt receipts from letting furnished accommodation in an individuals own home of up to £7,500 per year
- Rental income from furnished holiday accommodation is also taxed as property income but is not aggregated with rental income from non-furnished holiday accommodation
- For individuals, losses arising from a property business can, generally, only be relieved by carrying forward for offset against future profits of that property business
- Certain rules differ for rental income received by companies.

Questions for students

See Appendix 2 for a practice question relating to Chapter 5. Answers are available online.

CHAPTER 6

Trading profits

INTRODUCTION

This chapter looks at how business profits of a sole trader are calculated and assessed for income tax purposes.

Sole trader versus limited company

A sole trader is someone who carries on a trade, business or profession in their own and is entitled to all of the profits. In other words, no limited company is involved.

For example, John Smith may carry out his tax consultancy business in his own name or he may use a trading name such as "The Smith Tax Consultancy". In either case, there is no company is involved and Mr Smith is trading as a sole trader. As a consequence, any profits made from the business by Mr Smith are subject to income tax as non-savings income (and Class 4 NIC – see Chapter 20).

Accounting profit versus taxable profit

When preparing the financial statements or accounts for a sole trader business, generally accepted accountancy principles (GAAP/accruals rules) will apply.

However, *for tax purposes*, the rules which apply may not be the same as those which apply *for accountancy purposes*, and as a result, the accounts profit for a period is likely to be different from the taxable profit for the same period.

Where there is a specific tax rule which is different from the accountancy rule, the tax rule prevails. An example would be client entertaining expenditure. In determining a sole trader's accounts profit for a period, the costs of entertaining business clients would be deducted. However, for tax purposes, such costs are *not* deductible. It is necessary in this case to disallow these costs and add-back this item to the accounts profit to arrive at the correct taxable profit of the business for the relevant period.

As will be seen below other adjustments to the accounts profit may also be necessary to obtain the taxable profit.

The starting point in ascertaining the taxable profit for a period is always the accounts profit i.e. the net profit as shown by the accounts.

Trading allowance

The trading allowance was introduced from 6 April 2017, to help very small businesses. The trading allowance provides an exemption from income tax for traders with trading income of £1,000 or less in a tax year, in total from all of their businesses.

Alternatively, partial relief is available where trading income exceeds £1,000. In these circumstances, the trader has the choice to deduct their allowable business expenses when calculating their taxable profits, as detailed below, or elect to deduct the £1,000 trading allowance instead.

The trading allowance cannot be claimed by partnerships and cannot be claimed if any of the trading income is received from an employer, spouse, civil partner, partnership in which they are a partner or a close company in which they are a participator.

The trading allowance may be used in conjunction with the cash basis.

Period of account

The period for which accounts are prepared for a sole trader is referred to as a *period of account* (companies are taxed on profits of an *accounting period,* rather than *periods of account,* which for tax purposes cannot be longer than 12 months; see Chapter 16).

A period of account for a sole trader, for tax purposes, is typically for 12 months but may be longer or shorter.

Tax adjusted profit

To work out the tax adjusted profit for a period of account there are *four* types of adjustment which need to be made to the corresponding net profit of the accounts.

Two adjustments involve *adding back* items to the net profit per the accounts and two adjustments involve *deducting* items from the net profit shown in the accounts.

Adding back items
- *expenditure* deducted in the accounts but not deductible for tax purposes
- *income* assessable as trading income but not shown in the accounts.

Deduction items
- *expenditure* not shown in the accounts but deductible in arriving at the trading profit
- *income* shown in the accounts but not assessable as trading income, for example, interest received on the business bank account.

Typically, most adjustments will arise from the need to disallow and add back expenses which have been deducted in arriving at the net profit for accounts purposes which are not, for various reasons, tax deductible.

Allowable expenses for tax purposes

In calculating the tax adjusted profits of a trade, no deduction is allowed for items of a capital nature.

In addition, for an expense to be allowable in computing a sole trader's taxable business profit it must be:

wholly and exclusively incurred for the purpose of the trade.

In other words, if an expense has a private purpose it is not a tax-deductible business expense. For example, travel expenses paid from the business bank account incurred by a sole trader for a private holiday would not be deductible.

However, if the expense is incurred for more than one purpose, any identifiable proportion of the expenditure may be allowable. As an example, where a sole trader uses a motor car for both business and private purposes it is possible to agree with the tax authorities an appropriate percentage split between business and private usage so that the business proportion of the costs of running the car can be deducted in computing taxable profit (ITTOIA 2005[1] section 34 sets this out in a surprisingly clear and understandable manner!).

If the expense has a dual purpose and cannot be easily separated, then no relief is due. The leading example would be an item of clothing purchased to wear for business. As well as being suitable for work, the clothes also provide normal "warmth and decency" and therefore would not be allowable expenditure.

Finally, certain expenditure is specifically disallowed as a deduction by the tax legislation and will need to be added back to find the tax adjusted profit.

Specific disallowed expenses

The following is a summary of some of the main items of expenditure shown in the accounts but *not deductible* for tax purposes either due to the general rules above or specifically detailed by legislation (All references are to ITTOIA 2005). These items are disallowed and added back to the profit.

Donations: no deduction is allowed for political or charitable donations. Trade subscriptions are generally deductible e.g. an accountant's subscription to the ACCA; small donations to a local charity are also normally deductible. Note, however, if the payment to charity constitutes a gift aid payment then higher and additional rate relief may be available (see Chapter 4).

Fines and/or penalties: e.g. fine for breach of health regulations; car parking fine for a sole trader; (however, car parking fines paid by a sole trader on

---

[1] Income Tax (Trading and Other Income) Act 2005

behalf of an employee whilst on employer's business are usually allowable). Fines would cover illegal payments and payments for bribery.

Entertaining: only employee entertaining is deductible; add back client or supplier entertaining.

Gifts to clients: for a gift to a client to be deductible the gift must cost less than £50 per client per year, the gift must carry a conspicuous advertisement for the business *and* the gift must not be of food, drink or tobacco (although gifts to employees are normally deductible) (sections 45-47).

Capital improvements: a capital improvement could be the purchase of a capital asset (e.g. a piece of equipment or machinery or building; note that in some cases capital allowances may be available; see Chapter 7). Alternatively if, for example, the roof of a factory was in need of repair then the expenditure to repair or replace it would be deductible. However, if in replacing the roof it was substantially improved at the same time then such expenditure is likely to be regarded as capital and therefore not deductible.

Depreciation: the depreciation of a capital asset is not deductible. However, instead, capital allowances may be permitted (see Chapter 7).

Legal and professional fees: e.g. solicitors' fees etc incurred in relation to the acquisition of capital or non-trading items (e.g. fees associated with acquiring an item of plant or machinery, a building or the granting of a lease). However, other legal and professional fees charged concerning trading (e.g. legal fees for the collection of trade debts, accountants' fees for the preparation of accounts and tax computation) are deductible. Legal costs associated with the *renewal* of a lease of 50 years or less are also deductible.

General provisions of any sort: disallow general provisions for potential future costs.

Unpaid remuneration: no deduction is allowed for unpaid employee remuneration (e.g. a bonus) unless it is paid within nine months from the end of the period of account (section 36).

Salary or interest on capital paid to the sole trader: this would be treated as drawings. In addition, a salary which is paid to the sole trader's spouse or child, who is an employee, is deductible if it is at the same rate as would be paid to an unconnected employee – disallow any excessive proportion of such payment.

Private expenses of the sole trader: disallow payments by the business of the sole trader's private expenses or private proportion if this can be ascertained, for example, the private proportion of motor expenses (such payments on behalf of employees are deductible. However, see Chapter 10 for impact on employee's tax position).

Interest: disallow interest payable on loans not incurred for trade purposes e.g. a loan which the sole trader used to buy a property for renting to third parties (see Chapter 5).

Expenditure incurred more than seven years prior to the commencement of trading: expenditure incurred within seven years before the commencement of the sole trader's trade is deductible if it would have been deductible if it had been incurred after commencement; it is assumed to have been incurred on the first day of actual trade.

A proportion of any car hire payments paid in relation to the lease of a car with CO_2 emissions in excess of 110 g/km (130g/km for contracts entered into before 6 April 2018/1 April 2018 for companies). 15% of the car hire or lease charges are disallowed. There is no restriction for lower emission motor cars (section 48).

Educational/training courses for the sole trader where the course is in relation to the sole trader acquiring new skills or knowledge are disallowed. However, if the course merely updates existing skills or knowledge the cost will be deductible and educational courses for employees are deductible.

Income assessable as trading income but not shown in the accounts

An addition to profit is necessary where the sole trade takes items from the inventory of the business for personal consumption and either not paying for the stock or paying less than the full value. For example, a wine trader may take some of his stock of wine for his personal consumption without paying for it.

In such cases, the full market value of the items taken (basically, their selling price) must be added to the net profit as shown by the accounts (i.e. simply increases income by this amount) less any amount actually paid by the owner (which may be zero).

Deductions from profit

Income shown in the accounts but not assessable as trading income

This refers to any item of *non-trading* income.

Typically such items would include:
- interest income, rental income and dividend income (these items are assessable but not as trading income); and
- capital profits (e.g. profit on the sale of fixed assets is normally a capital gains tax not income tax issue).

Expenditure not shown in the accounts but deductible in arriving at the trading profit

Two types of expense fall into this category:
- capital allowances (see Chapter 7) which may be claimed on items of plant and machinery; and

- a part of any premium which may be payable under a lease of 50 years or shorter (see Chapter 5).

Therefore, to work out a sole trader's taxable profit for a period of account, the net profit shown in the accounts for that period must be adjusted for each of the above four potential adjustments. Not all adjustments will be necessary in every case.

Remember the purpose of this exercise is to arrive at the taxable trading profit of the sole trader for the period of account. The fact that, for example, bank interest is deducted does not mean that such interest is not liable to income tax but merely that it is not liable to tax as trading profit.

The following somewhat long example highlights many of the issues just raised.

Example 6.1

Omar started trading as a wine merchant on 1 April 2015, preparing annual accounts to 31 March each year. His accounts for the year ended 31 March 2021 show the following:

	£	
INCOME		
Gross profit		250,000
Bank interest received		8,000
Dividends received		3,500
Rental income		4,000
Profit on sale of capital items		2,500
		268,000
EXPENSES		
Salaries: staff	65,000	
wife	25,000	
Shop premises:		
repairs and maintenance	6,600	
rent & business rates	7,500	
council tax	850	
water rates	225	
buildings insurance	1,500	
gas and electricity	2,600	
telephone	1,275	
Motor expenses	9,000	
Depreciation	12,700	
Professional charges	1,000	
Advertising, promotion and gifts	7,600	
Sundry expenses	12,000	
		(152,850)
Net profit		115,150

Notes

1. Omar's wife only works part-time for the business and if Omar was to employ someone other than his wife he would only need to pay a salary of £15,000.
2. Omar and his wife occupy a flat above the shop. It has been agreed that this flat represents 40% of the overall premises (i.e. flat plus shop). Business rates are £2,500.
3. Repairs and maintenance of the premises include £1,600 of improvements and the redecoration of Omar's flat at a cost of £750.
4. The telephone charge of £1,275 includes private business calls of £650.
5. Omar is leasing his car. The car has CO_2 emissions of 155 g/km. His private use has been agreed as 30%. The leasing cost included is £3,000. The balance of motor expenses, £6,000, represents normal running costs.
6. Professional charges include legal fees of £375 in connection with a new 5-year lease; accountancy fees of £500 and £125 for legal fees in connection with pursuing a trade debt.
7. The gifts amounted in total to £1,200 and consisted of food hampers for clients.
8. Sundry expenses include client entertaining of £5,000; a donation to a local charity of £350; car park fines of £250 for Omar. The balance of the expenses are in connection with printing costs for business cards, stationery and invoices plus postage costs.
9. Over the Christmas period, Omar took wine for his family consumption which had cost him £800. His normal gross profit percentage of sales is 60%.
10. Available Capital allowances have been calculated as £8,260.

Calculate Omar's adjusted trading profit for the year ended 31 March 2021.

Answer

Omar Adjusted trading profit		Year ended 31 March 2021	
		£	£
Net profit per accounts			115,150
Less:			
Capital allowances (Note 10)		8,260	
Bank interest		8,000	
Dividends		3,500	
Rents		4,000	
Capital profit		2,500	
			(26,260)
Add:			
Wages: wife	(25,000 – 15,000)		10,000
Premises:			
repairs & maintenance	(1,600 + 750)		2,350
rent & rates	40% x (7,500 – 2,500)		2,000
council tax			850
water rates	40% x 225		90
insurance	40% x 1,500		600
gas and electricity	40% x 2,600		1,040
telephone			650

Motoring:

Car leasing costs	Private use 3,000 x 30%	900
	Restriction 2,100 (3,000 - 900) x 15%	315
Running costs	Private use (30% × 6,000)	1,800
Depreciation		12,700
Professional charges		375
Advertising, gifts etc.		1,200
Sundry expenses	(5,000 + 250)	5,250
Goods for own use	(800/0.4)	2,000
Adjusted trading profit		**£131,610**

Notes

1. Wife's salary exceeds a normal arm's length amount by £10,000 which is therefore added back.
2. Repairs and maintenance include improvements of £1,600 which are not repairs but capital and are therefore not deductible. The repairs attributable to the private flat are not business expenses and so not deductible.
3. Only 60% of the costs of the premises are deductible. All the council tax has been added back is this is a personal cost of Omar and not a business cost.
4. The telephone call costs can be split; only the business-call costs are deductible.
5. 30% of the car leasing cost is added back for private use. The 15% restriction applies to the balance as the car has CO_2 emissions greater than 110 g/km.
6. Legal charges in connection with a new lease are capital and therefore not deductible.
7. The gifts comprise food and are therefore not deductible.
8. Client entertaining and car park fines for Omar are not deductible.
9. Goods taken for own use must be treated as if sold at their normal market price.
10. Although bank interest, dividends and rent received have been deducted, these items may still be taxable but not as trading income. Similarly, the capital profit may be subject to capital gains tax.

Cash basis

Normally the profits of a business must be calculated using the accruals basis. However small unincorporated businesses with a turnover of up to £150,000 may opt to calculate their profits using the cash basis.

This means that income is recognized when received and expenses when they are paid, including items of plant and machinery, excluding cars (but capital allowances can be claimed on cars – see Chapter 7). There is a limit on the amount of loan interest that may be deducted. This is restricted to £500 per year.

If a business using the cash basis incurs a trading loss, the loss can only be carried forward against future profits from that trade.

A sole trader can continue to use the cash basis until annual turnover exceeds £300,000.

Basis periods

Having calculated the taxable adjusted trading profit for a period of account it is then necessary to identify and determine the taxable profit which falls liable to income tax for a particular tax year. This requires a set of rules to determine the basis period for the relevant tax year. Once a business is running and preparing accounts for the same date each year, then this is straight forward but complications arise when a business commences or ceases.

For example, Tracy has been trading for many years and produces her accounts for the 12 months to 30 June each year. For the year to 30 June 2019 how much of these profits fall liable to income tax for the tax year 2019/20? To answer this requires a set of rules.

The normal rule

A sole trader is normally assessed on the taxable trading profit to the accounting date (i.e. the date to which accounts have been prepared) ending in the relevant tax year.

Thus, for Tracy in the above example, for the tax year 2020/21, the taxable trading profit is the profit for the 12 months ended 30 June 2020. The basis period is from 1 July 2019 to 30 June 2020.

If Jon prepared his accounts to 30 September each year, then the taxable trading profit for the tax year 2020/21 would be the taxable profit for the 12 months ended 30 September 2020. The basis period is from 1 October 2019 to 30 September 2020.

This is known as the current year basis (CYB).

Tax year of commencement of trade

Different rules apply when an individual starts to trade.

The taxable profit for the tax year in which a sole trader starts to trade is the taxable profit from the date of commencement of the trade to the end of that first tax year (i.e. 5 April).

The year of assessment for the first year of trading must be clearly identified.

Example 6.2

Eve commenced trading on 1 September 2019 and prepares her first set of accounts for 12 months to 31 August 2020 showing a tax adjusted profit of £36,000.

Therefore, the tax year to 5 April 2020 (2019/20) is the tax year in which Eve started to trade and her basis period for 2019/20 is 1 September 2019 to 5 April 2020. Her assessable profits for 2019/20 will be £36,000 x 7/12 months = £21,000.

Example 6.3

Simon started to trade on 1 October 2020 and prepared his first set of accounts for the nine months to 30 June 2021 showing a tax adjusted profit of £40,500.

Therefore, for the tax year 2020/21, the tax year in which Simon started to trade, the basis period is 1 October 2020 to 5 April 2021. Therefore, his assessable profits for his first year of trading, 2020/10 are £40,500 x 6/9 months = £27,000.

Second tax year of trading

Identifying the basis period for the second tax year can be more difficult.

For the second tax year, the amount of the taxable profit depends upon:
- whether or not there are accounts prepared to a date ending in the second tax year; and
- the length of the accounting period.

Taking each scenario in turn:

No accounting date ending in the second tax year
The basis period is the tax year itself (i.e. 6 April to following 5 April)

Accounting date ending in the second tax year and accounts are for less than 12 months
The basis period is the first 12 months of trading.

Accounting date ending in the second tax year and accounts are for exactly 12 months
The basis period is the period of 12 months to the end of the accounting period.

Accounting date ending in the second tax year accounts are for a period longer than 12 months
The basis period is the period of 12 months to the end of the accounting period.

Example 6.4

Geri started to trade on 1 January 2019. What are the basis periods for Geri's first two tax years of trading assuming that she prepares her first accounts as follows:
(a) 16 months to 30 April 2020
(b) 9 months 30 September 2019
(c) Year to 31 December 2019
(d) 15 months to 31 March 2020

Subsequent accounts will be prepared for 12 months. (i.e. to the end of the same month in the following year).

Answer

In each of the above four options (a) to (d), the *first* tax year is **2018/19** i.e. the tax year in which Geri started to trade.

Therefore, the basis period for the tax year 2018/19 is the period 1 January 2019 (i.e. the date the trade started) to 5 April 2019 (i.e. the end of that tax year in which the trade started) in all four cases. However, the actual profits apportioned may be different depending on the overall tax adjusted profits shown in the first set of accounts.

The basis period for the second year of trading, **2019/20**, will be different in each case due to the choice of accounting date.

(a) 2019/20 is the second tax year of trade. In this case, there is no accounting date ending in 2019/20. Therefore, the basis period for the tax year 2019/20 is the period 6 April 2019 to 5 April 2020.

(b) In this case, there is an accounting date ending in the tax year but it is for a period of less than 12 months. Therefore, the basis period for the tax year 2019/20 is the period 1 January 2019 to 31 December 2019, the first 12 months of trading.

(c) In this case, there is an accounting date in the tax year of exactly 12 months and this will form the basis period. Therefore, the basis period for 2019/20 is the period 1 January 2019 to 31 December 2019.

(d) In this case, there is an accounting date in the tax year and the period from commencement to this date is more than 12 months. Therefore, the basis period for tax year 2019/20 is 12 months to the end of the accounting period, 1 April 2019 to 31 March 2020.

Third tax year of trade

The basis period for the third year of trading is the 12 months to the accounting date ending in this tax year.

Example 6.5

Continuing from 6.4 above, Geri started to trade on 1 January 2019. She prepared her first set of accounts as follows:

(a) 16 months to 30 April 2020

(b) 9 months 30 September 2019

(c) Year to 31 December 2019

(d) 15 months to 31 March 2020.

Subsequent accounts will be prepared for 12 months. (ie to the end of the same month in the next year).

What are the basis periods for the third year of trading, **2020/21**?

(a) 2019/20 is the third tax year of trading. The accounting period to 30 April 2020 ends during this tax year. Therefore, the basis period will be the 12 months to 30 April 2020.

(b) In this case, there will be accounts for the year to 30 September 2020. As this ends during 2020/21 and is for 12 months, this will form the basis period.

(c) In this case, there will be accounts for the year to 31 December 2020. As this ends during 2020/21 and is for 12 months, this will form the basis period.

(d) In this case, there will be accounts for the year to 31 March 2021. As this ends during 2020/21 and is for 12 months, this will form the basis period.

Overlap profit

It may have become clear from the examples above that in most cases some taxable profit is in fact assessed twice. Such profits are referred to as *overlap profits*. Relief for overlap profits will be provided when a business ceases or possibly on a change of accounting date. As a result over the life of a business, the tax adjusted profits arising will be equal to the profits taxed, although the timing may differ.

Example 6.6

Bernie started to trade on 1 July 2018. He prepares his accounts to 30 June each year.

What are the base periods for the first three tax years and identify the overlap profits?

Answer

2018/19

Taxable profit for period 1 July 2018 to 5 April 2019.

2019/20

Taxable profit for period 1 July 2018 to 30 June 2019.

2020/21

Taxable profit for period 1 July 2019 to 30 June 2020.

The taxable profit attributable to the period 1 July 2018 to 5 April 2019 is taxed twice and is thus overlap profit. This profit is taxed in the tax years 2018/19 *and* 2019/20.

Trading profit allocated to basis periods

Having ascertained the basis periods for the relevant tax years it is then necessary is to work out the actual amount of taxable profits allocated to each year and the overlap profits.

Example 6.7

Returning to Geri in examples 6.4 and 6.5, let's show the tax adjusted profits for each accounting period and then we can calculate the assessable profits for each tax year and overlap profits.

Geri started to trade on 1 January 2019. You will recall that we examined four possible year end scenarios. Her tax adjusted profits as per her accounts are as follows:

(a)	16 months to 30 April 2020	Profit £24,600
(b)	9 months 30 September 2019	Profit £11,100.
	Year to 30 September 2020	Profit £24,300.
(c)	Year to 31 December 2019	Profit £16,500.
	Year to 31 December 2020	Profit £25,800.
(d)	15 months to 31 March 2020	Profit £22,500.
	Year to 31 March 2021	Profit £27,000.

For each scenario, calculate Geri's assessable profits for 2018/19, 2019/20, 2020/21 and her overlap profits.

Answer

(a)

2018/19 Basis period 1 January 2019 to 5 April 2019
        Profits £24,600 x 3/16 months = £4,613

2019/20 Basis period 6 April 2019 to 5 April 2020
        Profits £24,600 x 12/16 months = £18,450

2020/21 Basis period 12 months to 30 April 2020
        Profits £24,600 x 12/16 months = £18,450

Overlap profits:

Period 1 May 2019 to 5 April 2020 11 months = £16,913

(Reconciliation £4,613+£18,450+£18,450-£24,600 = £16,913)

(b)

2018/19 Basis period 1 January 2019 to 5 April 2019
        Profits £11,100 x 3/9 months = £3,700

2019/20 Basis period 1 January 2019 to 31 December 2019

   Profits to 30/9/19 £11,100 plus to 30/9/20 £24,300 x 3/12 months = £17,175
2020/21 Basis period 12 months to 30 September 2020
   Profits £24,300
Overlap profits:
Period 1 January 2019 to 5 April 2019 and 1 October 2019 to 31 December 2019 (To 30/9/19 x 3/9 months plus to 30/9/20 x 3/12 months) = £9,775
(Reconciliation £3,700+£17,175+£24,300-£11,100-£24,300 = £9,775)

(c)
2018/19 Basis period 1 January 2019 to 5 April 2019
   Profits £16,500 x 3/12 months = £4,125
2019/20 Basis period year to 31 December 2019
   Profits £16,500
2020/21 Basis period year to 31 December 2020
   Profits £25,800
Overlap profits
Period 1 January 2019 to 5 April 2019 3 months = £4,125
(Reconciliation £4,125+£16,500-16,500 = £4,125)

(d)
2018/19 Basis period 1 January 2019 to 5 April 2019
   Profits £22,500 x 3/15 months = £4,500
2019/20 Basis period 1 April 2019 to 31 March 2020
   Profits £22,500 x 12/15 months = £18,000
2020/21 Basis period year to 31 March 2021
   Profits £27,000
Overlap profits
None
(Reconciliation £4,500+£18,000-22,500 = £0)

Notes
The overlap profit can be reconciled (or calculated) by adding the assessable profits for each of the tax years deducting the adjusted profits for the accounting periods involved.

Example 6.8
Karl is a self-employed electrician. He started to trade on 1 September 2017 and prepared his first set of accounts to 31 December 2018.

His adjusted profits (i.e. his taxable trading profits) are as follows:

1 September 2017 to 31 December 2018 (16 months)	£160,000
1 January 2019 to 31 December 2019	£320,000
1 January 2020 to 31 December 2020	£264,000

What is Karl's taxable trading profit for each tax year?

Answer
2017/18
The tax year in which trade started.
Basis period is 1 September 2017 to 5 April 2018
Assessable profits are £160,000 x 7/16 = £70,000

Note

1 September 2017 to 5 April 2018 is seven months; the first five days of April are ignored. Period 1 September 2017 to 31 December 2018 is 16 months. Hence, for 1 September 2017 to 5 April 2018 taxable profit allocated to this period is going to be £160,000 x 12/16 = £70,000.

2018/19

Second tax year of trading.

Basis period is 1 January 2018 to 31 December 2018 (i.e. 12 months to account date 31 December 2018 as there *is* an accounting date (31 December 2018) ending in the second tax year but first set of accounts are for a period longer than 12 months).

Assessable profits are £160,000 x 12/16 = £120,000.

Overlap profits

The 16-month accounting period to 31 December 2018 has formed the basis periods for each of the two years to 5 April 2019. The total profits assessed are for 19 months (7 + 12 months). Therefore, there is a three-month overlap (19 less 16 months) and the overlap profits are therefore £30,000. This can be simply proved by adding the assessable profits together for 2018/19 and 2019/20 and deducting the accounting profits (70,000+120,000-160,000).

2019/20

Third tax year of trading.

Basis period is 1 January 2019 to 31 December 2019 (Current year basis)

Assessable profits are £320,000.

2020/21

Fourth tax year of trading.

Basis period is 1 January 2020 to 31 December 2020 (Current year basis)

Assessable profits are £264,000

Overlap profit relief

There is no relief for overlap profits until either the sole trader changes their accounting date in the future (see Example 6.13 below) and/or ceases to trade (see Example 6.9 below).

On either of these occasions, some relief may be available. This relief is obtained by deducting some or all of the overlap profit from the taxable profit of the tax year of cessation or accounting date change.

Cessation of trading

This occurs when a sole trader no longer continues to trade.

Basis of assessment

In the tax year in which the trade ceases the taxable trading profit for that tax year is the taxable profit for the period from the end of the basis period of the tax year prior to the tax year of cessation to the date of cessation.

Example 6.9

Tracey has been trading for many years. She prepares her accounts to 30 November each year. She ceased to trade on 30 June 2020.

What is the basis period for the tax year 2020/21?

Answer

The date of cessation is 30 June 2020.

The tax year of cessation is 2020/21.

The tax year prior to the tax year of cessation is therefore 2019/20.

The basis period for 2019/20 is the year to 30 November 2019.

Therefore, for the tax year 2020/21, the basis period is 1 December 2019 to 30 June 2020.

When calculating the assessable profits for the year of cessation, any unused overlap profits may be deducted.

Example 6.10

Henry has been trading for several years. He prepares his accounts to 30 November each year. He ceased to trade on 31 December 2020. He has overlap profits brought forward of £50,000. His taxable profits for his last three tax years of trading are as follows:

1 December 2018 to 30 November 2019: £400,000

1 December 2019 to 30 November 2020: £500,000

1 December 2020 to 31 December 2020: £100,000

What is the assessment for the tax year of cessation?

Answer

The tax year of cessation is 2020/21.

The basis period for the tax year prior to cessation (2019/20) is 1 December 2018 to 30 November 2019 (Normal current year basis).

The taxable profit for the tax year 2020/21 (the tax year of cessation) is therefore for the period 1 December 2019 to 31 December 2020
i.e. £500,000 + £100,000 = £600,000

However, relief for the overlap profit is available in the tax year of cessation.
Therefore, the assessable profit for 2020/21 is £600,000 - £50,000 = £550,000

Change of accounting date

A sole trader may decide for various reasons to change their accounting date.

When this occurs, new rules are used to determine the relevant basis period for the tax year of the change.

Any change of accounting date in the first three tax years is automatically valid.

Otherwise, for a change of accounting date to be valid:

- the change of accounting date must be notified to the HMRC by 31 January following the tax year in which the change is made;
- the first accounts to the new date must not exceed 18 months in length; and

- there must not have been a change of accounting date within the previous five tax years (this condition does not apply if the change is made for genuine commercial reasons).

When a change of accounting date occurs the first step is to identify the year of the change. The tax year of the change is the earlier of the tax year in which accounts are first made up to the new accounts date or the tax year in which the accounts have not been made up to the old date.

It is then necessary to identify the basis periods for the tax year either side of the year of change. Before the year of change, this will be the "old" accounting date ending in that tax year and after the change, it will be the 12 months to the "new" accounting date.

Example 6.11

Cat prepares her accounts to the 30 September each year the last being to 30 September 2019. She then changed her accounting date and prepared her next set of accounts to 31 March 2020.

The first accounts to the new date are to 31 March 2020 – 2019/20.

The first year where accounts are not made up to the old date i.e. to 30/9/2020 – 2020/21.

The tax year of change is the earlier of the two years – 2019/20.

There are two accounting dates ending in this tax year i.e. 30.9.19 and 31.03.20.

Therefore, the basis period for tax year 2019/20 is 1 October 2018 to 31 March 2020. The assessable profits will be the sum of the profits for these two periods. However as this is longer than 12 months, overlap relief will be available to reduce this.

Example 6.12

Harry prepares his accounts to 31 December each year, the last being to 31 December 2019. He then changed his accounting date to 30 June and prepared his next set of accounts for the six months to 30 June 2020.

The first accounts to the new date are to 30 June 2020 – 2020/21.

The first year where accounts are not made up to the old date i.e. to 31 December 2020 – 2020/21.

The tax year of change is 2020/21.

The profits falling into 2020/21 are for the six months to 30 June 2020. However, as this is less than 12 months, this must be increased to 12 months by calculating a 12 month period to the new date by including the appropriate proportion of the profits of the previous accounting period.

Therefore, the basis period for tax year 2019/20 is 1 July 2019 to 31 June 2020.

This would be calculated as profits to 31 December 2019 x 6/12 plus profits for the six months to 30 June 2020.

In this case, as the profits for the six months to 31 December 2019 have already been assessed in the previous tax year, this will increase the overlap profits to carry forward.

Overlap profits and change of accounting date

As was indicated earlier in the chapter overlap profits (i.e. those profits taxed twice) which arise when a sole trader starts to trade (see Example 6.6 above) may be relievable when the sole trader changes accounting date. The overlap profits relieved will in effect reduce the basis period to 12 months as illustrated by Example 6.13 below.

However, for this to occur the change of accounting date must give rise to a basis period of more than 12 months, as illustrated by Example 6.11 above. If the change of accounting date requires profits to be assessed again, then this increases the overlap relief to carry forward,(see Example 6.12).

Example 6.13

Steph prepares her accounts to the 30 September each year the last being to 30 September 2019. She then changed her accounting date and prepared her next set of accounts to 31 December 2019. Her tax adjusted profits were as follows:

Year to 30 September 2018   £70,500
Year to 30 September 2019   £82,100
3 months to 31 December 2019   £12,600

Steph has overlap profits brought forward for 6 months of £50,000

The first accounts to the new date are to 31 December 2019 – 2019/20

The first year where accounts are not made up to the old date i.e. to 30 September 2020 - 2020/21

The tax year of change is the earlier of the two - 2019/20.

There are two accounting dates in this tax year i.e. to 30.9.19 and 31.12.19.

Therefore, the basis period for tax year 2019/20 is 1 October 2018 to 31 December 2019 i.e. 15 months long.

Therefore, three months' worth of overlap profits are available (the three months being the excess over 12 months of the new set of accounts).

The assessable profits for 2019/20 will be

Year to 30 September 2019   82,100
Period to 31 December 2019   12,600
Less: Overlap profits 50,000 x 3/6   (25,000)
Assessable profits 2019/20   69,700

Notes

It should be noted that if the accounting date had remained as 30 September 2019, then the assessable profits for 2019/20 would be £82,100. In this case, by changing the accounting date and "triggering" the release of part of the overlap profits, the assessable profits for 2019/20 have reduced.

SUMMARY

The starting point for working out a sole trader's taxable profit for a period of account is the accounts profit prepared according to generally accepted accounting principles.

Adjustments are necessary to the accounts profit as in certain cases there is a clash between the rules for tax and those for accountancy; where this arises the tax rules prevail.

In general expenses of a capital nature and revenue expenditure not *wholly and exclusively incurred for the purpose of the trade* are disallowed and added back to determine the tax adjusted profits. In addition, a number of specific rules will disallow certain other expenses and any non-trading income must be deducted. Capital allowances may be available to reduce taxable profit.

Before the taxable profits for a tax year can be determined it is necessary to establish the basis period and match the period of account to the appropriate tax year.

The date to which a sole trader prepares their accounts will affect the basis periods for each tax year. In particular, the extent of any overlap profits will be affected by the date to which the first set of accounts are prepared.

The rules for determining the appropriate basis period for a tax year are extremely important (Unfortunately many students find the opening year calculations to be one of the most difficult areas of taxation!).

APPENDIX

The Badges of trade – is a transaction trading?

At times, it is necessary to consider whether a transaction should be treated as a trading transaction, with the appropriate income tax and NIC liabilities or perhaps should be treated as a capital gain or non-taxable. For example, the sale of a rental property after nine years of ownership and generating rental income for the owner, would not normally suggest trading as a property dealer. However, a property purchased, renovated and sold after a short period of letting may be more indicative of trading.

The usual starting place is by reference to the "badges of trade" as listed by the Royal Commission of 1955. Each badge should be considered in turn and a decision made based on the overall picture that they present. The badges are:

1. The subject matter – is the item sold something that could be used or enjoyed by the owner or realistically is the only reason to own the item to later sell it?
2. Length of ownership – acquiring an asset and selling it shortly afterwards can suggest trading.

3. The frequency of transactions – a one off transaction may not suggest trading but a volume of transactions can indicate trading.
4. Additional work – improvements or repairs to an item with a view to a sale may increase the probability of trading.
5. Circumstances for the sale – a forced sale due to a change of circumstances may not suggest trading.
6. Motive – the purchase of an item with a clear intention to sell it on can be a pointer to the conclusion that a trade is being carried on.

Over the decades since the Royal Commission, a number of other considerations have been adopted by the courts including:

*   The source of finance – a short term loan may suggest trading.
*   Similar or existing trade – trading can be suggested if the individual is involved in a similar business.
*   Method of acquisition – the acquisition of an asset by inheritance, or as a gift, is less likely to suggest trading.

In conclusion, when considering whether a specific transaction has the character of trading income or not, all of the above factors should be considered and weighed up to give an overall picture of the transaction. The decision will be based on the specific facts for each transaction. Some factors may not be present in every case.

Even a one-off transaction may be deemed to be "an adventure in the nature of trade" if the circumstances support this conclusion.

(The badges of trade are Subject matter, Length of ownership, Frequency, Circumstances, Additional work, and Profit motive – more than twenty years ago I used the mnemonic Sam Likes Fish Chips And Peas to remember this for my final exams and it's still there!)

CHAPTER 7

Capital Allowances

INTRODUCTION

This chapter considers the tax equivalent of the accountant's depreciation - capital allowances. Capital allowances allow the cost of certain capital assets to be written off against taxable profits.

As noted in Chapter 6, depreciation charged in a sole trader's accounts is not a tax-deductible item in computing taxable trading profit as it is capital in nature. Instead, capital allowances are claimed which are treated as a trading expense. There are two types of capital allowances claims – on plant and machinery and on structures and buildings (SBA).

Trading expense

Capital allowances are treated as a trading expense when computing a sole trader's taxable trading profit (See Example 7.1).

Chargeable period

Capital allowances are computed for a chargeable period which, for income tax purposes, is any period of account (assuming such period is 18 months or shorter).

Capital items

Capital allowances are available for items of plant and machinery and on construction expenditure on buildings and structures incurred on or after 29 October 2018.

Plant and machinery (P & M)

Simply put, P&M are items or apparatus used by a sole trader in carrying out their business, but not the setting in which the business is carried on. Such apparatus is of a permanent nature and therefore does not include the sole trader's stock in trade which is bought and sold.

P&M can include:
- cars and other motor vehicles
- office furniture
- fixtures and fittings
- light fittings
- computers and software
- fire regulation expenditure
- thermal insulation expenditure in industrial buildings
- air conditioning equipment

Items which have been held by the Courts not to qualify as P&M include:
- football stand
- a canopy over a petrol station forecourt

- false ceilings used to hide electrical wiring

Types of allowance

Capital allowances are available to a sole trader who incurs capital expenditure on P&M which is used for the purposes of their business.

There are three main types of capital allowance:
- writing down allowance;
- annual investment allowance; and
- enhanced capital allowances.

Writing down allowance (WDA)

A writing down allowance (WDA) is available for *each* period of account *including* the period of account in which the expenditure on the P&M is first incurred. Normally, no account is taken of when the expenditure is incurred during the period – the full WDA would apply if the expenditure was incurred on the first or the last day of the period. The annual rate of WDA is 18% on the balance of the main pool and 6% of the special rate pool. The annual rate of WDA on the special rate pool was reduced from 8% to 6% from 6 April 2019 (1 April 2019 for corporation tax). Where an accounting period straddles 6 April 2019 a hybrid rate applied to the special rate pool, calculated on a time basis.

A WDA is an allowance *per annum* and therefore depends upon the length of the period of account. If the period of account is shorter or longer than 12 months the WDA is then adjusted either down or up respectively (e.g. period of account is 9 months – WDA will be (18%/6% x 9/12) of the relevant balance).

Most expenditure on P&M is allocated to the main pool. However, expenditure on the following items is allocated to the special rate pool:

- P& M that form part of a building – referred to as 'integral features';
- items with a long life (25 years or more);
- thermal insulation of buildings; and
- motor cars with CO_2 emissions of more than 110g/km (130g/km before 6/4/18 (1/4/18 for companies)).

Integral features include:
- lifts, escalators and moving walkways
- space and water heating systems
- air-conditioning and air cooling systems
- hot and cold water systems (but not toilet and kitchen facilities)
- electrical systems, including lighting systems and
- external solar shading.

All other expenditure on P&M is allocated to the general pool.

The WDA for each period of account for P&M is based on the pool's *tax written down value* (TWDV) (i.e. original cost less allowances claimed previously) at the end of the previous period of account and is calculated on what is referred to as a *reducing balance basis*. (For the first period of trading, there will be no brought forward amount and any allowances will be based on the asset cost).

The value of the pool of P&M expenditure may be increased when items of P&M are purchased and decreased when items of P&M are sold. The WDA for any period of account is calculated on the balance of the pool i.e. after taking into account asset purchases and sales.

Example 7.1

Ben prepares his business accounts to 31 December each year. As at 31 December 2018, the TWDV on the pools are as follows:

Main pool   £24,000
Special rate pool   £10,000

Calculate Ben's capital allowances (CA) for each of the years ended 31 December 2019 and 20, assuming no new purchases or sales of P & M.

Answer

Year ended 31.12.19

	Main Pool	Special rate Pool		Allowances or Claim
TWDV brought forward	24,000	10,000		
WDA @ 18%	(4,320)			4,320
WDA @ (8% x 3/12 + 6% x 9/12)		(650)		650
			CA claimed	4,970
TWDV carried forward	19,680	9,350		
Year ended 31.12.20				
WDA @ 18%	(3,542)			3,542
WDA @ 6%		(561)		561
			CA claimed	4,103
TWDV carried forward	16,138	8,789		

Notes
1. The WDA for the year ended 31 December 2020 is calculated based on the TWDV carried forward. The WDA is, therefore, lower as it is based on a reducing tax written down value.
2. Note the hybrid rate of WDA on the special rate pool in the year to 31 December 2019, as the period spans the date of reduction on 6 April 2019.
3. Note the basic template used for calculating capital allowances. Usually, the calculation will only cover one period of account.

Annual Investment Allowance (AIA)

AIA was introduced as an incentive for businesses to invest in additional plant and machinery (P & M).

AIA of 100% can be claimed for additions of P&M in an accounting period totalling up to the lower of the total expenditure on P&M and the annual maximum, currently £1,000,000, for expenditure incurred after 1 January 2019. Prior to this date, the maximum was £200,000 and the maximum will return to this from 1 January 2021. If the accounting period is less than or greater than 12 months a pro rata AIA will be available. See the appendix to this chapter where an accounting period straddles 1 January 2021.

AIA is available on all P&M except for motor cars.

If the expenditure on new P&M exceeds the annual limit, the balance of the expenditure falls into the appropriate pool and WDA may be claimed. If expenditure exceeds the annual limit, then the maximum claimed should be made for items falling into the special rate pool in priority to main pool items to maximise the capital allowances claim.

Example 7.2

Jenny, a sole trader, has been trading for several years and prepares her accounts to 31 December each year. During the year to 31 December 2020, Jenny purchased a new machine, a piece of P&M falling into the main pool, at a cost of £1,300,000. As at 31 December 2019, the TWDV on the pools are as follows:

Main pool   £40,000
Special rate pool   £8,000

Calculate the capital allowances to which Jenny is entitled to for the accounting period to 31 December 2020.

Answer

		Main	Special	Allowances
TWDV brought forward		40,000	8,000	
Additions qualifying for AIA				
Main pool	1,300,000			
AIA (Maximum)	(1,000,000)			1,000,000
Balance		300,000		
		340,000		
WDA @ 18%		(61,200)		61,200
WDA @ 6%			(480)	480
				CA Claimed 1,061,680
TWDV carried forward		278,800	7,520	

Notes

1. As the expenditure qualifying for AIA exceeds £1,000,000, the AIA claim is limited to £1,000,000. The remaining balance of expenditure is transferred to the main or special rate pool as appropriate. In this case, it is added to the main pool. The WDA on the main pool is therefore calculated on the TWDV brought forward and the £300,000 balance of expenditure on new equipment.
2. Note the template used for calculating capital allowances involving AIA.

Enhanced Capital Allowances or First Year Allowances

In place of AIA, certain assets qualify for 100% Enhanced Capital Allowances (ECA). Therefore, a business may claim 100% allowances on items qualifying for AIA up to the annual maximum plus an unlimited amount on items qualifying for 100% ECA. The following items can qualify for ECA:

- new cars with CO_2 emissions up to 50 g/km (75g/km up to 5 April 2018/ 1 April 2018 for companies);
- energy saving and water saving equipment (removed from eligibility from April 2020);
- gas, biogas and hydrogen refuelling equipment;
- electric charge point equipment; and
- new zero-emission goods vehicles and vans.

Example 7.3

Stephen a sole trader has been trading for many years and prepares his accounts to the 31 July each year. In the year to 31 July 2020, Stephen purchased a new machine, a piece of P&M falling into the main pool, at a cost of £1,175,000. In addition, he acquired new zero emission goods vehicles costing £54,000. As at 30 July 2019, the TWDV on the pools are as follows:

Main pool   £10,000
Special rate pool   £27,000

Calculate the capital allowances to which Stephen is entitled to for the accounting period to 31 July 2020.

Answer

		Main	Special	Allowances
TWDV brought forward		10,000	27,000	
Additions qualifying for AIA				
Main pool	1,175,000			
AIA	(1,000,000)			1,000,000
Balance		175,000		
		185,000		
WDA @ 18%		(33,300)		33,300
WDA @ 6%			(1,620)	1,620
Additions qualifying for ECA				
Main pool	54,000			
ECA	(54,000)			54,000
CA Claimed				1,088,920
TWDV carried forward		151,700	25,380	

Notes

Note the template used for calculating capital allowances involving AIA and ECA.

Small Pools Allowance

If the balance on the main pool or special rate pool before calculating WDA is £1,000 or less, then a WDA up to the whole amount may be claimed. This was introduced to simplify calculations by avoiding the requirement to calculate ever reducing small amounts of WDA.

Non-pooled assets

There are some assets which do not form part of the pool of P & M.

These assets are:

- assets with any private use by the sole trader; and
- short-life assets.

In each of these cases, each asset is treated separately and all allowances are computed separately.

Assets with private use

Any asset which is used partly for business and partly for private purposes by the owner (i.e. the sole trader) of the business is not pooled.

Capital allowances are computed individually for each such asset. However, although the capital allowances computation is carried out as normal, the amount of allowance which can actually be claimed is reduced by the private percentage usage i.e. only the percentage usage attributable to business can be deducted as a trading expense. The WDA is calculated and deducted from the pool in full but the amount claimed is reduced for private use.

If the asset is used partly privately by an employee of the business (i.e. not the business owner) then no restriction of allowances occurs.

Note that if there is more than one asset used privately each asset with private use is treated separately i.e. privately used assets are not pooled together.

Example 7.4

Gloria a sole trader has been trading for a number of years and prepares her accounts to 31 March each year. In the year to 31 March 2021, Gloria made no acquisitions or disposals of P & M. As at 31 March 2020 the TWDV are as follows:

Main pool	£24,600
Car with private use	£16,800

30% of Gloria's use of the motor car is private. The car has CO_2 emissions of 145 g/km.

Calculate the capital allowances to which Gloria is entitled to for the accounting period to 31 March 2021.

Answer

	Main Pool	Asset with Private Use		Allowances or Claim
TWDV Brought forward	24,600	16,800		
WDA @ 18%	(4,428)			4,428
WDA @ 6% (Note 1)	____	(1,008)	(less 30%)	705
			CA Claimed	5,133
TWDV Carried forward	20,172	15,792		

Notes

The WDA for the car with private use is calculated at the full 6% applicable for a high emissions motor car. However, the allowances *claimed* for the car are reduced to reflect the 30% private use.

Short-life assets

An election may be made for an asset to be treated as a short-life asset where it is anticipated that the asset is likely to be sold or scrapped within eight years of the end of the period of account in which the asset is acquired.

The advantage of short life asset treatment is that a balancing allowance (see below) can arise on sale which would not be the case if the asset had simply been added to the general pool.

If the asset is not in fact sold by the end of the period of account eight years after the end of the period when it was purchased, its tax written down value as at that time (i.e. end of eight years) is transferred to the general or special rate pool, if appropriate, at the commencement of the next period of account.

Note that if there is more than one short life asset each asset is treated separately i.e. short life assets are not pooled together.

Sales of assets

Balancing allowances and balancing charges

In the year of purchase AIA or ECA will normally be available on P&M and thereafter a WDA will be available.

If the asset is not sold or scrapped, eventually its original cost will be written down to zero.

If, however, an item of P&M is sold then in the period of account in which the sale occurs a deduction will be required from the pool.

In all cases, on the sale, the amount deducted from the pool is *the lower of* the actual sale proceeds or the asset's original cost.

Ongoing Businesses

Main or special rate pool

The sale of an asset out of the main pool or special rate pool simply means that the sale proceeds reduce the size of the pool i.e. the pool will decrease. However, if the amount brought into account on disposal exceeds the balance on the pool, then a balancing charge will arise. A balancing charge is treated as taxable trading income and thus increases the taxable trading profit.

Assets with private use or short life assets

In each of these cases, the sale of the asset will close the pool and lead to a balancing allowance or balancing charge depending upon whether the sale proceeds are respectively less than or more than the tax written down value of the asset at the time of sale. For assets with private use, any balancing adjustment is reduced for private use.

Note that where an asset is sold, the amount deducted from the pool is the *lower of original cost and sale proceeds*. This is because it is not possible to claw back more allowances than have been given for the asset.

Example 7.5

Malcolm a sole trader has been trading for a number of years and prepares his accounts to the 31 May each year. In the year to 31 May 2020, Malcolm made no acquisitions. As at 31 May 2019, the TWDV are as follows:

Main pool	£18,500
Car with private use	£15,250

An item in the main pool, which originally cost £1,000 was sold during the year for £1,500.

The car was also sold during the year for £12,000.

25% of Malcolm's use of the motor car is private. The car has CO_2 emissions of 105 g/km.

Calculate the capital allowances to which Malcolm is entitled to for the accounting period to 31 May 2020.

Answer

	Main Pool	Asset with Private Use		Allowances or Claim
TWDV Brought forward	18,500	15,250		
Disposals	(1,000)	(12,000)		
Balancing allowance		3,250	(Less 25%)	2,437
	17,500			
WDA @ 18%	(3,150)			3,150
			CA Claimed	5,587
TWDV Carried forward	14,350			

Notes

1. As the car with private use was sold during the year, there is no WDA.
2. On the sale of an asset with private use, a balancing allowance or charge can arise. In either case, the balancing amount is reduced for private use.
3. The disposal from the main pool does not create a balancing charge as there remains a balance to calculate WDA.
4. The deduction is the lower of proceeds and original cost. Therefore £1,000 is deducted from the main pool and not the proceeds of £1,500.

Cessation of a business

For the accounting period of cessation, there is no ECA, AIA or WDA. Additions are simply added to the appropriate pool. Disposal values are deducted from each pool and on each, a balancing charge or allowance can arise. If the business owner keeps any assets on cessation, they are treated as sold to them at market value at the cessation date.

Note that where an asset is sold the amount brought into account *is the lower of original cost and sale proceeds.* This is because it is not possible to claw back more allowances than have been given for the asset.

Example 7.6

Paula a sole trader has been trading for a number of years and prepares her final accounts to cessation on 14 August 2020. During the period to 14 August 2020, Paula acquired Main pool P&M for £3,000. As at the start of the accounting period, the TWDV are as follows:

Main pool	£6,200
Special rate pool	£12,090
Car with private use	£8,800

The sale proceeds for each pool were as follows:

Main pool	£8,000
Special rate pool	£14,000
Car	£6,000

In each case, the disposal proceeds were less than the original cost.

10% of Paula's use of the motor car is private. The car has CO_2 emissions of 140 g/km.

Calculate the capital allowances to which Paula is entitled to for the accounting period to 14 August 2020.

Answer

	Main Pool	Special Rate Pool	Asset with Private Use	Claim
TWDV Brought forward	6,200	12,090	8,800	
Additions	3,000			
Disposals	(8,000)	(14,000)	(6,000)	
Balancing allowance	1,200			1,200
Balancing allowance			2,800 less 10%	2,520
Balancing charge		(1,910)		(1,910)
			CA Claimed	1,810

Notes

1. As this is the period of cessation, there are no ECA, AIA or WDA.
2. On the sale of the asset with private use, the balancing allowance has been reduced for the 10% private use.
3. The disposal from the special rate pool creates a balancing charge which reduces the overall claim.

Hire purchase and leasing

Hire purchase

An asset bought on hire purchase is treated as if it had been purchased outright. As a consequence, capital allowances are available based on the purchase price.

Leased assets

Under a lease, the lessee merely hires the asset over the leased period. The hire charge is treated as a normal trading expense/deduction.

However, where the asset concerned is a motor car with CO_2 emissions of 110g/km or more (130g/km up to 6 April 2018), a 15% restriction is placed on the amount of the leasing costs which is eligible for treatment as a deductible trading expense (see Chapter 6).

Capital allowances for structures and buildings

Finance Act 2019 introduced a new type of capital allowances in respect of qualifying construction expenditure on buildings and structures incurred on or after 29 October 2018. Structures and Buildings Allowance (SBA) was introduced as the government believes there is a gap in the existing capital allowances system, where relief has not been given for buildings and structures other than for integral features. Relief is given for eligible expenditure at an annual rate of 2% on a straight-line basis per year. The rate is increased to 3% per annum from 6 April 2020 (1 April 2020 for corporation tax) until the full cost has been relieved. A hybrid rate will apply for accounting periods that straddle April 2020. There is no balancing allowance or charge on the disposal of a building on which SBA has been claimed – the purchaser will simply be entitled to continue to claim the 3% of the original cost for the balance of the unrelieved cost. However, when calculating the capital gain on the seller, the cost is reduced by the SBA claimed.

Relief is available for new commercial buildings and structures, including costs for conversions or renovations. Relief is available for UK and overseas buildings and structures where the business is subject to UK tax. Relief is limited to the construction costs and not for the cost of land. Expenditure on integral features will continue to qualify as P&M and will not be included in an SBA claim.

SBA is available when a structure or building is first brought into use for a qualifying activity. This includes a trade, profession or vocation or a property business. Relief is not available for residential property or other dwellings, such as student accommodation at a university but is available for hotels and care homes.

Example 7.7

Paul, a sole trader, buys a new office building from a developer at a cost of £12 million, of which £2 million has been identified as relating to integral features and £3 million relates to the land. Paul prepares his annual accounts to 31 December each year and starts to use the building in his trade from 1 January 2020.

Calculate the SBA for the year to 31 December 2020.

Answer

The expenditure eligible for SBA is calculated as follows:

Total expenditure	£12 million
Less: P&M - integral features	(£2 million)
Cost of land	(£3 million)
Eligible expenditure for SBA	£7 million
SBA 2020/21 (@2% x 3/12 + 3% x 9/12)	£192,500
SBA for subsequent years @3%	£210,000

SUMMARY

Capital allowances allow a tax deduction for the cost of certain capital items spread over the life of the asset. The following key points should be noted:

Plant and machinery

- AIA, ECAs and WDAs are computed for periods of account
- AIA and ECA are at the rate of 100%
- The maximum amount of AIA for a 12 month period is £1,000,000. This is reduced to £200,000 from 1 January 2021
- WDA is 18% per annum on a reducing balance basis on the main pool and 6% per annum on the special rate pool
- Not all P&M is pooled – assets with private use are separated
- A short life asset election may be made to de-pool such assets.
- Any capital allowances claim is reduced for private use
- A business is not required to claim the full AIA, ECA or WDA
- A balancing adjustment may be required when an asset is sold.

Structures and Buildings Allowance

- Applies to qualifying expenditure incurred on or after 29 October 2019
- SBA is calculated at 3% of the qualifying expenditure per year.
- Balancing allowances or charges do not apply on disposal.

Questions for students

See Appendix 2 for practice questions relating to Chapters 6 and 7. Answers are available online.

APPENDIX

Annual Investment Allowance Increase – periods straddling 1 January 2021

The AIA limit was temporarily increased from £200,000 to £1,000,000 for assets acquired on or after 1 January 2019. The AIA limit returns to £200,000 on 1 January 2021. Where a period of account straddles 1 January 2021, then the limits must be apportioned but care must be given to the overall limit for the period before the change. Regardless of the apportioned maximum for the accounting period, the maximum that can be claimed post to 1 January 2021 is £200,000.

This is illustrated as follows:

A business prepares accounts for the year to 31 March 2021. The maximum expenditure that can qualify for AIA is

To 31 December 2020 £1,000,000 x 9/12 = 750,000

To 31 March 2021   £200,000 x 3/12 =   50,000

Maximum for accounting period   800,000

However, the maximum that can be claimed in respect of qualifying expenditure incurred in the period 1 January 2021 to 31 March 2021 is limited to £50,000.

For example, consider a business preparing annual accounts to 31 March 2021, that purchases plant and machinery costing £400,000 in November 2020 and a further £400,000 in February 2021. It would appear that this would fully qualify for AIA. However, as the second item was purchased in the period £50,000. Therefore, the available AIA is £450,000, with the remaining £350,000 falling into the appropriate pool for the WDA claim.

CHAPTER 8

Sole Trader Business Losses

INTRODUCTION

In some years, rather than making a trading profit, a sole trader may incur a trading loss. This chapter looks at how a sole trader may utilise such losses when they arise.

Trading losses

There are various ways in which a sole trader may claim tax relief for a trading loss.

A trading loss can be:

- carried forward and offset against future profits from the same trade (section 83)
- offset against net income of the tax year of the trading loss and/or the previous tax year (section 64)
- after a claim against income, offset the remaining loss against chargeable gains (section 71).

Extended forms of trading loss relief are available in specific situations as follows:

- in the first four years of trade (section 72)
- upon cessation of a trade (section 89)
- following incorporation of a sole traders business (section 86).

It is usual to refer to the possible use of trading losses by the appropriate section number. Each of the above section numbers refers to sections of the Income Taxes Act 2007 (ITA 2007).

If the relevant conditions for a particular relief are satisfied a taxpayer can claim one or more of the various reliefs to use as appropriate.

Where for a period of account a trading loss arises the assessable trading profit for the relevant tax year is treated as "nil" (see Example 8.1 below).

Trading loss carry forward (section 83)

Any trading loss of a period of account can be carried forward indefinitely for offset against future profits from the same trade. The trading loss must be used against future trading profits as soon as possible. This relief is given automatically for any losses not subject to an alternative claim.

Example 8.1

John has been trading for a number of years and prepares his accounts to 31 December each year. He has the following results:

    Year ended 31.12.18 trading loss   £10,000
    Year ended 31.12.19 trading profit £3,000
    Year ended 31.12.20 trading profit £6,000

How can John use section 83 relief?

Answer

Tax year	2018/19	2019/20	2020/21
Basis period	31.12.18	31.12.19	31.12.20
Trading profit	0	3,000	6,000
Section 83 loss relief	____	(3,000)	(6,000)
Net trading profit	0	0	0

Note

There remains a balance of loss of £1,000 (10,000-3,000-6,000) to carry forward to 2021/22.

It is important to note the layout which should be used (i.e. tax years across the page). Where a trading loss occurs (e.g. in y/e 31.12.18 above), the assessment for the tax year for which this period of account is the basis period (i.e. 2018/19) is "0" and hence "0" appears under "Tax year 2018/19". The trading loss amount itself of £10,000 for y/e 31.12.18 only appears when it is being utilised against other trading profits (i.e. for tax years 2019/20 and 2020/21).

Trading loss offset against taxable income (ITA 2007 section 64)

A trading loss for a period of account can be offset against the net income of the tax year in which the loss arises and/or the net income of the immediately preceding tax year.

The taxpayer can choose which option to adopt. However, whichever option is chosen the trading loss must be offset to the maximum possible extent in the tax year of claim against that year's net income (i.e. before personal allowances).

There are effectively four possible options under this section:

- trading loss offset *only* against net income of the tax year of loss
- trading loss offset *only* against net income of the tax year prior to the tax year of loss
- trading loss offset against net income of the tax year of loss *and* then the net income of prior tax year
- trading loss offset against net income of prior tax year *and* then the net income of tax year of loss

The taxpayer can choose any of these four options. The loss must be claimed within one year of 31 January following the end of the tax year in which the loss arose.

Remember **net income** is **total income less reliefs** (see Chapter 2).

Where net income for a tax year exceeds the trading loss then the trading loss should be deducted in order, first from non-savings income, then any balance remaining from savings income and then dividend income for the relevant tax year.

Where a trading loss arises in two succeeding tax years the trading loss from the earlier tax year must be offset before the later trading loss may be offset.

Example 8.2

Aisha has been trading for a number of years and prepares her accounts to 31 December each year and has the following results:

Year ended 31.12.18   trading profit £34,000
Year ended 31.12.19   trading loss   £48,000
Year ended 31.12.20   trading profit £60,000

Aisha also has other income for 2018/19 and 2019/20 of £5,000 and £6,000 respectively.

How should Aisha utilise the loss to 31.12.19?

Answer

	2018/19	2019/20	2020/21
Trading profit/loss	34,000	nil	60,000
Less:			
Section 83 relief	nil	nil	(9,000)
Net trading profit/loss	34,000	nil	51,000
Other income	5,000	6,000	nil
Total income	39,000	6,000	51,000
Less:			
Section 64 relief	(39,000)	nil	nil
	nil	6,000	51,000
Less:			
Personal allowance	nil	(6,000)	(12,500)
Taxable income	nil	nil	38,500

Notes

1. The trading loss for y/e 31.12.19 is a trading loss for tax year 2019/20. Any of the four options described above may be chosen.
2. It can be seen however that to offset any part of the trading loss in tax year 2019/20 would not make sense as Taxable income for that year is in any event "nil" even without using the trading loss due to the personal allowance. Therefore under section 64, the only effective option is to offset the 2019/20 trading loss against net income of the prior tax year 2018/19 namely £39,000.
3. It should be noted that as a result of the section 64 loss claim, the personal allowance for 2018/19 is wasted.
4. After this offset 48,000 - 39,000 = 9,000 of trading loss remains unrelieved. This must then be carried forward under section 83 against future *trading profits* (not net income) of future tax years (i.e. in this example 2020/21).

In general, the most tax efficient way to utilise section 64 relief is to offset the trading loss against the prior tax year's net income and then if any unused trading loss remains, then claim against the net income of the tax year of the loss. In other words, in most cases, the sooner tax relief can be obtained the better. However, if the rate of tax charged on other income of the year of loss is higher than the previous year, then a current year claim should be prioritised.

Cap on income tax reliefs

From 6 April 2013, there has been a restriction on the maximum relief that can be claimed against other income under section 64 or section 72. The loss claim against other income is restricted to the greater of £50,000 and 25% of adjusted total income. There is no cap on the loss that can be claimed against profits of the same trade. Adjusted total income is total income less gross personal pension contributions paid. The cap also applies to allowable loan interest.

Example 8.3

Greg has been trading for a number of years and prepares his accounts to 30 September each year and has the following results:

Year ended 30.09.19 trading profit   £28,000
Year ended 30.09.20 trading loss   £100,000
Greg also has rental income for 2019/20 of £60,000.

What is the maximum loss that Greg can claim for 2019/20 under section 64?

Before the loss claim Greg's tax position for 2019/20 is as follows:

Trading profits	(to 30/9/19)	28,000
Rental income		60,000
Net Income		88,000

Greg may claim, under section 64, the loss to 30.09.20 to be utilised against the trading profits of the previous year, without restriction. However, the claim against other income is limited to the greater of £50,000 and 25% of adjusted total income. The loss claim against 2019/20 will be:

Trading profits	28,000
Rental Income	60,000
Less s64 loss	(78,000)
Net income	10,000

Notes

1. The maximum loss available against trading profits is the full amount of the trading profits of £28,000, without restriction.
The maximum loss available against other income is restricted to the greater of:
(a)   £50,000, and
(b)   25% of adjusted total income (i.e. 88,000 x 25% = 22,000)
Therefore, the claim is limited to £50,000.
The total s64 loss claim will be £78,000 (£28,000 + £50,000).
2. The personal allowance would then be deducted from net income to calculate taxable income. As net income is less than the personal allowance, the balance of the personal allowance will be wasted.

Trading loss offset against capital gains (ITA 2007 section 71)

It may make sense to return to study this part after a study of capital gains in Chapter 13 has been undertaken.

This relief is a little unusual as it permits an *income* loss to be offset against a *capital* gain. Normally, income losses may only be offset against income and capital losses only against capital gains.

This loss relief is only available for any tax year after loss relief against other income, under section 64, has been claimed.

The trading loss for the tax year must first be offset against net income of the same tax year and assuming a part of the trading loss still remains unrelieved this surplus may then be offset against any capital gains less capital losses of the same tax year.

However, although the trading loss is offset against current tax year net gains the actual amount of the surplus trading loss available for relief is, in fact, the *lower* of the unrelieved trading loss and net capital gains less capital losses brought forward.

Example 8.4

Lucy has the following income and gains arising for 2020/21:

Trading loss	£30,000
Net other income	£20,000
Capital gain	£40,000
Capital loss	£16,000
Unrelieved capital loss brought forward from earlier years	£9,000

The capital gains annual exemption for 2020/21 is £12,300.

Calculate for 2020/21:
(a) the section 64 loss relief against net income, and
(b) the additional section 71 loss relief against chargeable gains.

Answer

(a) Income tax computation, 2020/21

Net income	20,000
Less: section 64 loss relief	(20,000)
Taxable income	nil

Therefore, unrelieved trading loss for 2020/21 is 30,000 less 20,000 = 10,000.

(b) Capital gains computation 2020/21

Current year gain		40,000
Less: current year capital loss		(16,000)
		24,000
Less: section 71 trading loss relief – *lower* of:		
(i) Unrelieved trading loss after s.64 relief	10,000	
(ii) Net current year gains	24,000	
Less: b/f capital loss	(9,000)	
	15,000	(10,000)
		14,000
Less capital loss b/f		(1,700)
		12,300
Less: annual exemption		(12,300)

Taxable amount   nil

Notes

1. Before section 71 relief could be claimed for the tax year of the trading loss (i.e. 2020/21) the 30,000 trading loss must be relieved under section 64 against net income for tax year 2020/21.
2. As the net income is reduced by the section 64 loss to £0, the personal allowance is wasted.
3. As a surplus trading loss of 10,000 arose after section 64 relief then section 72 could be claimed.
4. The amount of the surplus trading loss of 10,000 which is available to be offset against net current year capital gains (i.e. 24,000) is the *lower* of the surplus trading loss (i.e. 10,000) and net current tax year capital gains (i.e. 24,000) less any capital losses brought forward (i.e. 9,000) i.e. 15,000. In this case, the whole of the surplus trading loss of 10,000 is available for offset against the capital gains for the tax year 2020/21.
5. Having offset the trading loss against net capital gains under section 72 the resulting 14,000 of net capital gains remaining can then be reduced by using a part of the capital loss brought forward.
6. The amount used under point 5. above is restricted to leave in charge to CGT an amount equal to the annual exemption for 2020/21 i.e. 12,300 (see Chapter 13). The final chargeable gains amount is then "nil".
7. 7,300 of the capital loss b/f (i.e. 9,000 – 1,700) can then be carried forward for offset against future capital gains.

Trading losses offset in the early years of trade (section 72)

In the early years of a sole trader's trade, where trading losses arise there may be no other income to claim these against. However, a special loss relief is available in the first four tax years of trading.

Any trading loss arising in the first four tax years of a trade may be claimed against net income of the three tax years immediately preceding the tax year of the trading loss beginning with the earliest and ending with the latest tax year (i.e. a so-called First in First Out (FIFO) basis). The loss must be claimed within one year of 31 January following the end of the tax year in which the loss arose.

Although section 72 only applies in these particular circumstances, a sole trader may still choose to utilise either sections 64, 83 and/or section 71 if preferred. Generally speaking, however, in these circumstances section 72 is likely to give maximum tax relief soonest.

A typical scenario might be where an employee decides to leave employment and set up their own sole trader business. Under section 72 any early tax year trading losses might be carried back and offset against earlier tax year's net income, which will, of course, include the person's salary. It may then be possible to obtain a tax refund for some or all those earlier tax years.

Example 8.5

Tim started in business on 1 July 2018 (i.e. 2018/19) and prepares his accounts to 30 June each year. His results are as follows:

y/e 30 June 2019 Trading loss	£30,000
y/e 30 June 2020 Trading profit	£15,500

Before setting up his own business Tim was an employee and received the following salary:

2017/18	£11,000
2016/17	£28,000
2015/16	£21,000

Tim also receives savings income of £500 each tax year.

Show Tim's tax position if loss relief under section 72 is claimed.

Answer

First, it is necessary to calculate Tim's trading profit/loss for each tax year. This involves using the basis period rules discussed in Chapter 6.

First tax year is 2018/19 and produces a trading loss of 9/12 x 30,000 = 22,500

Second tax year is 2019/20 and produces a trading loss of 30,000 - 22,500 = 7,500

However, if a trading loss arises in the first period of trading, relief for the loss cannot be given twice (i.e. overlap profits are possible but not overlap losses). Thus, for 2019/20 the normal basis period of 1.7.18 to 30.6.19, which gives a trading loss of 30,000, needs to be reduced by the trading loss of 22,500 (for 1.7.18 to 5.4.19) for the tax year 2018/19.

	2015/16	2016/17	2017/18	2018/19	2019/20	2020/21
Trading income	n/a	n/a	n/a	nil	nil	15,500
Salary	21,000	28,000	11,000	nil	nil	nil
Savings income	500	500	500	500	500	500
Net income	21,500	28,500	11,500	500	500	16,000
Less:						
Section 72 relief	(21,500)	(1,000)				
Section 72 relief		(7,500)				
Revised net income	0	20,000	11,500	500	500	16,000

Notes

1. For each year the revised Net income would be reduced by the personal allowance available.
2. The trading loss of 2018/19 must be considered first i.e. before the later trading loss of 2019/20.
3. Under section 72 this loss is carried back three preceding tax years to 2015/16 and offset against that tax year's net income first and then any remaining loss against 2016/17.
4. The trading loss of 7,500 for 2019/20 can similarly be carried back under section 72 to the preceding three tax years and thus in this case to 2016/17 first where the remaining net income after relief for the 27,500 (i.e. 28,500 - 1,000) can be offset by the 7,500.
5. Note, however, that the use of the 2018/19 trading loss in 2015/16 resulted in a loss of the personal allowance for that tax year.
6. The cap of income tax reliefs must be considered in all section 72 claims.

How would the above position compare if Tim had instead decided to utilise section 64 relief rather than section 72 relief?

	2015/16	2016/17	2017/18	2018/19	2019/20	2020/21
Trading income	n/a	n/a	n/a	nil	nil	15,500
Less:						
Section 83	-	-	-	-	-	(15,500)
Salary	21,000	28,000	11,000	nil	nil	nil
Other income	500	500	500	500	500	500
Net income	21,500	28,500	11,500	500	500	500
Less:						
Section 64 relief	nil	nil	(11,500)	nil	nil	nil
Revised net income	21,500	28,500	nil	500	500	500

Notes

1. Under section 64 £11,500 of the trading loss of 2018/19 has been claimed against the previous tax year's (i.e. 2017/18) net income reducing it to nil. The balance (i.e. 22,500 - 11,500) 11,000 could be offset against net income for 2018/19 under section 64. However, the income for 2018/19 would be covered by the personal allowance and this claim is not made, leaving 11,000 of 2018/19 trading loss which can only now be carried forward under section 83.
2. The trading loss of 2019/20 of £7,500 could be claimed under section 64 to offset the net income for that tax year. However, the income for 2019/20 is covered by the personal allowance and this claim is not made, leaving the loss of 7,500 also to be carried forward under section 83.
3. In 2019/20 the loss of £15,500 offset under section 83 comprises the balance of 11,000 from 2018/19 and 4,500 from 2012/20, leaving 3,000 to carry forward to 2021/22.

Comparing the taxable income under each option shows that where earlier tax relief is obtained using section 72 i.e. 2015/16 and 2016/17 the overall taxable income is lower and therefore less tax would be paid for those tax years. Full calculations including personal allowances would be required to make a final decision for the optimum loss claim.

Trading losses in the closing year (section 89 terminal loss relief)

Terminal loss relief only arises when a sole trader ceases to trade.

A terminal loss is the trading loss of the last 12 months of trading.

Under section 89 such a loss may be claimed against any trading profits of the three tax years preceding the tax year of cessation (taking the later tax years first; i.e. a LIFO basis approach). The loss must be claimed within four years from the end of the tax year in which the trade ceased.

The terminal loss is calculated as the trading loss of the last 12 months of trading less any part of which may have been relieved first under section 64. The terminal loss is calculated by adding together the following components:

(i) the actual trading loss from 6 April to the date of cessation

(ii) the actual trading loss incurred from a date 12 months before the date of cessation to the following 5 April.

If either (i) or (ii) produces a profit then it is assumed to be nil for the purpose of calculating the terminal loss.

Any overlap profits still unrelieved are added to the amount under (i) above.

Remember from Chapter 6 that on a sole trader's cessation the basis period for the final tax year is from the end of the basis period of the immediately preceding tax year prior to cessation to the date of cessation.

Example 8.6

Lynn prepares her accounts to 30 June each year. Lynn ceased to trade on 31 May 2020. Her trading profits and losses are as follows:

Year ended 30 June 2017 Trading profit £70,000
Year ended 30 June 2018 Trading profit £36,000
Year ended 30 June 2019 Trading profit £12,000

The 11 month period ended 31 May 2020 produced a trading loss of £44,000.

Lynn has overlap profits unrelieved of £15,000.

Show Lynn's position assuming a section 89 terminal loss claim is made.

Answer

The terminal loss is the trading loss for the 12 months 1.6.19 to 31.5.20 (date of cessation).
This period is split:
2020/21 *(6/4/20 to 31/5/20)*
Trading loss for this period

Loss to 31/5/20 44,000 x 2/11 months =	(8,000)
Overlap profits unrelieved	(15,000)
	(23,000)

2019/20 *(1.6.19 to 5.4.20)*
Trading loss for this period

Loss to 31/5/20 44,000 x 9/11 =	(36,000)	
Profit to 30/6/19 12,000 x 1/12	1,000	
	(35,000)	
Therefore terminal loss		(58,000)

	2017/18	2018/19	2019/20	2020/21
Trading profit	70,000	36,000	12,000	nil
Less:				
Section 89 relief	(10,000)	(36,000)	(12,000)	nil
Trading profit	60,000	nil	nil	nil

Notes
1. For the tax year of cessation i.e. 2020/21, a trading loss of 44,000 arose plus unrelieved overlap profits of 15,000 i.e. 59,000. However, the terminal loss relief claim is restricted to 58,000 as shown.
2. The terminal loss has been relieved first against the trading profit for tax year 2019/20 then carried back to 2018/19 and then to 2017/18.

Trading loss relief following incorporation of a sole trader business (section 86)

It is not unusual for a sole trader after having traded for a while to contemplate converting their business into a limited company. Normally, any losses are personal to the trader and cannot be transferred. However, subject to the satisfaction of certain conditions, unrelieved accumulated trading losses arising at the date of incorporation from the sole-tradership may be carried forward to be offset against the first available income of the former proprietor which he or she receives from the company provided the shares allotted are still held. Available income includes salary and dividends. This relief will only apply where the business is transferred to a limited company and the whole or main consideration is the allotment of shares to the former sole trader.

The trading losses unrelieved and carried forward are offset first against earned income (i.e. salaries and directors' fees) and then against unearned income (i.e. dividends).

Example 8.7

On the advice of his accountant, Vlad transferred his sole trader business to a limited company, VC Ltd, on 1 July 2019. The consideration for the transfer was an issue of ordinary shares. As at the date of the transfer of the business Vlad had unrelieved trading losses of £55,000. Vlad's salary from the company is £16,000 per annum and dividends of £5,000 per annum are received in December each year.

Show how Vlad will obtain relief under section 86 for the trading losses from his business.

Answer

	2019/20	2020/21	2021/22
Employment income	12,000	16,000	16,000
S86 loss relief	(12,000)	(16,000)	(16,000)
Dividends	5,000	5,000	5,000
S86 loss relief	(5,000)	(5,000)	(1,000)
Net income	nil	nil	4,000

Notes

1. The trading loss of 55,000 has been offset in each tax year, commencing with tax year 2019/20, first against the salary Vlad draws and then against any dividends received.
2. The salary of 12,000 for 2019/20 arises because Vlad only worked for VC Ltd in that tax year for nine months i.e. 1.7.18 to 5.4.19 giving 9/12 x 16,000 = 12,000.
3. The trading loss of 55,000 is exhausted in tax year 2021/22.
4. There is no loss relief against National Insurance Contributions, so Vlad will have a Class 1 NIC liability for all years on his salary.

SUMMARY

Utilising trading losses in the most tax efficient manner may require several "what if" calculations to be prepared to review the various options.

In general, it will be beneficial to claim losses against income that attracts a tax charge at the highest rate and as far as possible avoids wasting personal allowances.

Assuming that none of the special circumstances arise (e.g. trade cessation; incorporation; etc.) then, generally speaking, trading losses of a tax year should be offset under section 64 against the prior tax year's net income and any surplus loss remaining unrelieved should then be offset under section 64 against current tax year net income. Any remaining unrelieved trading loss can then be carried forward under section 83 for offset against future trading profits.

Questions for students

See Appendix 2 for practice questions relating to Chapter 8. Answers are available online.

CHAPTER 9

Partnerships

INTRODUCTION

This chapter examines how partners in a trading partnership are taxed.

General

The first thing to note is that a partnership is not a separate taxpayer. Whereas a company is a taxpayer in its own right separate from its shareholders, directors and employees, a partnership is not.

As a consequence, it is the individual partners, and not the partnership itself, who are taxed.

Basis of assessment

Although a partnership is not a separate taxpayer, an overall partnership trading profit is computed for a period of account adopting the same rules as apply to a sole trader (see Chapter 6).

This overall partnership trading profit is then allocated amongst the partners according to the profit sharing ratios laid down in the partnership agreement and each partner is then subject to income tax accordingly on their share of the profits. A partnership tax return is required each tax year to supply this information to HMRC with filing penalties for each partner for late submission.

Each partner is effectively treated as if he or she is, in fact, a sole trader, applying all of the normal rules to identify their basis period (see Chapter 6). In addition, all the ways in which a sole trader may offset a trading loss (e.g. section 64; section 83 etc.; see Chapter 8) also apply to each individual partner.

Partnership profit sharing arrangements

Each partner in a partnership is entitled to a share of the partnership profit for a period of account.

In a simple partnership, each partner will be entitled to a percentage share of the profits (or using partnership share ratios). However, other prior allocations may be made. For example, partners may be entitled to a "salary" before the remaining profits are shared (these amounts are not, however, salaries in the employment income sense; see Chapter 10).

It is also not unusual for a partner to receive interest on any capital which they may have contributed to the partnership. Again, this is a share of the profits and not assessed as savings income.

Therefore, in sharing out any partnership profit for a period of account, any interest paid on capital during that period of account and any "salaries" already paid again during that period of account must be taken into consideration, before profit shares.

Example 9.1

John, Jackie and James commenced trading as a partnership on 1 January 2019. They share profits in the ratios of 3:2:1. They each contributed capital as follows and each receives interest thereon at 5%:

John	£50,000
Jackie	£45,000
James	£30,000

Each partner is to receive a salary of £25,000 per annum.

The partnership accounts are prepared to 31 December each year and the adjusted taxable trading profits for the partnership are as follows:

Year ended 31 December 2019 £125,000

Year ended 31 December 2020 £200,000

Calculate each partner's trading profit assessment for the tax years 2017/18, 2018/19, and 2019/20.

Answer

	John	Jackie	James	Total
Period of account:				
1/1/19 to 31/12/19:				
Salary	25,000	25,000	25,000	75,000
Interest on capital:				
5% of £50,000	2,500			2,500
5% of £45,000		2,250		2,250
5% of £30,000			1,500	1,500
Balance of profit share				
3:2:1	21,875	14,583	7,292	**43,750**
Total	49,375	41,833	33,792	125,000
Period of account:				
1/1/20 to 31/12/20:				
Salary	25,000	25,000	25,000	75,000
Interest on capital:				
5% of £50,000	2,500			2,500
5% of £45,000		2,250		2,250
5% of £30,000			1,500	1,500
Balance of profit share				
3:2:1	59,375	39,583	19,792	**118,750**
Total	86,875	66,833	46,292	200,000

Notes

1. The steps in the calculation for each period of account are as follows:

   First, salary and interest on capital are calculated for each partner and then aggregated;

   Second, the total balance of profit share (the figure in bold above i.e. **43,750**) is calculated by deducting the total salaries plus total interest on capital from the trading profit for that period of account (i.e. for 1.1.19 to 31.12.19 125,000 − (75,000 + 2,500 + 2,250 + 1,500) = 43,750

Third, this total balance profit share figure (i.e. 43,750) is then divided according to the profit share ratios (i.e. 3:2:1) to give the figures *21,875 14,583 and 7,292* for John, Jackie and James respectively.

Finally, salary, interest on capital and profit share are added to find the total share of the profits for each individual partner.

2. The above steps are then repeated for each subsequent period of account.

It now becomes necessary to work out each partner's individual trading profit assessment for each tax year.

Remember that to do this the normal sole trader basis period rules apply. Thus:

Name of partner	Tax year	Basis period	Assessment	
John	2018/19	1/1/19 to 5/4/19	3/12 x 49,375 =	12,344
	2019/20	1/1/19 to 31/12/19		49,375
	2020/21	1/1/20 to 31/12/20		86,875
Jackie	2018/19	1/1/19 to 5/4/19	3/12 x 41,833 =	10,458
	2019/20	1/1/19 to 31/12/19		41,833
	2020/21	1/1/20 to 31/12/20		66,833
James	2018/19	1/1/19 to 5/4/19	3/12 x 33,792 =	8,448
	2019/20	1/1/19 to 31/12/19		33,792
	2020/21	1/1/20 to 31/12/20		46,292

Notes

1. As the partnership started to trade on 1 January 2019 then the tax year 2018/19 is the first tax year of trading and the opening year basis period rules apply.
2. Each partner is treated as a sole trader and their assessable profits are computed accordingly.
3. Overlap profits also arise for each partner. The overlap period is in each case the period 1.1.19 to 5.4.19.

Changes during a period of account

It may be that either or all of salaries, interest on capital and balance of profit shares may change during a period of account. In this case, this needs to be taken into account. Nevertheless, the above approach is still adopted.

Example 9.2

Sally and Emma have been in partnership for a number of years preparing their partnership accounts to 30 September each year. For the year ended 30 September 2020 the partnership adjusted taxable trading profit is £60,000.

With effect from 1 July 2020 Sally and Emma agreed to change their profit shares and the salaries each receive. Up to 30 June 2020, the salaries for Sally and Emma were £15,000 p.a. and £20,000 p.a. respectively and from 1 July 2020 were changed to £18,000 p.a. and £25,000 p.a.

Profit shares were also changed from 3:2 to 2:1 from 1 July 2020

Show the allocations for the period of account 1.10.19 to 30.9.20.

Answer

	Sally	Emma	Total
Period of account 1/10/19 to 30/9/20			
1/10/19 to 30/6/20			
Salary			
9/12 x 15,000	11,250		11,250
9/12 x 20,000		15,000	15,000
Balance of profit share			
3:2	11,250	7,500	**18,750**
Total (9/12 x 60,000)	22,500	22,500	45,000
1/7/20 to 30/9/20			
Salary			
3/12 x 18,000	4,500		4,500
3/12 x 25,000		6,250	6,250
Balance of profit share			
2:1	2,833	1,417	**4,250**
Total (3/12 x 60,000)	7,333	7,667	15,000
Total for year	29,833	30,167	60,000

Notes

1. As the profit share ratios change *during* (and not at the end of a period of account) it is necessary to split the period of account (i.e. 1/10/19 to 30/9/20) into separate periods; one period from the start of the period of account to the date of the changes (i.e. 1/10/19 to 30/6/20) and one from that date to the end of the period of account (i.e. 1/7/20 to 30/9/20). The adjusted profit for the period of account is then split into these two periods (i.e. 45,000 and 15,000 each respectively 9/12ths and 3/12ths of 60,000).
2. The salaries etc. for each partner have also changed and account needs to be taken of these changes also.
3. A simple time apportionment approach is taken.
4. Also, note that interest on capital is not always paid.

Changes in the partnership

Typically during the lifetime of a partnership, some partners will leave the partnership and new partners will join.

For those who leave they will be treated as ceasing to trade. Similarly, for those who join they will be treated as commencing to trade.

For the partners who continue to trade both before and after such changes, there are no tax effects upon them; they will simply continue to be assessed on the relevant basis.

In other words, for any partnership it may be that for a particular tax year some partners (i.e. those just joining) will be assessed using the commencement rules; some will be assessed using the cessation rules (i.e. those leaving); whilst the remaining partners will be assessed on the usual CYB basis (see Chapter 6).

Example 9.3

John and Kevin have been in partnership since they started trading on 1 July 2016. The partnership accounts are prepared to 30 June each year. On 1 July 2017, Lisa joins the partnership. On 30 June 2019 Kevin retires from the partnership leaving John and Lisa as partners.

For simplicity, assume that profits are always shared equally and that no salaries or interest on capital are paid.

Adjusted profits are:

Year ended 30 June 2017	£50,000
Year ended 30 June 2018	£60,000
Year ended 30 June 2019	£120,000
Year ended 30 June 2020	£200,000

Show the assessments for each partner for the relevant tax years.

Answer

Period of account	John	Kevin	Lisa	Total
1/7/16 to 30/6/17				
Profit share				
1:1	25,000	25,000	nil	50,000
Period of account				
1/7/17 to 30/6/18				
Profit share				
1:1:1	20,000	20,000	20,000	60,000
Period of account				
1/7/18 to 30/6/19				
Profit share				
1:1:1	40,000	40,000	40,000	120,000
Period of account				
1/7/19 to 30/6/20				
Profit share				
1:1	100,000	nil	100,000	200,000

Name of partner	Tax year	Basis period	Assessment
John	2016/17	1/7/16 to 5/4/17	9/12 x 25,000 = 18,750
	2017/18	1/7/16 to 30/6/17	25,000
	2018/19	1/7/17 to 30/6/18	20,000
	2019/20	1/7/18 to 30/6/19	40,000
	2020/21	1/7/19 to 30/6/20	100,000
Kevin	2016/17	1/7/16 to 5/4/17	9/12 x 25,000 =18,750
	2017/18	1/7/16 to 30/6/17	25,000
	2018/19	1/7/17 to 30/6/18	20,000
	2019/20	1/7/18 to 30/6/19	40,000
		Less: Overlap relief	(18,750)
			21,250
	2020/21 (Not a partner after 30/6/19)		Nil

Lisa	2016/17 (Not a partner until 1/7/17)	Nil
	2017/18	1/7/17 to 5/4/18 9/12 x 20,000= 15,000
	2018/19	1/7/17 to 30/6/18	20,000
	2019/20	1/7/18 to 30/6/19	40,000
	2020/21	1/7/19 to 30/6/20	100,000

Note

1. The opening tax year basis rules applied to John and Kevin for tax year 2016/17 but to 2017/18 for Lisa. For 2019/20 when Kevin left the partnership, the cessation basis rules applied to Kevin for that tax year. This happened to be the same basis period as for John and Lisa for 2019/20 because Kevin left on the last day of the period of account. However, unlike John and Lisa, Kevin can obtain relief for his overlap profits of 18,750 in his tax year of cessation.
2. You will note that if you total Kevin's profit share for each accounting period, this is equal to his total assessable profits for all years.

Capital allowances

As in the case of the sole trader, capital allowances are treated as a tax-deductible trading expense.

However, it may be that some assets are owned by the partnership as a whole, for example, office equipment and furniture (both qualifying as plant and machinery for capital allowance purposes; see Chapter 7) whereas some assets are owned by the individual partners, for example, motor cars.

In such cases, capital allowances are computed on all assets for the relevant period of account of the partnership as normal. Individual partners cannot claim capital allowances on their own behalf.

Example 9.4

John and Jane are in a partnership which owns all the assets except for two cars which they each own individually.

For the year ended 31 December 2020 the partnership adjusted trading profit *before* capital allowances is £175,000. John and Jane share profits 3:2 respectively. John's salary is £20,000 p.a. and that of Jane £25,000 p.a.

The main pool partnership assets have a tax written down value as at 1 January 2020 of £100,000.

John's car has a tax written down value at this time of £20,000 and Jane's £10,000. Both cars have CO_2 emissions of less than 110g/km.

John uses his car 70% for business; Jane uses her car 60% for business.

Calculate John and Jane's profit allocations.

Answer

Capital allowances for the period of account 1/1/20 to 31/12/20

INCOME TAX

	General Pool	Private use cars		CA Claimed
		John	Jane	
TWDV 1/1/20	100,000	20,000	10,000	
WDA (18% p.a.)	(18,000)	(3,600)	(1,800)	18,000
		John 3,600 x 70% =		2,520
		Jane 1,800 x 60% =		1,080
		Capital allowances claim		21,600
TWDV 31/12/20	82,000	16,400	8,200	

Therefore partnership adjusted taxable trading profit for year ended 31.12.20 is:

Trading profit pre CAs	175,000
Less CAs	(21,600)
Trading profit post CAs	153,400

Partnership Profit Allocation for Period of account 1.1.20 to 31.12.20

	John	Jane	Total
Salary	20,000	25,000	45,000
Balance of profit share			
3:2	65,040	43,360	108,400
Profit share	85,040	68,360	153,400

Trading losses

Trading losses are allocated to individual partners in the same manner in which partnership profits are allocated.

Once allocated each partner may then individually utilise any of the loss reliefs available to a sole trader (see Chapter 8).

If as a result of the profit allocation some partners have losses and some profits, then the losses must first be reallocated against the profit-making partners.

Limited liability partnerships

Such partnerships are a relatively new vehicle.

The basic concept is that under such partnerships each partner's liability to contribute to, for example, third parties claims against the partnership and partnership losses is limited by agreement. Normally, a partner's exposure to such items is joint and unlimited.

For tax purposes, the partner's taxable profits are as calculated above. However, the one difference is in connection with losses.

The amount of any trading loss which may be offset against a partner's other income is limited to the amount of capital the partner has contributed to the partnership.

SUMMARY

The key issue to note in connection with partnerships is that the partnership as a whole is not itself taxed. Instead, the individual partners are taxed on their share of the partnership profit.

However, to ascertain a partner's share of the partnership profit requires that the partnership's overall taxable profit be computed. This is done in the same manner as for a sole trader. The profits are then divided between the individual partners following the partnership agreement and each partner is then effectively assessed to income tax on their share of the profits following the basis of assessment for sole traders.

Relief for trading losses is available to each partner as they are to a sole trader.

CHAPTER 10

Employee Taxation

INTRODUCTION

This chapter considers the tax aspects associated with employees including the taxation of non-cash benefits provided by an employer to an employee, such as a company car.

General

Employment income is taxed under the Income Tax (Earnings and Pensions) Act 2003 (ITEPA 2003).

Employed or self-employed

Identifying whether an individual is an employee (i.e. works for an employer under a contract of employment) or is self-employed (i.e. works for himself/herself in his/her own business) is important as the tax treatments are different in each case. Currently, this question is often in the news in connection with workers within the "gig economy".

An employee is taxed under ITEPA 2003 whereas a self-employed individual is taxed under the provisions of ITTOIA 2017 (see Chapter 6).

The basic division between the two is that an employee has a contract *of* service whereas a self-employed individual will have a contract *for* services.

Although there are no exact rules for determining whether an individual is self-employed or an employee, factors which would be taken into account include:

- control over how the work is to be done
- whether the individual provides their own equipment
- whether the individual can hire helpers or a substitute when unavailable
- who bears the financial risk
- the degree of management exercised
- the extent to which the individual can profit from their works
- whether work is carried out for only one client/customer
- the mutual obligation to provide work and perform work
- method of payment for work done
- holiday/sick pay entitlement

As indicated above usually no one single factor determines the issue. All of the factors must be reviewed and then a decision is taken based on the overall picture.

Some of the main differences between the self-employed and an employee are:

- a self-employed person is liable to income tax under the self assessment provisions and may be required to make two payments on account of the tax year's liability and a balancing payment (see Chapter 21) whereas an employee pays income tax on earnings each month (or week) under Pay As You Earn Regulations (PAYE) i.e. self-employed income tax payments are made later;

- the expense rules (i.e. those expenses which are tax deductible) for an employee are more rigorous than for the self-employed i.e. more difficult to satisfy; and
- a self-employed person pays Class 2 and 4 National Insurance Contributions (NICs) whereas an employee pays Class 1; the latter is greater than the former (see Chapter 20).

Personal Service Companies

Many individuals choose to work for their clients using their own limited companies, referred to by HMRC as 'personal service companies' and in recent years there have been a number of high profile cases considering this area.

Limited companies can be a tax efficient way for individuals to work. The individual may divide the income that they take from their company between salary and dividends, with a resulting saving as NICs are not charged on dividends. By using a limited liability company, individuals are also protected to a certain extent from business risk.

The term 'personal service companies' was introduced from April 2000 under the so-called IR35 legislation. The legislation applies to relevant engagements, where a "worker" provides services to a client through an intermediary, usually a company, where, if the intermediary company did not exist, this individual providing services to a client would be treated as an employee and not as self-employed.

In effect, the personal service company rules treat almost all income from relevant engagements during a tax year as a deemed salary. The deemed payment is subject to both income tax and NICs, removing any benefits of drawing income as a dividend or simply leaving profits in the company.

There are detailed rules for these calculations which are beyond the scope of this text.

Employment income

An individual is liable under ITEPA 2003 to income tax on employment income. This may include salary, wages, tips/gratuities and so-called money's worth (i.e. something capable of being converted into money) plus amounts treated as earnings (i.e. benefits in kind as detailed below).

Basis of assessment

Receipt of money earnings

Earnings are taxable when received not when earned even if they are not for that tax year. Receipt occurs at the earlier of the following:

- when payment is made of or on account of earnings, or
- when a person becomes entitled to payment.

For directors, receipt can occur earlier:

- at the date when a sum is agreed or credited in the company's accounts or records (e.g. crediting the director's account will constitute receipt);
- the end of a period of account if the amount of the director's income is determined for that period before it ends;
- the date that the director's income for a period of account is determined if after the period ends.

Example 10.1

Peter receives an annual bonus based on the results of his employer. For the year to 31 March 2020, Peter was entitled to a bonus of £12,500 and this was made available to him on 1 July 2020. For the year to 31 March 2021, Peter is due a bonus of £15,600 and he was entitled to this on 14 August 2021. How much bonus will be assessable on Peter during the year to 5 April 2021?

Answer

It is irrelevant which period the bonus relates to. Using the rules above, Peter became entitled to the bonus of £12,500 on 1 July 2020 and this will be included in his taxable income to 5 April 2021. The bonus of £15,600 will fall to be assessed in the following tax year.

Receipt of non-money earnings

Benefits (other than non-cash vouchers)

Earnings not consisting of money or cash are normally treated as received in the tax year when the benefit is provided. This rule applies to the provision of:

- cash vouchers;
- credit tokens;
- living accommodation;
- cars, vans and related benefits;
- loans;
- other benefits in kind;
- use of an asset without transfer; and
- transfer of used asset.

Non-cash vouchers

For non-cash vouchers receipt occurs:

- in the tax year in which cost of provision is incurred; or
- if later, the tax year in which voucher received by the employee.

Otherwise, receipt occurs when the benefit is provided to the employee.

Vouchers and credit tokens

Non Cash vouchers (i.e. one exchangeable for goods or services but not cash) give a benefit equivalent to the expense incurred by the employer in providing the vouchers (i.e. not on its exchange value).

Cash vouchers (i.e. vouchers which can be exchanged for cash) are treated as pay and therefore are treated as income equal to the cash exchange value.

Credit tokens (e.g. a company credit card) give rise to a benefit equal to the cost to the employer of providing the goods, services etc. obtained using the credit token.

Benefits in kind

In addition to receiving a salary, an employee may also receive benefits in kind or "perks". Benefits in kind refer to items of additional remuneration that are not in the form of cash, such as a company car, an interest-free loan or provision of private health insurance etc.

Although these are not rewards in the form of monetary consideration they are provided in return for work done or services provided by the employee. They are therefore in principle subject to income tax in the same way that an employee's salary is.

The legislation sets out how benefits in kind are to be valued for income tax.

However, not all benefits are subject to income tax – some benefits are exempt from income tax; see below.

Approach to use when working out the value of a benefit

When working out the value of a benefit for a tax year the general approach is:

STEP 1: Work out the value of the benefit for the whole tax year according to the relevant provision.

STEP 2: Reduce the value in Step 1 to the extent that the benefit is not available for any part of the tax year (e.g. because it was provided part way through tax year).

STEP 3: Deduct from the value arrived at in Step 2 any deductible employee contributions towards the benefit (e.g. because the employee may contribute to the cost of the benefit). Any amounts made good must be paid by 6 July following the end of the tax year to be deductible.

Taxable value of benefits in kind

General rule

Where a benefit in kind is provided or given to an employee, the general rule is that the taxable value of the benefit is the cost to the employer, unless a specific statutory rule applies, for example for company cars.

The cost to the employer will be the marginal or additional cost where "in-house" benefits are provided, such as free flights for staff by an airline.

Example 10.2

ABM Ltd pays private medical insurance premiums for its employee Alan. The cost to the employer is £500. The insurance would cost Alan £650 personally.

Alan's taxable benefit is the cost to his employer of £500.

In other words, Alan's total employment income will be increased by £500.

Assets made available for private use

A taxable benefit arises where an employee is permitted to use an asset without ownership being transferred to the employee from the employer. In other words, the asset continues to belong to the employer.

In general, the measure of the benefit is the higher of:
- the annual value of the use of the asset; and
- the annual amount paid by the employer as rent or hire charges.

The annual value is equal to 20% of the asset's market value on the date that it is first provided to the employee.

The benefit is reduced by employee contributions and time apportionment where the asset is provided for part of tax year only.

Example 10.3

Janet is provided by her employer with a television for her personal use. It is provided on 6 July 2020 at which time it's market value is £700.

Calculate the benefit to Janet for the tax year 2020/21.

Answer

The annual benefit = 20% x 700 = 140

However as Janet only had the use of the television from 6 July 2020, the benefit in kind for 2020/21 will be 140 x 9/12 months = 105

These general rules do not apply, however, where a benefit is taxed according to its own specific statutory rule including living accommodation; company cars; vans; and beneficial loans.

Transfer of asset following use

If an asset, other than a car, owned by the employer and previously made available to an employee for use, is subsequently transferred to an employee the benefit arising from the transfer of title of the asset from employer to employee is the *greater* of:
- the market value of the asset at the date of transfer; and
- the market value of the asset when first made available for the employee's use less the aggregate of the use benefits assessed on the employee.

Example 10.4

Ollie has been using an asset provided by his employer from 6 April 2018 until 6 October 2020. On 6 October 2020, Ollie was given the asset by his employer when it's market value at that date was £2,750.

On 6 April 2018, the market value of the asset was £6,000.

Calculate Ollie's benefit for each relevant tax year.

Answer

The use benefit will be as follows:

2018/19	20% x 6,000	=	1,200
2019/20	20% x 6,000	=	1,200
2020/21	20% x 6,000 x 6/12 =		600

On 6 October 2020 Ollie was given a previously used asset.
The benefit of the purchase will be the greater of:
1. 2,750 (i.e. market value of the asset at the date of purchase), and
2. 6,000 – [1,200 + 1,200 + 600] (i.e. market value when first made available less use benefit) = 3,000

Therefore, Ollie will be assessed on the benefits as follows:

2018/19	1,200
2019/20	1,200
2020/21 600 + 3,000 =	3,600

Note

If Ollie had been given the asset outright on 6 April 2018, the benefit in kind would have been £6,000, being the market value of the asset at that time. You will note that the aggregate of the benefits in kind in the above example is also £6,000.

Living accommodation

The measure of the taxable benefit for the provision of living accommodation depends upon whether the accommodation is job or non-job related.

Not job-related accommodation

The benefit for the provision of accommodation comprises two parts:
Firstly, the *greater* of:
- the annual rateable value of the accommodation, *and*
- the rent paid by the employer

plus an additional charge where the cost of providing the accommodation exceeds £75,000. The additional charge is:

(Cost of provision - £75,000) x appropriate percentage.

The cost of provision is found by adding the original expenditure incurred by the employer to acquire the property and the cost of any improvements incurred *before* the tax year in question.

The *appropriate percentage* is the official interest rate applying to beneficial loans at the beginning of the relevant fiscal year for which the benefit is being valued (currently 2.25% for tax year 2020/21).

Cost of provision versus market value

"Market value" is substituted for "cost of provision" if the property has been owned by the employer for more than six years *at the date of the employee taking up occupation.*

Improvement expenditure incurred on the property *prior to the beginning of a tax year* increases the cost or market value as appropriate for that tax year. Note, however, that unless the cost of the accommodation is £75,000 or greater, market value cannot apply. Thus, if the original cost of providing the accommodation is less than £75,000 no additional charge can apply even if market value exceeds this cost.

Deductions from the additional charge occur for *bona fide* business use of the accommodation and/or for rent paid by the employee that exceeds the benefit under the normal charge (i.e. any rent paid by the employee is first offset against the basic charge and then against the additional charge).

Example 10.5

Dougie is provided with a house on 6 April 2020 which was purchased by his employer, DMP plc, for £550,000 in January 2017. The annual value of the house is £2,000 and Dougie pays rent of £500 a month to the company.

Calculate Dougie's assessable benefit for 2020/21, assuming the official rate of interest is 2.25%.

Answer

Benefit equals:

Annual value	2,000
Additional benefit 2.25% x (550,000 – 75,000)	10,687
	12,687
Less: Employee contribution (i.e. 500 x 12)	(6,000)
	6,687

Assuming the house had in fact been purchased before 6 April 2014 then the market value on 6 April 2020 would be substituted for the cost of the accommodation.

Example 10.6

MBT Ltd purchased a flat in 2006 for £100,000. Expenditure was subsequently incurred by MBT Ltd on property improvements of £60,000 in 2012 and a further £50,000 in December 2020. MBT Ltd made the property available, rent-free, to an employee, Michelle, on 6 April 2020.

The market value of the property was £250,000 on 6 April 2020 and £320,000 on 6 April 2021.

The annual rateable value of the property is £2,000.

Calculate Michelle's assessable benefit for 2020/21, assuming the official rate of interest is 2.25%.

Answer

Benefit equals:

Annual value	2,000
Additional benefit 2.25% x (250,000 – 75,000)	3,937
	5,937
Less: Contribution by employee	nil
	5,937

Notes

1. Additional benefit - at the date of the first occupation by Michelle the flat has been owned by MBT Ltd for more than six years after purchase; therefore, market value is substituted for cost i.e. 250,000 is used to determine the additional benefit.

2. The improvements in December 2010 (i.e. during the tax year 2020/21) will not affect the computation of the benefit for the tax year 2020/21 but will impact the benefit for the tax year 2021/22. For tax year 2021/22, the additional charge will be based upon the market value of 250,000 plus 50,000 i.e. 300,000.

Job-related accommodation

No benefit arises if the occupation of the property is 'job-related' i.e.

- where it is necessary for the employee to reside there to perform his or her duties e.g. a caretaker; *or*
- where it is customary to occupy it for the better performance of his or her duties; *or*
- if it is provided for the employee's personal security.

The first two exceptions do not apply to directors, other than full time working directors who do not own more than 5% of the employing company's ordinary share capital (i.e. have a material interest).

Ancillary expenses connected with living accommodation

Ancillary expenses of accommodation include:

- heating
- lighting
- cleaning
- repair and maintenance
- provision of furniture (at 20% of market value – see below)

Telephone costs (i.e. calls and line rental) are *not* regarded as "ancillary expenses" although they are treated as a benefit and taxable.

Where the accommodation is "job-related" the amount of the "ancillary expenses" which are treated as a benefit are normally restricted to 10% of "net earnings" i.e. salary plus benefits (other than ancillary benefits in question) less certain expenses (primarily, pension contributions to the employer's pension scheme and any own car mileage allowance expense claims). Note also that there is no assessment on council tax or rates paid by an employer where the accommodation is job-related.

INCOME TAX

The 10% restriction does not apply to directors, other than to full-time working directors without a material interest.

Example 10.7

Peter's employer PVP Ltd provides him with accommodation which cost £70,000 and has an annual rateable value of £1,000. In addition to providing the accommodation PVP Ltd also bears the costs of the accommodation during tax year 2020/21 as follows:

Electricity	1,340
Gas	1,200
Cleaning and maintenance	2,500
Telephone	850
Structural repairs	3,000

It has been agreed with the tax authorities that 70% of the telephone call charges relate to business use. The line rental included in the telephone costs is £50.

Calculate the assessable benefit for 2020/21 in respect of the ancillary expenses.

Answer

Benefits are taxable as follows:

Ancillary expenses:

Electricity	1,340
Gas	1,200
Cleaning and maintenance	2,500
	5,040
Telephone: line rental	50
Call costs	800
Less: business calls	(560)
	5,330

Notes

1. The accommodation benefit itself would simply be £1,000.
2. Ancillary expenses exclude telephone costs.
3. Line rental cannot be split into business and private elements; as a consequence all of the line rental cost is taxable.
4. Structural repairs are not taxable as they are the liability of the landlord and not the employee occupying the property.
5. If the accommodation had been job-related and Peter's salary had been £35,000 then the expenses benefit would have been the lower of 5,040 (total ancillary expenses) or 10% of (35,000 + 290) = 3,529.

Motor cars

Motor cars remain one of the most popular benefits provided to employees.

Not only is the provision of a car (a so-called company car) a taxable benefit but where any fuel (i.e. petrol or diesel) is paid for by the employer this gives rise to an additional benefit (see below).

Where a company car is made available for private use by an employee, the annual benefit in kind is calculated as follows:

(List price – capital contribution paid by the employee) x   % (based upon CO_2 emissions)

List price includes the original list price of the car (as published by the manufacturer at the time of the car's original registration), delivery charges (excluding road fund licence) and standard accessories fitted at the time of purchase. This may not be the actual price paid by the employer when purchasing the car, particularly if second hand (In fact, the car could be leased by the employer). Optional accessories fitted at the time of delivery are added to the list price.

Capital contribution by the employee applies where the employee contributes to the purchase price of the car. However, this figure is capped with a maximum deduction of £5,000.

% refers to the percentage which is determined according to the CO_2 emissions of the car as follows:

CO_2 Emissions	2020/21 Cars registered from 6 April 2020	2020/21 Older cars
Zero emissions	0%	0%
1g/km to 50g/km		
Electric range:		
130 miles or more	0%	2%
70 -129 miles	3%	5%
40 -69 miles	6%	8%
30-39 miles	10%	12%
Less than 30 miles	12%	14%
51g/km to 54g/km	13%	15%
55g/km to 59g/km	14%	16%
60g/km to 64 g/km	15%	17%
65g/km to 69 g/km	16%	18%
70g/km to 74 g/km	17%	19%

For each complete 5g/km above 70 g/km the % increases by 1% (an overall cap of 37% applies). Note that for electric or hybrid cars with CO_2 emissions below 50 g/km, lower percentages apply based on the electric driving range in miles.

The CO_2 rule above also applies to diesel cars but in this case, the % worked out as above is then increased by 4% (but again subject to a maximum of 37%). Diesel cars that meet the RDE2 standard will not be subject to this extra charge.

Where any accessory is added after delivery of the car has been taken, for the tax year in which they are fitted (and any subsequent tax years) the list price is increased by the cost of such items except that any individual accessory fitted at a cost of below £100 is ignored.

The benefit in kind calculated as above is regarded as taking into account various costs such as road tax, repairs and maintenance, insurance etc. (other than car fuel which as noted above is taxed as a benefit separately).

If the employee is required to make a payment towards the private use of the car, then this is deducted from the calculated benefit in kind.

If the car is not provided for the full tax year, the car benefit is apportioned on a time basis. In addition, the car must be unavailable for a continuous period of at least 30 days for a reduction to apply, for example, due to a repair.

Example 10.8

Graham is provided with a company car by his employer on 6 April 2020. The car has a CO_2 emission of 148g/km. The car cost Graham's employer £16,750, has a list price of £25,000 and was registered *before 6 April 2020*. Graham would like to know the likely benefit if the car is petrol and if it is diesel (Not RDE2 standard).

Answer

The base % is 19%

For each complete 5g/km above 70g/km the % increases by 1%

148g/km rounded down to 145 less base 70 = 75 above

75/5 increases the percentage by 15%

The % is therefore 19% + 15% = 34%

The benefit in kind is £25,000 x 34% = £8,500

If the car is a diesel car then the benefit is as above i.e. 34% but plus 4% = 38%. However, the maximum is 37%. Therefore, if the car has a diesel engine the benefit in kind would be increased to £25,000 x 37% = £9,250

Notes

1. The cost of the car is completely ignored. The benefit in kind is calculated on the list price of the car.

2. Graham will continue to be assessed to income tax on the benefit in kind for the car in subsequent years where the car remains available to him.

Example 10.9

Julia is provided with a petrol company car by her employer on 6 October 2020. The car has a CO_2 emission of 157 g/km, a list price of £19,000 and was registered *after 6 April 2020*.

Accessories were fitted in December 2020 costing £65, after Julia took delivery, and for £150 in May 2021.

Julia is required to contribute £30 per month towards the running costs of the car.

Calculate Julia's taxable car benefit.

Answer

The base % is 17%

For each complete 5g/km above 70g/km the % increases by 1%

157g/km rounded down to 155 less base 70 = 85 above

85/5 increases the percentage by 17%

The % is therefore 17% + 17% = 34%

The annual benefit in kind is £19,000 x 34% = £6,460. However, the car was only available to Julia for six months of this tax year.

Therefore, the benefit = 6/12 x 6,460 = £3,230. From this, Julia's contribution of £30 per month can be deducted (6 x £30) giving a net taxable benefit for 2020/21 of £3,050 (£3,230 - £180).

Note

The accessory fitted after delivery of £65 in 2020/21 is below the £100 threshold and thus ignored; the accessory fitted in 2021/22 tax year of £150 will be taken into account for 2021/22 and later tax years.

Example 10.10

Simon is a director of SBF Ltd. The company provided him with a company car with CO_2 emissions of 127g/km throughout 2020/21. The list price of the car was £36,000 and cost the company £25,000. The car was first registered *before 6 April 2020.*

Simon provided a capital contribution of £6,000. Simon's total mileage for the tax year was 12,500 miles of which 9,000 miles were on business.

Car tax, repairs and maintenance and car insurance paid by the employer for the tax year 2020/21 amounted to £2,750.

Calculate Simon's car benefit for 2020/21.

Answer

The base % is 19%

For each complete 5g/km above 70g/km the % increases by 1%

127g/km rounded down to 125 less base = 55 above

55/5 increases the percentage by 11%

The % is therefore 19% +11% = 30%

The list price of £36,000 is reduced by £5,000 in respect of the capital contribution (Any additional contribution above £5,000 is ignored).

The annual benefit in kind is (£36,000-£5,000) x 30% = £9,300

Notes

1. The cost of the car to the employer is irrelevant.
2. Simon's capital contribution is capped at £5,000.
3. The various expenses of the car are ignored as, other than fuel, such expenses are included in the car benefit.
4. Car mileage is also totally irrelevant.

Pool cars

There is no benefit for an employee provided with the use of a pool car.

A pool car is a car which meets *all* of the following conditions:
- the car is used by more than one employee or director, *and*
- there is no (or merely incidental) private use, *and*
- the car is not kept at or near the home of the employee overnight.

Car fuel benefit

A car fuel benefit arises where any private fuel is made available to an employee with a company car by reason of his or her employment.

The car fuel benefit is based upon the same CO_2 emissions as is the car benefit itself (see above). The same percentage figure will be used for both purposes (i.e. car benefit and fuel). Again the maximum percentage is 37%.

To calculate the benefit on the provision of fuel the relevant percentage figure will be multiplied by a set figure for the year. For the year 2020/21, the set figure is £24,500.

Therefore, if the car has a list price of less than £24,100, the fuel benefit will be higher than the car benefit.

Unlike the general rule for benefits under which an employee's contributions reduce the value of any benefit (See Step 3 of the general approach), where an employee makes any contributions towards car fuel costs these contributions do *not* reduce the benefit *unless* the employee contributes the full cost of their private fuel usage in which case no fuel benefit arises.

Example 10.11

Stephen is provided with a petrol-fuelled company car throughout the tax year 2020/21. The car has CO_2 emissions of 160g/km and was registered before 6 April 2020.

Stephen's employer pays for all the running expenses of the car including fuel for private purposes.

Stephen pays £20 per month towards the cost of private fuel.

Calculate Stephen's car fuel benefit for the tax year 2020/21.

Answer

% used to calculate the company car tax benefit itself for 2020/21 is:
[[19% + [(160 − 70)/5 x 1%]] = 37%.

The fuel scale charge for 2020/21 will therefore be:
24,500 x 37% = 9,065.

Notes
1. There is no reduction for the £20 contribution as Stephen does not pay for ALL private fuel.
2. As with other benefits, the benefit would be reduced on a time basis if the car is unavailable for use.

Example 10.12

Liz is employed by LSS Ltd. The company provided her with a diesel company car (Not RDE2 standard) with CO_2 emissions of 150 g/km.

The list price of the car is £25,000, cost her employer £8,700 and was registered before 6 April 2020. All car fuel is paid for by Liz's employer.

Liz's business mileage for the tax year 2020/21 was 20,000 miles and running costs of the car for this period (excluding car fuel costs) were £1,650.

Calculate Liz's benefits for the tax year 2020/21.

Answer

Car benefit

Benefit % = [[19% + [150 – 70]/5]] = 35% +4% diesel supplement but capped at 37%

Benefit 37% x 25,000 = 9,250

Fuel benefit

Benefit = 37% x 24,500 = 9,065

Total benefit = 9,250 + 9,065 = 18,315

Note

The cost of the car, the mileage and actual running costs have no impact on the calculation of the taxable benefits.

Car park space and chauffeur

The provision of a personal chauffeur creates an additional taxable benefit but the provision of a car park space at or close to the workplace does not.

Car transferred to an employee

If a car is transferred to an employer, a benefit in kind will arise equal to the market value of the car at the date of transfer less any amount paid for the car by the employee. Any amounts previously assessed on the employee as a benefit in kind in respect of the car have no impact on the taxable amount.

Vans

Vans are treated differently and, possibly, more favourably than motor cars.

Where a van is provided to an employee, with no restriction on private use, for 2020/21 the benefit in kind is £3,490, regardless of engine capacity and list price (a reduced benefit in kind applies to zero emission vans).

However, the benefit is nil, where the van is made available to the employee mainly for business travel and private use by the employee is prohibited, although ordinary commuting (travel from home to work) and insignificant private mileage are acceptable (for example a trip to the rubbish tip once or twice a year and regular slight detours to stop at a shop on the way to work).

There is an additional van fuel benefit of £666, for the tax year 2020/21, where private fuel is provided.

Beneficial loans

Interest-free or cheap loans to employees can give rise to a taxable benefit.

INCOME TAX

Loans which are caught are those where the interest paid by the employee in a tax year is less than that which should have been paid according to the official rate of interest (2.25% per annum at the time of publication).

However, if throughout a tax year the total value of all such loans does not exceed £10,000, there is no taxable benefit in kind. If an individual has multiple loans at any time then these must be aggregated.

A loan used for a qualifying purpose, that would be eligible for income tax relief, is excluded (see Chapter 3).

The measure of the benefit is calculated either using the normal (or averaging) *or* alternative method and is the difference between the interest actually paid and that given using the official rate.

The alternative method gives a more accurate figure and may be used if either the employee or the HMRC so elect.

Example 10.13

On 6 April 2020, Marion borrowed £10,500 from her employer for a family holiday. Her employer charged interest at the rate of 1% per annum. The loan is still outstanding on 5 April 2021.

Calculate Marion's benefit for the tax year 2020/21 using the normal method.

Answer

Average debt = [[Amount outstanding at 6.4.20 + Amount outstanding at 5.4.21]/2]

= [[10,500 + 10,500]/2] = 10,500

Benefit = 10,500 x 2.25%	236
Less the interest paid by Marion £10,500 x 1%	(105)
Taxable benefit	131

In this example the benefit in kind would be identical under the alternative method.

Note

If Marion had borrowed £10,000 only, then there would have been no benefit in kind.

Example 10.14

If Marion repaid £4,000 on 5 December 2020, what would her taxable benefit under the average method be?

Average debt = [[10,500 + [10,500 - 4,000]/2] = 8,500

Benefit = 8,500 x 2.25%	191
Less the interest paid by Marion	(91)
(see Example 10.14 below)	
Taxable benefit	100

Note

Although the average debt was less than the £10,000 limit, the maximum debt during the tax year was £10,500, therefore, in excess of the limit.

Example 10.15

If Marion repaid £4,000 on 5 December 2020 what would her taxable benefit under the alternative method be?

Answer

Under the alternative method the benefit would be:

	10,500 x 2.25% x 8/12 (April to November)	157
plus	(10,500-4,000) x 2.25% x 4/12 (December to April)	49
		206

Less: Interest paid

	10,500 x 1% x 8/12 (April to November)	70
plus	(10,500-4,000) x 1% x 4/12 (December to April)	21
		(91)
Taxable benefit		115

In this case, the HMRC would elect to tax Marion on the benefit as calculated under the alternative method as this provides a greater taxable amount.

Note

Under the alternative method, interest is calculated on the exact amount of loan outstanding. Therefore, in the above example, £10,500 was outstanding from 6.4.20 to 5.12.20 (i.e. eight months) and then after Marion's repayment of £4,000, only £6,500 was then outstanding from 6.12.20 to 5.4.21 (i.e. four months).

Example 10.16

Jeff, an employee, borrows £12,000, from his employer, on 6 October 2020, for a family holiday. His employer does not charge interest on the loan. The full amount of the loan is still outstanding on 5 April 2021.

Calculate Jeff's taxable benefit for the tax year 2020/21 using the average method.

Answer

Benefit = [[Amount outstanding at 6.10.20 + Amount outstanding at 5.4.21]/2] x [2.25% x 6/12

= [[12,000 + 12,000]/2] x 2.25% x 6/12 = 135

Note

As the loan is only outstanding for six months i.e. 6 October to 5 April in 2020/21 then interest is calculated only for this period; hence the use of 6/12ths.

Loan written off

Where an employee loan is written off either in whole or in part, the amount written off is taxable.

Exempt benefits

As mentioned above, a number of benefits in kind do not give rise to an income tax charge on the employee. The main exempt benefits include:

- provision of one mobile phone (Payment of an employee's own mobile phone contract would not be exempt);
- free or subsidised canteen meals if available to *all* employees;
- employer contributions to approved pension plans;

- provision of car park space at or near the place of work (or reimbursement to the employee of costs in paying for such a car park place);
- certain gifts and entertainment provided by third parties; non-cash gifts from a third party up to £250 in a tax year are exempt;
- an annual party or function if the cost to the employer per employee does not exceed £150/year (If the cost is more than £150, the full amount is taxable);
- up to £6 per week (£4 per week up to 5 April 2020) as payment towards additional household costs incurred by employees who are required to work from home;
- welfare counselling;
- provision of in-house sports and recreational facilities;
- the first £8,000 of removal or relocation expenses (any excess is taxable);
- work-related training;
- workplace nurseries;
- childcare vouchers up to the relevant exempt amount (£55 per week for basic rate taxpayers, reduced for higher/additional rate taxpayers);
- job-related accommodation;
- interest-free or cheap loans not exceeding £10,000 in a tax year;
- trivial benefits that cost less than £50 (£300 limit per tax years for some directors);
- incidental personal expenses when required to stay away from home on business overnight (up to £5 per night in the UK or £10 if overseas);
- provision of vehicle-battery charging at a workplace;
- provision of work buses; and
- non-cash long service awards after at least 20 years' service (Gifts valued up to £50 per year can be tax free).

Salary sacrifice (optional remuneration arrangements)

Many employers offer their employees the opportunity to take a reduced salary in exchange for a benefit in kind. Where an employee takes a benefit in kind and forgoes pay, the benefit in kind will be calculated as the higher of the cash foregone or the current taxable value of the benefit in question. Certain benefits that were provided under such a scheme prior to 5 April 2017 may be protected from this treatment until 5 April 2021.

Example 10.17

Jonathan accepts an offer to take a reduction in his gross pay of £250 per year and in return is provided with a mobile phone, with unlimited private use. What is the income tax position?

Answer

This is an example of an optional remuneration agreement. Jonathan will be assessable on the greater of the pay foregone and the taxable value of the benefit in kind received. The taxable benefit in kind in respect of one mobile phone is £nil. Therefore, Jonathan will be assessable on £250 as additional employment income (i.e. exactly the same as before the salary sacrifice).

Lump sum payments on termination or variation of employment

Such payments may be tax free, partially taxable or fully taxable as detailed below.

Where a taxable payment is made in connection with a person leaving an employment it is taxed in the year of *receipt,* not the year of leaving.

Example 10.18

Jill has her contract of employment terminated on 31 December 2019. She receives a compensation payment on 30 June 2020.

If the compensation payment is subject to income tax it will be liable in the tax year of receipt i.e. 2020/21 not in the tax year in which Jill's contract was terminated i.e. 2019/20.

It should be noted that any taxable termination payment is assessed as non-savings income but as the highest slice of income, after dividend income.

Tax free payments

Where a lump sum payment is made:

- under an approved pension scheme; and/or
- made on account of injury, accidental death or disability,

it is exempt from income tax.

Taxable payments

Contractual entitlement

Payments to which an employee is contractually entitled (i.e. are provided for in the contract of employment) are taxable in full e.g. terminal bonuses.

Payments in lieu of notice

If an employer makes a payment in lieu of notice (i.e. a payment made by the employer where the employer has not given the employee the required period of notice specified in the contract of employment) then such payment will be fully taxed as earned income whether contractually entitled or not.

Redundancy payments and ex gratia payments

Payments which are made at the discretion of the employer (so-called *ex gratia* payments; i.e. employer not legally required to make such payments) to compensate an employee for loss of employment are exempt up to £30,000; any excess is taxable (The excess is also subject to Class 1A NIC).

Any statutory redundancy payment (a statutory redundancy payment is a payment which is legally required to made by the employer by law when an employee is made redundant) made to an employee will also count as part of the tax free £30,000 mentioned above.

HMRC may argue that an *ex gratia* payment made at or near retirement, is an unapproved pension payment and would, therefore, be taxable in full.

Other payments

The cost of the provision of counselling and helping an employee to find new employment (or self-employment) is not a taxable benefit.

A departing employee may be paid an amount in return for agreeing to limit his or her future activities, for example not to compete with an ex-employer; such an amount is fully taxable.

Expenses deductible from employment income

In arriving at the net taxable earnings of an employee certain deductions may be made.

General rule

The general rule is that an employee may deduct an expense if the expense has been incurred *wholly, exclusively and necessarily in* the performance of their employment duties (ITEPA 2003 section 336).

For example, no deduction is allowed for expenses which have not been incurred *in* the performance of the duties but in order to carry the duties out e.g. payment of a fee to an employment agency used to find a job; similarly, the costs of newspapers could not be deducted from a journalist's salary as the reading of such newspapers merely prepared the journalist to carry out their duties.

The need to meet the wholly, exclusively *and* necessarily test has resulted in few expenses being eligible for deduction mainly on the grounds that very few expenses are actually necessarily incurred. By "necessary" it is inferred that the duties of the employment require that the expenses be incurred; it is not sufficient that the expenses are incurred due to the personal choice of the employee and/or because the employer requires the employee to incur the expense.

By way of example, a bank manager who was required by their employer to join a London club was not able to deduct the expense from their earnings. The reason was that the expense had not been incurred *necessarily*.

Similarly, the wholly and exclusively part of the test requires that the expense is incurred solely for purposes of the employment. As a consequence, if the expense has been incurred partly for business and partly for private purposes then no part of it will be deductible by the employee. In some situations, however, where it is possible to split an expense into a business and private element the former will be deductible. This will generally not be possible or very often is likely to prove very difficult.

Business entertainment expenses are specifically denied as a deductible expense for an employee. In other words, an employee cannot deduct expenses he may decide to incur himself on business entertaining. However, the more likely situation would be where an employer reimburses the employee for such expenses. In this situation, the reimbursement is taxable on the employee but in this case, the employee is allowed an equal deduction for the expenses (Remember that the employer is likely to be required to disallow the entertaining expenses incurred in their adjusted profits computation – see Chapter 6).

Travel expenses

Travel expenses are allowed as a deduction if the employee is required to incur the expenses in the course of their employment and the expenses are necessarily incurred on travelling in the performance of their employment duties.

Travel costs incurred in travelling from home to work are not incurred in the performance of the employee's duties and are therefore not deductible. However, where an employee travels, for example, from one office of their employer to another office, or to visit a customer, such travel expenses are deductible. Travelling sales employees will also be able to deduct their travel expenses as they travel from customer to customer typically but not always by car.

There are detailed rules regarding costs incurred by travelling to a temporary workplace. The general rule is that travel costs to a temporary workplace are deductible. A temporary workplace is one in which an employee attends or intends to attend for no more than 24 months.

If an employee receives a sum to cover travel expenses but chooses does not actually incur a similar liability, then the excess will be taxable.

Example 10.19

Lorna is provided with £150 to purchase a first-class train ticket to attend a business meeting. Lorna only spends £85 on a second class ticket. What is Lorna's income tax position?

Answer

The expense payment of £150 by Lorna's employer is treated as earnings. From that amount, she can deduct the £85 that she actually incurred and is charged on a net amount of £65.

Business use of own vehicle– approved mileage allowance payments

A company car is a car made available to an employee by their employer. Any benefit associated with the car is calculated as described above.

However, in some cases, an employee may use their own car for business travel.

Where this happens the employee may be reimbursed by their employer without such reimbursement falling to be treated as a taxable income *if* the amounts paid by the employer to the employee are no greater than the approved mileage allowances provided by statute.

The approved mileage allowances are as follows:
- 45p per business mile for the first 10,000 business miles per annum
- 25p per business mile for business mileage above 10,000 business miles.

Where the payment by the employer is *less* than the above allowances the difference may be claimed by the employee as additional tax-deductible expenses against employment income.

If the allowances paid by the employer *exceed* these allowances then the excess is taxable on the employee.

Example 10.20

Gareth uses his car on business as his employer does not provide its employees with company cars.

During the tax year 2020/21, Gareth travelled 22,000 miles of which 12,000 miles were on business.

Gareth's employer pays a flat business mileage allowance of 50p per mile.

Calculate Gareth's tax position in respect of the mileage allowance.

Answer

Approved mileage allowance	= 10,000 x 45p + 2,000 x 25p	=	5,000
Employer payment	= 12,000 x 50p	=	6,000

Gareth will therefore be treated as receiving taxable income of 6,000 - 5,000 = £1,000

Example 10.21

If, instead, Gareth's employer had only provided a payment of 10p per mile

What would be his income tax position?

Answer

Of the approved amount calculated above of 5,000, Gareth will have received only 12,000 x 10p i.e. 1,200.

Thus, Gareth will not have any taxable mileage and will be able to claim a deduction against his employment income of 5,000 - 1,200 = £3,800

Reduced mileage rates of 24p and 20p per mile apply to business use of own motorcycles and bikes respectively.

Professional subscriptions

A deduction is allowed for any approved professional membership fees or subscriptions that an employee pays that relate to the work carried out in the employment. HMRC provide a regularly updated list of professional bodies approved for tax relief (referred to as List 3).

Specifically authorised deductible expenditure

Certain expenditure if incurred by an employee is specifically authorised as deductible from employment income.

This includes:

- contributions to an approved occupational pension scheme;
- fees and subscriptions to prescribed professional bodies;
- payments to charity under a payroll deduction scheme operated by an employer;
- The difference between car mileage payments at the approved mileage allowance rates and the mileage payments received;
- certain industry-specific flat-rate expenses, for example, nurses and police officers; and
- £6 per week (£4 per week up to 6 April 2020) to cover additional household costs when required to work from home.

Reimbursed expenditure

No liability to income tax arises where allowable expenses are reimbursed by the employer to the employee.

An exemption applies for round sum allowances or reimbursement of actual expenses incurred in connection with incidental overnight expenses up to the maximum of £5 per night in the UK (£10 non-UK). If these limits are exceeded no part of the exemption applies.

Employment income computation – a comprehensive example

Example 10.22
During the tax year 2020/21, Dilip was paid a gross annual salary of £48,500 by ARL plc. Income tax of £8,100 was deducted under PAYE.
On 1 January 2021, Dilip personally paid a professional subscription of £320 to an HMRC approved professional body.
During 2020/21 ARL plc paid private medical insurance of £400 on behalf of Dilip.
In July 2020 ARL plc gave Dilip £100 to take a client to dinner to discuss their business plans. The actual cost of the meal was £120 and Dilip was not reimbursed for the additional cost.
ARL plc provided Dilip with a mobile phone that he could use for private calls; the cost to ARL plc was £30 per month.
Dilip used his private motor car for business purposes. He drove 6,500 miles in the performance of his duties for ARL plc during 2020/21 for which the company paid him an allowance of 50 pence per mile.
During the tax year, Dilip contributed 4% of his salary into ARL plc's HMRC registered occupational pension scheme and this was matched by his employer.
What is Dilip's taxable employment income for the year to 5 April 2021?

Answer

	£
Salary	48,500
Professional subscriptions paid	(320)
BIK – Private medical insurance	400
Entertaining	0
BIK – Mobile phone	Exempt
Business mileage	
- received (6,500 @ 50p)	3,250
- allowable (6,500 @ 45p)	(2,925)
Occupational pension (48,500 x 4%)	(1,940)
Occupational pension employer's contribution	Exempt
Assessable employment income	46,965

Notes

1. As the cost of entertaining covers the amount received, there is no assessable amount. However, Dilip is not allowed a deduction for the extra expenditure.

2. One mobile phone is exempt.

3. The PAYE deducted of £8,100 would be deducted from Dilip's income tax liability to find the income tax payable.

SUMMARY

An individual's employment income can typically comprise of salary plus any benefits in kind less any allowable expenses.

Employment income is taxable as non-savings income.

Different rules apply to certain benefits. If there is no specific rule, then the general rule of "cost to the employer" is applicable or 20% of the market value for the private use of an asset.

Specific rules apply to cars, vans, accommodation and loans.

Some benefits are tax free.

Expenses may be deducted in arriving at an employee's taxable earnings although generally speaking allowable expense deductions are limited.

Questions for students

See Appendix 2 for practice questions relating to Chapter 10. Answers are available online.

CHAPTER 11

Personal Tax: Overseas Aspects

INTRODUCTION

This chapter takes a brief look at some international aspects of UK taxation for individuals. For many years the concept of UK tax residence was based on case law and guidance notes. However, following some high-profile cases, the statutory residence test was introduced by Finance Act 2013. This chapter also looks at income arising overseas and introduces the concept of double taxation relief.

A UK resident individual is, generally, subject to UK income tax and capital gains tax on their worldwide income and gains.

A non-UK resident may still be liable to UK income tax on profits arising from a trade or profession carried on in the UK, and a UK property business. Non-residents are generally exempt from UK capital gains tax except for gains arising on the sale of UK properties.

The statutory residence test

An individual is a resident in the UK for UK tax purposes if they meet:

- one of the automatic UK tests; or
- the sufficient ties test

for any tax year (6 April to the following 5 April).

There are three steps to the statutory residence test.

Step one – if the individual meets any one of the three **automatic overseas tests**, they will be considered to be a non-UK resident. Otherwise, go to step two.

Step two – if the individual meets any of the **UK tests** they will be considered a UK resident. Otherwise, go to step three.

Step three – if the steps above prove to be inconclusive, then, the individual must consider the **sufficient ties test** to determine their UK tax residence status.

When considering the number of days in the UK, an individual will be considered to be in the UK for any day that they remain in the UK at midnight.

Automatic overseas tests

If an individual meets any one of the three automatic overseas tests, they are considered non-resident for the tax year.

The three tests are as follow:

(1) An individual who was a UK resident for one or more of the previous three years spends less than 16 days in the UK during a tax year.

(2) An individual who was not a UK resident for any of the previous three years spends less than 46 days in the UK during a tax year.

(3) An individual working full-time overseas. In addition, the individual may only work up 31 days in the UK, for more than three hours, and they must spend less than 91 days in the UK overall (HMRC has provided comprehensive guidance on the meaning of "working full time" in their booklet RDR3).

Automatic UK tests

The three automatic UK tests are:

(1) An individual will automatically be considered UK resident if they are in the UK for 183 days or more during a tax year.

(2) An individual's only home is in the UK. They must stay there for at least 30 days during the tax year and the property must be available for 91 consecutive days or more (or they also have an overseas home but live in that property for less than 30 days in the tax year).

(3) An individual is considered a UK resident if they work full time in the UK for any period of 365 days if all or part of that period falls within the tax year.

Sufficient ties test

If an individual did not meet any of the tests detailed above, the sufficient ties tests should be used to determine UK residence status for the tax year.

The number of ties that are needed to be considered a UK resident, is determined by the number of days spent in the UK during a tax year.

There are two tables. The first is for individuals who have been UK resident for one or more of the previous three tax years.

Days spent in UK during tax year	UK ties needed
Up to 15	Automatically non-resident
16 – 45	At least 4 ties
46-90	At least 3 ties
91-120	At least 2 ties
121 -182	At least 1 tie
183 or more	Automatically resident

The second table is for individuals who have not been resident in any of the previous three tax years.

Days spent in UK during tax year	UK ties needed
Up to 15	Automatically non-resident
16 – 45	Automatically non-resident
46-90	At least 4 ties
91-120	At least 3 ties
121 -182	At least 2 ties
183 or more	Automatically resident

The possible ties referred to above are as follows:

(1) Your spouse, civil partner or child under 18 years old are UK resident.

(2) You have accommodation available in the UK available for a continuous period of at least 91 days and you spend at least one night there during the tax year.

(3) You work in the UK on at least 40 days during the tax year.

(4) You have spent 90 days or more in the UK in either or both of the previous two tax years.

A final fifth test only applies to individuals that have been resident for one or more of the previous three tax years. This test is that the UK is the country in which you were present for the greatest number of days in that tax year.

Example 11.1

Bruce is visiting the UK for the first time in his lifetime, for a holiday and remains in the UK from 1 May 2020 until he leaves on 8 June 2020, a total of 38 days.

Answer

As Bruce was not a UK resident for any of the previous three years and spends less than 46 days in the UK during the tax year, he meets one of the automatic overseas tests and is not a UK tax resident for 2020/21.

Example 11.2

Connie has always been resident in the UK, spending at least 320 days in the UK every year, until she buys a property in Spain and moves there to live on 6 April 2020. She keeps her home in the UK where her husband continues to live for the majority of the time. Connie visits her husband, staying in her UK home for 80 days during 2020/21. Connie is retired and does not work. What is Connie's UK tax residence status?

Answer

When looking at the automatic overseas tests, Connie fails as she has previously been resident and is in the UK for more than 16 days during 2020/21.

Next, we need to consider the automatic UK residence tests. Connie does not meet any of these as she was in the UK for less than 183 days, has an overseas home and is not working during 2020/21.

Therefore, we must consider the sufficient ties tests. As Connie is a "leaver" and was in the UK for 80 days, she will be considered UK resident if she has three or more ties.

Connie has three ties (out of the five possible ties) as follows:

1. Connie's spouse is a UK resident.
2. Connie has accommodation available in the UK.
3. Connie spent more than 90 days in the UK in both of the previous two tax years.

Therefore, Connie will continue to be treated as a UK tax resident for 2020/21.

Notes

Connie's tax status in Spain will not impact the ruling on her UK tax status. By 2022/23 the third tie above may not be applicable and Connie would no longer be a UK resident.

Alternatively, Connie could reduce the number of days that she spends in the UK to 45, during 2020/21, in which case she would need four ties to be considered a UK resident.

Strictly an individual is resident or not for a complete tax year. However, a tax year may be split where, for example:

- an individual comes to the UK for permanent residence or starts to have a home in the UK;
- comes to the UK to work full time;
- leaves the UK for permanent residence abroad and ceases to have a UK home; or
- leaves the UK to take up full-time employment abroad.

In these "split year" cases, a tax year is apportioned into periods of residence and non-residence.

Domicile

Domicile is a legal term and may not be the same as an individual's country of residence. A person's country of domicile is generally where they regard as their permanent home and have the closest ties.

A child acquires the domicile of their father at birth (domicile of origin) unless their parents are not married when they acquire their mother's domicile at birth.

An individual can only have one domicile for UK tax purposes. Nationality and residence are irrelevant in determining domicile status. Until aged 16 if the father or mother's domicile changes so does the child's; this is known as a domicile of dependency.

From age 16 an individual can acquire a domicile of choice which is independent of their father/mother's domicile. This is not easy to do and may require that all links with the former country of domicile are severed and, after moving to a new country, new links are set up in the newly chosen country with the intention of making a new permanent home there.

From 6 April 2017, an individual will be deemed UK domiciled for income tax and capital gains tax purposes if they have been UK resident for more than 15 out of the previous 20 tax years or if they were born in the UK with a UK domicile of origin and are resident in the UK, even if they have obtained a domicile of choice elsewhere.

Non-UK income

The basis of assessment for income arising outside of the UK is the "arising" basis; income arises when received or when credited. A UK resident individual is taxable in the UK on their worldwide income, subject to the points detailed below.

The remittance basis of assessment

For income tax and capital gains tax, the importance of domicile is that a non-UK domiciled UK resident individual (a so-called "Non-Dom") may claim for non-UK income and gains to be taxed only when remitted to the UK rather than the normal arising basis but the claimant will not be entitled to a personal allowance.

There are detailed rules on the meaning of remitted to the UK and the claimant must pay an annual remittance basis charge. The remittance basis charge for 2020/21 is £30,000 if the individual has been UK resident for seven out of the last nine tax years, increasing to £60,000 if they have been UK resident for 12 out of the last 14 tax years. As mentioned above, an individual is deemed UK domiciled for income tax and capital gains tax purposes after 15 years of UK residence. If the unremitted income and gains are less than £2,000 in any tax year, then the remittance basis may automatically apply, without loss of personal allowance.

Double tax relief

An individual may be a tax resident in more than one country and, therefore, may be taxed twice on the same income. The UK has entered into bilateral double tax treaties with many countries, which typically exempt such income from taxation in one of the countries, as specified in the individual treaty.

Otherwise, relief will be provided for overseas tax suffered against an individual's UK income tax liability. Such double tax relief (DTR) may be available either unilaterally (i.e. under the UK's domestic tax laws) or under a double tax treaty.

Any overseas income liable to UK tax is included "gross" (i.e. before foreign taxes are deducted).

In ascertaining the extent of any DTR, the credit for any foreign tax will be the lower of:
- the foreign tax paid on the foreign income; and
- the UK tax on that foreign income.

Example 11.3

John, a UK resident and domiciled individual received a salary of £25,000 for the tax year 2020/21.

In addition during that tax year John also receives overseas rental income of £1,950 after foreign tax of £1,050 had been deducted and interest on a foreign bank account of £8,000 after local foreign tax of £1,500 had been deducted.

Calculate John's income tax liability for 2020/21.

Answer

John is entitled to DTR on the two sources of overseas income.

First, it is necessary to calculate John's income tax liability on *all* (i.e. his UK and foreign source) income before being able to determine the amount of his DTR.

	Non-Savings	Savings	Dividends
Employee income	25,000		
Relevant foreign income:			
Rental income (Gross)	3,000		
Bank interest (Gross)		9,500	
Less:			
Personal allowance	(12,500)		
Taxable income	15,500	9,500	Nil

	Taxable income	Rate of tax	Tax liability
NSI	15,500	20%	3,100
SI	1,000	0%	0
	8,500	20%	1,700
	26,000		4,800

Therefore, income tax liability before DTR = 4,800

This amount is reduced by any foreign tax credit i.e. foreign tax paid on overseas income.

UK income tax charged on the foreign rental income = 3000 x 20%	=	600
Foreign tax paid on rental income		= 1,050

Therefore, DTR is the lower of the two figures i.e.600.

This procedure is now repeated for the foreign bank interest

The UK income tax charged on the foreign bank income	= 1,700
Foreign tax paid on bank income	= 1,500

Therefore DTR is the lower of the two figures i.e. 1,500

Therefore:

Income tax liability (pre-DTR)	= 4,800
Less:	
DTR on rental income	600
DTR on bank income	1,500
Total DTR	(2,100)
Net UK income tax liability	2,700

Note

In the case of the foreign rental income, the UK income tax liability was less than the foreign tax paid on that income. As a consequence, any surplus foreign tax unutilised is simply lost.

SUMMARY

An individual's UK tax residence status is determined by the statutory residence tests.

UK resident individuals are liable to UK income tax on their worldwide income (i.e. UK source income and overseas income).

Non-domiciled individuals who are UK resident are liable to UK income tax on UK source income and may claim for unremitted foreign income to be taxed when remitted to the UK.

Double tax relief (DTR) is available to reduce the UK income tax liability on the relevant overseas income but such DTR cannot exceed the UK income tax liability on that particular source of relevant foreign income.

CHAPTER 12

Pensions

INTRODUCTION

This chapter looks at the income tax relief for payments by individuals into pension schemes and the limits on contributions attracting relief.

Occupational pensions or defined benefit schemes

A defined benefit scheme is one which is run by an employer to provide its employees with a pension on retirement. Normally, the pension scheme will be approved by the HMRC which means that a number of tax benefits accrue.

Under this type of scheme, the amount of pension payable on retirement to an employee depends upon the amount of the employee's remuneration prior to retirement together with the employee's length of service. Therefore, these schemes are often referred to as final salary schemes. In this text, these schemes are referred to as occupational pension schemes, although some occupational schemes could, in fact, be defined contribution schemes.

A typical final salary occupational pension scheme will require the employee to make contributions to the pension fund out of their salary whilst working for the employer. The employer will then deduct each month (or week) this level of contribution from the employee's gross salary before the calculation of income tax under PAYE, therefore immediately giving income tax relief on the contributions (See Chapter 10).

The employer will also contribute to this fund on behalf of its employees.

Most occupational pension schemes are approved by HMRC. The approval means that several tax advantages are available to both employer and employee. Unless a scheme is approved such tax advantages are not available.

For the employer, any tax contributions made on behalf of employees are tax deductible in computing trading profits. There is also no upper limit on employer contributions, although in certain circumstances relief may be spread over a number of years.

For the employee, the contributions made on their behalf by their employer are not taxable as benefits for income tax purposes (see Chapter 10). As mentioned above, an employee's own contributions to an occupational pension scheme are tax deductible in arriving at taxable employment income.

At retirement, pensions are taxable even when payable under an approved scheme. However, an employee may commute a part of their pension entitlement into a tax free cash lump sum. After any such commutation, the remaining pension payable will be reduced.

Personal pensions or defined contribution schemes

Personal pension schemes were originally primarily for those who are self-employed. In addition, some employees, whether or not a member of an occupational pension scheme, may also take out a personal pension. As mentioned above, employers may establish defined contribution schemes on behalf of their employees.

Personal pension schemes are basically money purchase schemes i.e. the benefits payable on retirement are dependent upon the amount of the contributions and any investment returns and not on the employee's final salary.

At retirement, a number of options are available, for example drawing 25% of the fund as a tax free lump sum and purchasing a pension (referred to as an annuity) with the balance. This annuity is taxable.

As with occupational pension schemes, there are tax benefits available for personal pension schemes assuming the scheme is approved by HMRC (see below).

Unlike occupational schemes, where an employee contributes to a personal pension it is unusual for an employer to also contribute. However, where the employer does make a contribution a tax deduction in computing the employer's trading profits will normally be given. The employer's contribution will not be treated as a taxable benefit on the part of the employee.

Contributions by an individual are made net of basic rate tax (i.e. net of 20%). In other words on making the contribution the individual deducts income tax at source at the rate of 20%. The pension fund itself may then claim back from HMRC the tax so deducted which is then added to the individual's fund.

However, the individual is entitled to tax relief at their highest rate of tax i.e. 40% or 45%. Where, for example, a self-employed individual or employee is liable to income tax at 40% the extra 20% of tax relief (i.e. 40% less 20%) is obtained by extending their basic and higher rate bands by the gross allowable personal pension contributions(see Chapter 4).

Example 12.1

Sandra makes a gross contribution of £10,000 in tax year 2020/21 to a personal pension scheme.

On making the payment Sandra is entitled to withhold income tax at the basic rate of 20% from the gross payment. Therefore, Sandra will pay the net amount of £8,000 (£10,000 less 20%) to the pension scheme.

If Sandra is a higher or additional rate taxpayer (i.e. she pays tax at the 40% or 45% rate) then she will be entitled to higher rate tax relief which will be obtained by extending the basic rate and higher rate bands by her gross contribution of £10,000. Therefore, Sandra's basic rate band will be extended from £37,500 to £47,500, with a similar extension to the higher rate band (See Chapter 4).

Pension contribution limits

There are two limits to the pension contributions that may be relieved in any tax year. First, a limit on the amount that qualifies for income tax relief and secondly a check to see if the annual allowance has been exceeded.

The limit on pension contributions that qualify for income tax relief is an amount equal to greater of £3,600 gross and the individuals relevant UK earnings for the tax year. Relevant UK earnings include employment income, self-employed profits, partnership trading profit shares and profits from furnished holiday lettings. Where an individual has low or no UK relevant earnings, their maximum limit is £3,600 (£2,880 net) per year. Non-taxpayers may also make use of this lower limit to obtain basic rate tax relief on pension contributions.

However, pension contributions over an upper limit or annual allowance, currently £40,000 per year (subject to a restriction for individuals with adjusted income in excess of £240,000 (£150,000 for 2019/20)) will give rise to an annual allowance charge. For this calculation, all tax allowable pension contributions of the individual are added to any employer contributions.

Where an individual does not fully use their annual allowance, any balance is carried forward for up to three years and may be utilised after the current year's allowance on the basis of the earliest year first ("FIFO"). This unused amount may only be carried forward where the individual was a member of a pension scheme for the earlier year.

Example 12.2

Ian has taxable profits from his self-employment for 2020/21 of £75,000. Ian first joined a personal pension scheme in 2019/20 when he contributed £10,000.

What is the maximum amount of pension contributions that Ian can obtain income tax relief on for 2020/21 and how much could be paid without exceeding his available annual allowance?

Answer

Ian's maximum limit for tax relief on pensions for 2020/21 is £75,000, equal to his relevant earnings. However, if contributions exceed his annual allowance plus any unused allowances brought forward, he will be subject to an annual allowance charge.

Annual allowance for 2020/21   40,000

Unused annual allowance brought forward:

2017/18   Not available as not a member of a pension scheme

2018/19   Not available as not a member of a pension scheme

2019/20	Annual allowance	40,000
	Used	(10,000)
	Balance to carry forward	30,000
Maximum annual allowance for 2020/21		70,000

Ian may, therefore, make pension contributions of £70,000 gross (£56,000 net) without incurring an annual allowance charge.

Basic rate tax relief is obtained by paying the contributions net and any higher rate relief will be obtained by extending his basic rate band by the gross amount of his contributions.

Where an individual's adjusted income exceeds £240,000 (£150,000 for 2019/20), the annual allowance is reduced. The reduction is £1 for every £2 above £240,000 subject to a minimum allowance of £4,000 (£10,000 for 2019/20). Adjusted income is usually calculated as total income plus any occupational pension contributions paid personally and by their employer. This restriction will only apply where an individual has threshold income above £200,000 (£110,000 for 2019/20). The threshold income is net income less any personal pension contributions. This threshold test ensures that a one-off increase in employer contributions does not lead to the individual coming into the charge.

Annual allowance charge

Where contributions exceed the annual allowance, an annual allowance charge will apply. The individual will receive income tax relief as normal on the full contributions up to the relevant earnings but the contributions over the annual allowance will be charged to income tax as the highest slice of the income. This charge does not form part of the calculation of the individual's income, it just gives rise to a charge, therefore, for example, it is not included when calculating adjusted net income to establish the personal allowance.

Example 12.3

Erica has a total income for 2020/21 of £110,000. All of her income is non-savings earned income. Her annual allowance, including unused allowances brought forward, has been calculated at £45,000. However, she has made a pension contribution of £56,000 net.

What is her total income tax liability for 2020/21?

Answer

Erica's net pension contributions are grossed up £56,000 x 100/80 = £70,000.

As the gross contributions are less than Erica's relevant earnings, she is entitled to income tax relief on the full amount of the contributions.

Erica's basic rate band is extended by her gross personal pension contributions, from £37,500 to £ 107,500.

Non- savings income	110,000
Less: Personal allowance	(12,500)
Taxable income	97,500

INCOME TAX

Income tax	97,500 @ 20% =	19,500
Plus		
Annual allowance charge		
Pension contribution	70,000	
Less: Annual allowance	(45,000)	
Excess charge	25,000	
Income tax	10,000 @ 20% =	2,000
	15,000 @ 40% =	6,000
Total income tax liability		27,500

Note

The excess annual allowance is charged at the marginal rates of income tax. In this example, part of the charge uses up the balance of the extended basic rate band and the balance falls into the higher rate band.

Erica is entitled to the full personal allowance as her adjusted net income is less than £100,000 (£110,000 less pension contributions) (See Chapter 3).

If the tax charge on the excess annual allowance charge is more than £2,000 then it is possible to make an election requiring the pension scheme to meet the annual allowance charge liability relating to that scheme in return for a reduction in pension benefits.

Lifetime allowance

In addition to the annual limits, an overall lifetime allowance or limit has been introduced. This must be considered when benefits are taken from a pension. The lifetime allowance is £1,073,100 (£1,055,000 for 2019/20). The allowances for earlier years are provided in the rates and allowances at the front of this book. It was initially £1,600,000 when introduced for 2005/6.

Whenever part of a pension fund is crystallized, for example, to pay out a lump sum or an annuity, if the total fund is in excess of the limit then a charge will apply. The charge will depend on how the money is paid out. The rate is:

- 55% on a lump sum; or
- 25% other withdrawals, for example, an annuity.

If a fund is partially crystallized, it must be established what percentage of the lifetime allowance remains for later events.

Normally the lifetime allowance tax charge is deducted by the pension scheme administrator before pension benefits are paid out.

Example 12.4

Ben was entitled to access his pension fund in 2012/13 and withdrew a tax free lump sum of £600,000. At that date, the lifetime allowance was £1,500,000. Therefore, Ben has used 40% of his lifetime allowance (600,000/1,500,000 x 100 = 40%).

In 2019/20 Ben crystallizes the balance of his fund by way of an annuity. The fund was valued at £2,000,000. What is his lifetime allowance charge?

Answer

Value of the pension fund		2,000,000
Lifetime allowance 2020/21	1,073,100	
Less: Already utilised – 40%	(492,240)	
Net lifetime allowance		(643,860)
Amount subject to lifetime allowance tax charge		1,356,140

As the pension was drawn as an annuity, the lifetime tax charge will be at 25%.

SUMMARY

Pensions, whether state, occupational or personal, are taxable on the recipient as non-savings income.

Contributions to occupational or personal pension funds attract income tax relief for individuals. How income tax relief is granted, however, differs.

Tax relief for contributions to an occupational pension scheme is obtained by the employee deducting the contributions from his or her salary.

In the case of personal pension contributions tax relief is obtained by way of tax deducted at source plus an extension of the basic and higher rate bands.

When making contributions, individuals must be aware of the annual limits for tax relief and the lifetime limit when taking pension benefits.

Questions for students

See Appendix 2 for practice questions relating to Chapter 12. Answers are available online.

CHAPTER 13

Capital Gains Tax: General Principles

INTRODUCTION

This chapter introduces capital gains tax and considers how an individual's capital gains and losses are calculated; the rates of capital gains tax; and some of the reliefs that may enable a capital gains tax liability to be reduced or avoided.

Basic principles

Capital gains tax (CGT) is a tax on the profit made on the disposal of *capital* assets, for example, shares, properties and antiques. If the sale is in the course of a trade, then it would be subject to income tax as trading income. For example, the one-off sale of a painting by an individual may give rise to a capital gain but the sale of the same painting by an art dealer is likely to be trading income. The badges of trade (Chapter 6 Appendix) would be used to consider trading or one off transaction.

Only *individuals* are liable to capital gains tax. Companies are not liable to capital gains tax although they are liable to corporation tax on capital gains (see Chapter 17). Partnerships are not chargeable – any gain is divided between the individual partners.

However, not all capital assets are liable to capital gains tax when disposed of (see below).

Technically speaking, a liability to capital gains tax arises when a chargeable person (e.g. an individual) makes a chargeable disposal (e.g. a sale) of a chargeable asset (e.g. a painting).

At its simplest a capital gain on the sale of a capital asset is computed as follows:

Sale proceeds	£35,000
Less:	
Cost of asset	£15,000
Capital gain	£20,000

As will be seen below, the actual computation can be a little more complicated.

For example, the "Cost of asset" may include elements of expenditure other than simply the original cost of the asset.

In any tax year, capital gains from the sales of assets are aggregated and any capital losses are offset giving, for any individual, either a net capital gain or net capital loss (note that the manner in which losses are offset can be very important; see below).

The annual exemption

Every individual is entitled to an annual CGT exemption which is £12,300 for the tax year to 5 April 2021.

This represents the value of gains which an individual can make in the tax year CGT free. It is the last item to be deducted when calculating an individual's capital gains for a tax year. It cannot be carried forward or backwards if unused and it cannot be surrendered to any other individual (for example, a husband cannot surrender any unused portion to his wife or vice versa).

It is not available to companies and special rules apply to trusts.

Chargeable assets

All assets are liable to CGT unless they are exempt.

Examples of capital or more correctly chargeable assets include:
- paintings
- jewellery
- listed and unlisted shares
- goodwill of a business
- plant and machinery
- land and buildings
- leases

Exempt capital assets include:
- National Savings certificates and premium bonds
- motor vehicles suitable for private use (but not personalised number plates)
- most government securities
- decorations for valour, unless acquired through purchase
- life assurance policies when held by the original beneficial owner
- investments held within Individual Savings Accounts (ISAs)
- foreign currency for the individual's private use
- pension rights
- prizes and betting winnings
- tangible movable property (chattels) with a life of 50 years or less (wasting chattels)
- a house occupied exclusively throughout the period of ownership as a main residence.

Any disposals to a charity are also exempt.

Chargeable disposal

A charge to CGT can arise whenever there is a disposal. The main types of disposal are:

- a sale, *or*
- a gift.

Other types of disposal include:
- the loss or destruction of an asset;
- the creation of one asset out of another e.g. the grant of a lease out of a freehold;
- the receipt of compensation (e.g. insurance proceeds; other than for personal injury or wrongs).

Disposal proceeds are usually the amount received less any incidental costs of sale, for example, auctioneers fees. In the case of a gift to anyone, or a sale at undervalue to a connected person, the sale proceeds are replaced by market value at the time of the disposal. This market value will be treated as the cost for the recipient of the gift.

Connected persons
An individual is connected with:
- their spouse or civil partner;
- their relatives (in this case meaning brothers, sisters, ancestors (i.e. parents) and lineal descendants (i.e., children, grandchildren etc.));
- the relatives of their spouse or civil partner; and
- the spouses/civil partners of their relatives and of their spouse/civil partner's relatives.

Transactions between connected persons are treated as if any gift or sale is, in fact, at the market value of the asset at the appropriate date. The actual price paid, if any, is irrelevant.

Also, any capital loss arising on a connected person transaction can only be offset against capital gains of the same or future tax years on disposals to the same person.

Inter-spouse transfers
Spouses and civil partners are treated as two separate persons for CGT (and indeed for income tax purposes) and each is therefore entitled to their own annual exemption.

Losses of one spouse/civil partner cannot be offset against the gains of the other.

However, disposals between spouses or civil partners living together do not give rise to chargeable gains or allowable losses. At the date of the transfer, the asset is assumed to have been transferred at its cost. This will then give neither a gain nor loss to the transferor.

The cost of the asset to the recipient is the same as the cost to the donor.

On a subsequent sale of the asset, the calculation would follow the normal rules.

Example 13.1

Colin purchased an asset in April 2007 for £13,000. He transferred it to his wife Mary on 16 July 2014 when it had a market value of £18,000. Mary then sold it on 1 June 2020 for £30,000. Mary made no other disposals during 2020/21.

Show the CGT position for Colin and Mary.

Answer

When Colin transferred the asset to Mary no chargeable gain arises. Mary is assumed to have acquired the asset at no gain/no loss to Colin and her cost will, therefore, be £13,000. On the sale in 2020/21 Mary's CGT position would be as follows:

	£
Disposal proceeds	30,000
Less:	
Cost	(13,000)
Gain	17,000
Less:	
Annual exemption	(12,300)
Taxable gain	4,700

Note

If Colin and Mary were not married, Colin would have been treated as disposing of the asset on 16 July 2014 at its market value of £18,000 giving rise to a capital gain of £5,000 (£18,000 - £13,000). Mary would be treated as acquiring the asset at market value and therefore her gain on the sale on 1 June 2019 would have been £12,000 (£30,000 £18,000).

The timing of a disposal

This is normally the *date of an unconditional contract* for the disposal *not* the date of receipt of the proceeds. This is usually when legal ownership of the asset changes.

A gift is also made on the date when ownership of the asset changes hands.

An asset lost is disposed of at the time of loss but, if compensation is received (e.g. from an insurance company) the date of disposal is normally the date of receipt of the compensation.

Allowable expenditure

This comprises three elements:

- *cost*
  (i.e. the price paid or market value when an item is received as a gift or inherited (probate value))
- *the incidental costs of acquisition and disposal*
  (e.g. fees for professional services; advertising costs)

- *enhancement costs so long as they are reflected in the nature of the asset at the date of disposal*
  (e.g. an extension to a property)

The costs of defending the title to an asset (e.g. legal costs in defending the owner's title to the asset) would also be included as part of the cost of an asset.

It is *not* possible to deduct expenditure which is:

- deductible from trading income as a trading expense; *or*
- interest on a loan taken out to acquire the asset; *or*
- recoverable from a third party.

Example 13.2

Helen buys an asset in May 2018 for a cost of £15,000 plus incidental costs of acquisition of £500. She sells the asset two years later for £17,500 and incurs incidental costs of disposal of £250.

Calculate Helen's capital gain.

Answer

Gross sale proceeds	17,500
Less:	
Incidental costs of disposal	(250)
Net sale proceeds	17,250
Less:	
Cost of asset	(15,000)
Incidental costs of acquisition	(500)
Capital gain	1,750

If an asset was acquired on or before 31 March 1982, then the cost is replaced by the value of the asset at 31 March 1982.

Part disposals

There may be occasions where a disposal is made of only part of the original asset that was acquired. For example, an antique table and chairs could be acquired as a set at auction and at a later date, only the table is sold. More commonly this section will apply where a parcel of land is acquired, part is retained and part sold, for example, a 10-hectare field is acquired as pasture and subsequently two hectares are sold to a developer. These rules do not apply to shares.

In these circumstances, the cost of the part sold must be established. The cost of the part disposed of is determined by the formula A/A+B, where A represents the gross consideration for the disposal and B the market value of the remaining property.

Example 13.3

Ian buys a 10-hectare field in April 2005 for a total cost of £30,000 including incidental costs of acquisition. He sells two hectares to a developer in May 2020 for £25,000. As at May 2020, the remaining eight hectares have a market value of £40,000.

Calculate Ian's capital gain.

Answer

First, establish the "cost" of the part sold using A/A+B

A = the consideration for the disposal i.e. £25,000

B = the market value of the remaining property i.e. £40,000

Cost of land sold: Total cost £30,000 x (25,000/(25,000+40,000)) = 11,538

(The balance of the cost (£18,462) relates to the eight hectares retained)

Gain on disposal of 2 hectares May 2020

Sale proceeds	25,000
Cost (as calculated)	(11,538)
Gain	13,462

For small part disposals of land, the individual may elect to deduct the sale proceeds from the cost, so that no gain arises until a subsequent sale. For these purposes, small means that the proceeds of the part disposal do not exceed £20,000 and the consideration does not exceed one-fifth of the market value of the whole piece of land as it comprised immediately before the disposal.

Chattels

As noted above chattels (tangible moveable property – something that you can touch, move and legally own) that are wasting assets (with a life expectancy of 50 years or less) are usually exempt from capital gains tax. This would include, for example, boats, clocks and animals.

Any gain (or loss) arising on the sale of a chattel, that is not a wasting asset, for example, antique furniture or paintings, is exempt where the disposal proceeds and cost are up to £6,000.

If the proceeds exceed £6,000 but the cost was less than £6,000, any gain arising is restricted to 5/3 of the gross consideration less £6,000. Effectively the assessable gain will be the lower of this amount and the gain calculated under normal rules.

Finally, as the gains can be exempt or restricted, there is also a restriction on any losses arising. If a non-wasting chattel is acquired for more than £6,000 and the sale proceeds are £6,000 or less, the sale proceeds are deemed to be £6,000, therefore reducing any allowable loss.

Example 13.4

Donald sells four individual paintings that are not part of a set during 2020/21.

The first painting cost £2,500 and was sold for £5,800. As the cost and proceeds are both less than £6,000, the gain is exempt.

The second painting cost £3,000 and was sold for £9,000. The gain is calculated as £6,000 (£9,000-£3,000). However, the gain is restricted to 5/3 x the gross proceeds less £6,000. This is £5,000 (5/3 x (9,000-6,000)). The gain is therefore reduced to £5,000.

The third painting cost £7,000 and was sold for £10,000. As both of these amounts are above £6,000 there is no adjustment and the gain is £3,000.

The final painting was purchased for £7,000 and was sold for £5,000. As the painting cost more than £6,000 but was sold for less than this amount, then the loss is restricted by treating the sale proceeds as £6,000. This gives an allowable loss of £1,000 (£6,000-£7,000).

Private or main residence relief

For most individuals, the largest or perhaps only capital gain that they will make in their lifetime is on the sale of their main residence. Fortunately, if the property was occupied by the owner throughout their period of ownership as their main residence only, the gain is fully exempt from CGT. The exemption can include gardens or grounds usually up to 0.5 hectares.

If this is not the case the gain is apportioned on a time basis between periods of occupation as a main residence and other periods. The proportion of the gain apportioned to occupation as a main residence is exempt from CGT and the balance is chargeable.

However, the rules are even more generous and some periods of absence are deemed to be periods of occupation further reducing the chargeable gain.

First, the last nine months (18 months for disposals up to 5 April 2020) of ownership are treated as a period of occupation, whether so occupied or not, provided that the property has actually been the main residence at some time. (This was introduced, for example, to avoid a CGT liability when an individual acquires a new private residence but has a delay selling their old home).

Example 13.5

Sandra bought her house on 1 June 2010 for £70,000. She lived in the house until 30 December 2017 when she moved in to live with her parents. Sandra's house remained unoccupied until it was sold on 31 May 2020 for £160,000.

Calculate Sandra's capital gain.

Answer

Sale proceeds May 2020	160,000
Less: Cost June 2010	(70,000)
Gain	90,000
Main residence relief (100/120)	(75,000)
Taxable gain	15,000

Note

The house was owned for 120 months. Sandra occupied the house has her main residence for 91 months. In addition, the last nine months of ownership are treated as a period of deemed occupation. Therefore, 100 months of the gain is exempt. The exempt gain is calculated as 90,000 x 100/120 months.

In addition, certain other periods of absence will be treated as occupied. However, these rules require that the property is actually occupied as a main residence *both* before *and* after the period of absence. The periods that may be deemed to be periods of occupation are:

1. any period or periods of absence, for any reason, up to three years in total;

2. any period or periods up to four years in total where the owner was required to live elsewhere for reasons of work in the UK; and

3. any period where the owner works overseas.

These points above may be aggregated to cover a longer period.

Example 13.6

Lindsey bought a house in Birmingham in January 2007 for £105,000 and lived there as her main residence until June 2010. She decided to go travelling with a friend and remained outside the UK until she returned to her house at the end of December 2012. After living in the house for 15 months, Lindsey was seconded to work in Glasgow and lived there for five years, returning to her house in April 2019. After living in the house for eight months, Lindsey moved to live with a friend and the house was eventually sold for £240,000 in December 2020.

What is her chargeable gain?

Answer	£	
Sale proceeds	240,000	
Less: Cost	(105,000)	
Gain	135,000	
Main residence relief 158/168 months	(126,964)	See below
Chargeable gain	8,036	

Main residence relief calculation:

From January 2006 to June 2009	Actual occupation	42 months
July 2009 to December 2011	Absent	30 months
January 2012 to March 2013	Actual occupation	15 months
April 2013 to March 2018	Absent (Work in the UK)	60 months
April 2018 to November 2018	Actual occupation	8 months
December 2018 to December 2019	Absent	13 months
Total period of ownership		168 months

Lindsey had a total of 103 months (30+60+13) out of 168 months of total ownership when she was absent from the property but we must consider whether any of these months can be treated as occupied.

First, the last nine months of ownership are always treated as a period of occupation and this rule will, therefore, cover the nine months of the 13 month period of absence from December 2018 to December 2019.

Then we must look at the other periods of absence. The 30 month period commencing July 2009 was both preceded and followed by a period of actual occupation, therefore this can be treated as a period of occupation using up 30 months of the three-year limit, under condition 1) above.

The period of 60 months commencing April 2013 was again both preceded and followed by a period of actual occupation. As Lindsey was absent due to working elsewhere in the UK, four years or 48 months of this period can be treated as occupied under condition 2). However, in addition, the remaining six months of the three years for any reason may also be used, giving 54 months in total treated as occupied.

Therefore, Lindsey had 65 months of actual occupation (42+15+8) plus 93 months of deemed occupation (9+30+54) for a total of 158 months being treated as a main residence. Therefore, there are only 10 months during which Lindsey is not treated as occupying the house. Lindsey will therefore only be taxable on 10/168th of the gain.

If there is a delay in occupying a main residence following acquisition due to construction, redecoration or alteration, or the delay of the sale of a previous main residence, then provided that the period does not exceed 24 months, it will be treated as a period of occupation as a main residence.

An individual may only have one main residence. A taxpayer has two years from the date of first having two residences to elect for one of them to be treated as their main residence, otherwise, the question will be determined by HMRC based on the facts of each case. Such an election may then be altered at a subsequent date. A married couple may only have one main residence between them.

If part of a residence is used exclusively for business purposes, this proportion of the gain will not be eligible for main residence relief.

An additional relief arises when part of a main residence is let. The relief only applies to periods when the owner also continues to occupy part of the property as his or her main residence. The gain that is chargeable due to the period of letting is reduced by the lower of £40,000, the amount of main residence relief or the gain attributable to the period of letting.

Example 13.7

Rosie sold her main residence for a gain of £200,000 in May 2020. Throughout her 12 years of ownership, 25% of the property was let out, whilst Rosie remained in occupation.

The gain not covered by main residence relief is £200,000 x 25% = £50,000

However, lettings relief will be available. This will be limited to the lower of

1) £40,000; 2) £150,000; or 3) £50,000.

The taxable gain will £50,000 - £40,000 = £10,000

Calculating the capital gains tax liability

A capital gain is taxed as though it is the highest part of an individual's income (see Chapter 2).

In other words, *income tax* is charged on non-savings, savings and then dividend income as normal (see Chapter 2) and then any capital gains are treated as on top of these categories and taxed appropriately.

Any capital gains falling into the basic rate band are charged at 10%, or 18% if the gains relate to residential property. Any gains that exceed the basic rate band are charged at 20%, or 28% if the gain relates to residential property. The annual exemption and order that gains are taxed can be arranged to the taxpayer's advantage.

Note: Personal allowances *cannot* be deducted from capital gains.

Example 13.8

In the tax year 2020/21, David has made non-residential property capital gains of £14,500 before annual exemption. His taxable income for the tax year is £42,500 all of which is Non-savings income. Calculate David's CGT liability.

Answer

Capital gains	14,500
Less:	
Annual exemption	(12,300)
Taxable gains	2,200

As David's taxable income (42,500) exceeds the 37,500 basic rate band limit all of the taxable gains are taxed at the higher rate of 20%.

The CGT is therefore 2,200 x 20% = £440

Example 13.9

Heather makes a residential property capital gain, after the annual exemption, of £14,600 in 2020/21.

Her taxable income (all non-savings) for the tax year 2020/21 is £28,000.

Calculate Heather's CGT liability.

Answer

Taxable income	Rate	Tax
	%	£
28,000 (taxable income)		
9,500 (gain)	18	1,710
37,500 (The basic rate band)		
5,100 (gain: 14,600 – 9,500)	28	1,428
Total capital gains tax payable		3,138

Note that part (£9,500) of Heather's capital gain is taxed at the 18% rate with the balance of the gain (£5,100) then being taxed at the 28% rate.

Example 13.10

Keith makes a non-residential capital gain of £7,600 and a residential property capital gain of £16,000 in 2020/21.

His taxable income (all non-savings income) for the tax year 2020/21 is £32,000.

What is Keith's CGT liability for 2020/21?

Answer

	Residential Property	Other Gains
Gains	16,000	7,600
Annual exemption	(12,300)	0
Net gains	3,700	7,600

Taxable income	Rate %	Tax £
32,000 (taxable income)		
3,700 (residential property gain)	18	666
1,800 (other gains)	10	180
37,500		
5,800 (other gains: 7,600 – 1,800)	20	1,160

Therefore, capital gains tax payable = 666 + 180 + 1,160 = £2,006

Note

As the rates of tax are higher for residential property gains, the annual exemption and basic rate band are first allocated against the residential property gains.

Using capital losses

On any sale of a capital asset a capital loss, as opposed to a capital gain, may arise. This would, of course, occur if the sale proceeds were less than the original cost.

Example 13.11

Hugh bought an asset for a cost of £10,000 and sold it for sale proceeds of £8,000.

Answer

Capital gain = £8,000 - £10,000 = £2,000 capital loss.

Current year capital losses

Capital losses must be offset against other capital gains of the same tax year, before utilising the annual exemption.

In any tax year, the total capital losses may exceed the total capital gains. Where this arises the excess capital losses can be carried forward to the succeeding tax years but never carried back (except in the year of death (see below)).

Carried forward capital losses

Surplus capital losses in any tax year may only be carried forward for offset against any net capital gains of future tax years.

Net capital gains for a tax year refers to capital gains less capital losses for that year. Thus, *current* year capital losses are offset against *current* year capital gains *before* any capital losses brought forward may be used.

Any capital losses brought forward are deducted before the annual exemption. However, losses brought forward are only required to reduce the gains to an amount equal to the annual exemption. Therefore, the annual exemption need not be wasted.

Example 13.12

Alka has the following gains and losses:

	2018/19	2019/20	2020/21
Gains	4,000	7,000	15,000
Losses	8,000	2,000	1,000

Calculate Alka's capital gains/loss position for each of the above tax years.

Answer

	2018/19	2019/20	2020/21
Gains	4,000	7,000	15,000
Losses	(8,000)	(2,000)	(1,000)
Current Net gains/losses	(4,000)	5,000	14,000
Less:			
Capital loss b/f	0	0 (note 1)	(1,700) (note 2)
Net gains/losses	(4,000)	5,000	12,300

Notes

1. The capital loss brought forward from 2018/19 is £4,000. However, none of this is used in 2019/20 as current year net gains are less than the annual exemption for that year. Thus, the £4,000 loss of 2018/19 is carried forward to 2020/21.
2. It is only necessary to utilise capital losses brought forward to leave chargeable gains equal to the annual exemption. Therefore only £1,700 losses are utilised in 2020/21, leaving a balance of £2,300 (4,000 - 1,700) to carry forward against future gains.

Optimal usage of capital losses and annual exemption

There is little choice in how capital losses can be utilised. Losses arising in the year must be offset against current year gains, even if as a result the annual exemption is wasted. However, if overall there remain chargeable gains, then it will be beneficial to allocate losses against residential property gains first. Again, it will generally be beneficial to deduct the annual exemption from residential property gains in preference to other gains.

Year of death

Death does not give rise to a disposal of assets for CGT.

In the year of death any capital losses arising in that year, on disposals made before death, may be *carried back to the three tax years* preceding the tax year of death on a LIFO basis and offset against gains assessable in those years.

However, any losses in the year of death must be first offset against gains of that year to the fullest extent.

The losses carried back are relieved against the most recent tax year first but the losses so relieved must be such as to leave in charge sufficient gains equal to the annual exemption for that tax year and similarly for earlier tax years.

The cost of any assets inherited on the death of an individual is treated as the market value at the date of death (the probate value).

Date of payment of CGT

Normally CGT is payable on the 31 January following the tax year in which the gain arose with any income tax/NIC balancing payment. There are no interim or payments on account as is the case for income tax (see Chapter 21).

However, on residential property sales on or after 6 April 2020, the CGT is payable within 30 days of completion of the sale. As the individual's overall tax position for the year may not be known at the time, an estimate may be required.

SUMMARY

Only individuals are liable to capital gains tax. Companies are liable to corporation tax on chargeable gains.

A capital gain arises where a chargeable person makes a chargeable disposal of a chargeable asset.

Certain assets are exempt from capital gains tax.

Individuals are entitled to an annual capital gains tax exemption, £12,300 for 2020/21.

The rate of capital gains tax is determined by the individual's taxable income. Gains sit on top of income to determine the appropriate rate band. Any gains falling within the basic rate band are taxed at 10% or 18% if the gain relates to residential property or at 20% or 28% respectively if the basic rate band has been fully utilised. If the rate bands have been extended (see Chapter 4), then these extended rate bands apply.

Current year capital losses are offset against current year capital gains before any brought forward unused capital losses may be used and the annual exemption.

Usually, capital gains tax is due for payment in one lump sum on the 31 January following the tax year in which the gains arose. However, on gains relating to the sale of residential property, the capital gains tax liability is payable within 30 days of completion.

CHAPTER 14

CGT: Shares and securities

INTRODUCTION

This chapter follows on from Chapter 13 and looks at the capital gains tax position on the sale of shares and securities by individuals.

Securities

Government stocks and most commercial securities i.e. company loan notes (qualifying corporate bonds ("QCB")) etc. are *exempt* from capital gains tax when they are held by individuals.

Shares

There is no equivalent exemption from CGT in respect of share sales by individuals. Sales of shares, therefore, give rise to either capital gains and/or capital losses.

The main problem when working out the capital gain/loss which may arise on a share sale is identifying which shares of those acquired at various different times have in fact been sold.

Example 14.1

Joan has purchased the following ordinary shares in ABC plc:

100 shares on 1 March 2006 for £4,000

50 shares on 3 August 2008 for £1,400

350 shares on 6 October 2012 for £6,250

On 19 September 2019, Joan sold 380 shares.

The question is which of the shares has Joan sold?

Matching rules: for individuals

The tax legislation lays down the following so-called *matching rules* i.e. on any sale of shares of the *same class in the same company* the shares sold are to be matched as follows:

1. with shares acquired *on the same day*, then
2. with shares acquired *within 30 days after* the disposal on a FIFO basis, then
3. with shares acquired *before the date of disposal – the share pool*.

Same day

Any shares which have been acquired on the same day as any sales are assumed to have been sold first (even if the purchase takes place after the sale).

Following 30 days

This may seem strange and this rule was introduced to counter a practice known as "bed and breakfasting" used, for example, to trigger a loss, then reacquiring the same shares. Thus, any shares which have been acquired within 30 days after the date of any sales are assumed to have been sold next.

Share Pool

Any pool can only contain shares of the same class in the same company (e.g. ordinary shares in ABC plc; or ordinary shares in XYZ plc). In effect, all acquisitions in the pool are combined to establish an average price per share.

Computational procedure

To work out the capital gain/loss on a share sale a number of separate calculations may be necessary. In some circumstances, where the entire shareholding is sold and there are no purchases in the next 30 days, this may be a simple case of deducting the cost of all of the shares purchased from the sale proceeds.

However, when only part of the shareholding is sold, then the shares sold must be identified or matched with specific purchases.

The basic approach is to work through the matching rules, matching shares sold with those purchased.

STEP 1

Match shares sold with shares acquired on the same day.

Calculate capital gain/loss on these matched shares.

If the number of shares sold exceeds the shares acquired on the same day then continue to STEP 2 (if this is not the case no further computation is necessary).

STEP 2

Match the shares sold not already matched under STEP 1 with shares acquired in the next 30 days.

Calculate capital gain/loss on these matched shares.

If the number of shares sold exceeds the shares matched under STEPS 1 and 2 then continue to STEP 3.

STEP 3

Match the shares sold not already matched under STEPS 1 and 2 with the shares in the share pool.

Calculate capital gain/loss on these matched shares.

STEP 4

Aggregate the net gains and losses from STEPS 1 to 3 to produce one single capital gain or loss.

Example 14.1 continued from above
As there are no same day or next 30 day acquisitions, the shares sold will be matched with the share pool – effectively an average cost approach.

Example 14.2

On 1 March 2021, Mehvish sold 3,000 shares in XYZ Ltd for £21,000, after deducting any incidental costs of disposal. Mehvish had purchased shares in XYZ Ltd as follows:

	Shares	Cost
17 September 2002	2,000	£5,000
3 January 2018	1,500	£2,000
1 March 2021	400	£2,750
25 March 2021	300	£1,900

Calculate Mehvish's capital gain/loss position for tax year 2020/21.

Answer

STEP 1 [same day]

Of the shares sold on 1 March 2021, 400 are matched with the shares acquired on this date.

	£
Sale proceeds [400/3,000 x £21,000]	2,800
Less: Cost	(2,750)
Gain	50

STEP 2 [next 30 days]

Of the shares sold on 1 March 2021, 300 are matched with shares purchased in the following 30 days after this date, on 25 March 2021.

	£
Sale proceeds [300/3,000 x £21,000]	2,100
Less: Cost	(1,900)
Gain	200

STEP 3

The remaining 2,300 (3,000 – 400 – 300) shares are identified or matched against the pool. For this, the share pool must be established.

	Date	Number of shares	Cost £
Purchase	17/9/02	2,000	5,000
Purchase	3/1/18	1,500	2,000
		3,500	7,000

Therefore, prior to the sale, there are 3,500 shares in the pool at a total cost of £7,000. The cost of the shares sold from the pool is based on the average share price and can be calculated by using 2,300/3,500 x £7,000 = £4,600. It is important, for future disposals to record this "cost" used to calculate the gain and the number of shares and cost remaining in the pool.

	Date	Number of shares	Cost £
Pool balances from above		3,500	7,000
Sale	1/3/21	(2,300)	(4,600)
Balance		1,200	2,400

It is now possible to calculate the gain on the shares sold from the POOL

Sale proceeds	[2,300/3,000 x £21,000]	16,100
Less: Cost		(4,600)
Gain		11,500

STEP 4

Calculate the total gain arising on the sale

From STEP 1	400 shares sold	gain	50
From STEP 2	300 shares sold	gain	200
From STEP 3	2,300 shares sold	gain	11,500
Total	3,000	Total gain	11,750

In calculating the actual capital gains tax liability, the gain of £11,750 would be aggregated with any other gains or losses arising in the tax year before the annual exemption and any available losses are deducted to leave the net taxable amount.

Example 14.3

Joe sold 1,000 shares in JSP plc, on 31 January 2021 for £20,000. He bought 1,500 shares on 30 April 2014 for £18,000; 500 shares for £7,000 on 31 May 2017; and 200 shares for £3,600 on 10 February 2021.

Calculate Joe's chargeable gain.

Answer

Same day matching

No shares were bought on the sale date of 31 January 2021.

Following 30 days matching

200 shares were bought in this period on 10 February 2021. Thus 200 shares sold can be matched with the shares bought in this period.

	£
Sale proceeds [(200/1,000) x £20,000]	4,000
Less: Cost	(3,600)
Gain	400

Share Pool

The remaining 800 shares are to be identified or matched against the share pool.

	Date	Number of shares	Cost £
Purchase	30/4/14	1,500	18,000
Purchase	31/5/17	500	7,000
		2,000	25,000
Sale	31/1/21	(800)	(10,000)
Balance		1,200	15,000

Sale proceeds [(800/1,000) x £20,000]	16,000
Less: Cost	(10,000)
Gain	6,000

Joe's total chargeable gains = 400 + 6,000 = £6,400

Scrip and rights issues

Effect of bonus and/or rights issues

The effect of each type of issue is to increase the number of shares held and, in the case of a rights issue, the total cost of the shares held.

Before matching shares sold with shares purchased, if either a bonus and/or a rights issue occurs prior to any sale of shares, it is first necessary to adjust the original shares purchased for the bonus/rights issue. Only after these adjustments are made can shares sold be matched.

Bonus issues

Bonus or scrip issues are a free issue of shares. The shareholder receiving the bonus shares does not pay anything for them.

For tax purposes, the bonus shares are assumed to have been acquired at the same date as the original shares in respect of which they have been issued.

Rights issue

A rights issue is an issue of shares but unlike a bonus issue, the shares have to be paid for.

For matching purposes, the rights shares are deemed to be a new acquisition.

Example 14.4

Greta bought 1,500 ordinary shares in UTB plc for £4,000 on 7 February 2017.

On 30 March 2019, a bonus issue of ordinary shares was made of 1 for 2.

Thus, Greta will have acquired an extra 1,500/2, i.e. 750 ordinary shares.

These extra 750 shares will be deemed to have been acquired on 7 February 2017 for no cost.

Assuming, no share disposals, Greta's share pool will be:

	Date	Number of shares	Cost £
Purchase	7/2/17	1,500	4,000
Bonus issue 1:2	30/3/19	750	0
		2,250	4,000

Example 14.5

Ivan bought 1,500 ordinary shares in MKT plc for £5,000 on 12 June 2015.

On 15 May 2020, a rights issue of ordinary shares was offered of 1 for 5 at a cost of £2.50/share.

Ivan accepted the rights issue and acquired an extra 1,500/5 i.e. 300 ordinary shares.

These extra 300 shares will be treated as acquired on 15 May 2020 for £750 (300 x £2.50).

Ivan's share pool for MKT plc will be:

CAPITAL GAINS TAX

	Date	Number of shares	Cost £
Purchase	12/6/15	1,500	5,000
Rights issue 1:5	15/5/20	300	750
		1,800	5,750

Take-overs

A take-over occurs where one company acquires the shares of another company. In effect, the shareholder in, say, Company A swaps their shares for shares in Company B. Company B is the acquiring company and Company A is the target company or company being acquired.

Take-over bids can be:

- share for share, *or*
- cash for share, *or*
- a mixture of the two.

An entirely share for share bid (i.e. with no cash involved, sometimes referred to as paper for paper) is *not* a disposal for CGT purposes provided that as a result of the bid the acquiring company controls either:

- more than 25% of the ordinary share capital of the target company, *or*
- more than 50% of the voting power of the target company.

Share for share

The new shares received in the acquiring company will "step into the shoes" of those originally held in the target company and will take their costs and dates of acquisition and do not give rise to a CGT disposal on the takeover.

Cash for shares

If only cash is received (i.e. no shares are issued) there is a CGT disposal of the old holding in the normal manner with a resulting capital gain or loss.

Share plus cash for shares

Where there is a hybrid, i.e. the consideration for the old shares is a mixture of cash and new shares, the cost of the original shareholding must be split between the cash and value of the shares received and as cash has been received a CGT liability will arise.

The allocation of the cost of the original shareholding is done on a pro rata basis according to the market values of the new shares immediately following the successful acquisition, effectively following the part disposal rules (A/A+B).

The consideration taken in new shares will "step into the shoes" of those shares originally held.

If the cash received on a takeover is "small" then there will be no immediate liability to CGT and the cash received reduces the cost of the new shares etc.

received. It will be "small" where it does not exceed either 5% of the total value of the consideration received as a result of the take-over or £3,000.

Example 14.6

Oldco plc was acquired by Newco plc in December 2020. Newco plc offered the shareholders of Oldco plc two ordinary shares and £3.00 cash for every one ordinary share held in Oldco plc.

Trevor owned 2,100 ordinary shares in Oldco plc purchased in March 2007 for £6,000.

The market values of the shares in Newco plc on the day after the take-over were £4 per share.

Calculate Trevor's capital gain on this sale.

Answer

The take-over was made by way of an issue of shares and cash. Therefore, the receipt of cash will give rise to disposal for CGT. The receipt of Newco plc shares will not create an immediate CGT disposal and part of the original cost of Oldco plc shares will be attributed to these new shares.

First, it is necessary to work out the value of the total consideration received by Trevor:

Two ordinary Newco plc shares plus £3.00 cash for every one ordinary share held in Oldco plc.

Trevor held 2,100 Oldco plc shares. Therefore, he will receive:

4,200 Newco ordinary shares valued at	16,800	(4,200 x £4 per share)
Cash	6,300	(2,100 x £3 per share)
Total disposal consideration	23,100	

Second, it is necessary to allocate part of the original shareholding cost to the cash received

The original cost of shares in Oldco plc was £6,000.

Using (A/A+B) allocate (6,300/23,100) x 6,000 = £1,636 to the cash proceeds.

Therefore £1,636 of the cost relates to the cash and the balance is the cost of the Newco plc shares received.

Third, calculate capital gain on the cash received

Sale proceeds 2,100 x £3	6,300
Less:	
Cost	(1,636)
Gain	4,664

Finally, calculate the cost of the Newco Plc shares to carry forward

The original cost of Oldco shares	6,000
Cost of cash as calculated	(1,636)
Cost of Newco shares	4,364

If a takeover includes the issue of securities that meet the conditions to be treated as a qualifying corporate bond ("QCB"), then the gain attributable to the receipt of the QCB is calculated and crystallises when the QCB is disposed of.

SUMMARY

It is important when calculating a CGT liability on a sale of shares to:

- First, identify shares purchased in each of the categories (i.e. same day; next 30 days; share pool).
- Second, adjust the shares purchased in each of these categories for any bonus and/or rights issues.
- Third, match the shares sold with shares purchased in each of these categories until all shares sold have been matched, the cost identified and the gains or losses calculated.
- Fourth, aggregate the resulting gains and losses into a single result.

CHAPTER 15

CGT: Business Reliefs

INTRODUCTION

This chapter examines the main CGT reliefs available to individuals involving businesses and business assets. Some of these reliefs are also available to companies.

Replacement of business assets or rollover relief (also available to limited companies)

This relief allows taxpayers to replace business assets used in their trade/business without incurring a liability to CGT on the sale of the "old" business assets at the date of sale (i.e. new business assets are purchased to replace old business assets). Several conditions must be satisfied.

On the sale of a qualifying business asset, where *all* of the proceeds from the sale are reinvested in another qualifying business asset (or assets), any gain on the sale of the first asset is not taxed immediately but is *deferred* until the replacement asset is itself sold. (It is possible for a further rollover to be made and so on so that the gains are deferred for successive replacements).

This deferral is achieved by simply deducting the gain made on the sale of the old asset from the base cost of the replacement asset.

If all the sale proceeds from the sale of the old asset are not fully reinvested then only a partial roll-over arises (i.e. part of the gain is taxed immediately with part being deferred).

Conditions for roll-over relief to apply

The general conditions for roll-over relief are:

- both 'old' and 'new' assets must be used wholly for trade purposes, *and*
- both assets must be within the *qualifying classes of assets* but need not belong to the same class, *and*
- the 'new' asset must be acquired within *one year before to three years after* the disposal of the 'old' asset.

The words 'old' and 'new' relate to the asset's position in relation to the particular business. In other words, the asset may be bought as a second-hand asset from someone else but is still categorised as new for the business which is buying it.

Qualifying assets

The qualifying assets for roll-over relief include:

- land and buildings occupied and used for trading purposes;
- fixed (i.e. immovable) plant and machinery;
- goodwill (not for companies);
- ships, aeroplanes and hovercraft;

- milk quotas; and
- satellites, space stations and spacecraft.

Example 15.1

David sold land and buildings, which had been used in a trade carried on by him, for £140,000 in March 2015 which he had bought for £100,000 in July 2003.

In September 2015 he bought a qualifying replacement asset, for £200,000.

In June 2020 he sold the replacement asset for £220,000 without any further reinvestment.

Calculate David's CGT position (pre annual exemption).

Answer

Original asset sale 2014/15

Sale proceeds	140,000
Less:	
Cost	(100,000)
Gain	40,000
Roll-over relief	(40,000)
Taxable gain	Nil

Full roll-over relief is available as the full sale proceeds have been reinvested into the replacement building.

The gain of £40,000 is rolled-over against the cost of the replacement asset i.e. deducted from it:

Cost of replacement asset	200,000
Less:	
Rolled-over gain	(40,000)
New base cost	160,000

Sale of new asset June 2020

Sale proceeds	220,000
Less	
New base cost	(160,000)
Gain	60,000

Notes

1. Therefore no capital gain is taxed in tax year 2014/15 but a capital gain is taxed in tax year 2020/21. The rollover relief does not reduce the total gain but defers tax on the original sale until the later sale.
2. If the proceeds from the sale of the new asset are reinvested into new qualifying assets within the permitted time limit, then a further rollover may be claimed.

For individuals, the claim must be made for rollover relief within four years from the end of the tax year in which the disposal occurs or the replacement asset is acquired, whichever is later.

Only partial reinvestment

Where the disposal proceeds of the old asset are *not* fully reinvested the surplus cash retained reduces the gain allowed to be rolled over (and in fact if the surplus cash retained is greater than the gain there will be no rollover at all). In effect, a partial roll-over occurs whilst at the same time a CGT liability arises as illustrated in the following example.

Example 15.2

Adeline sold a qualifying business asset for £130,000 making a gain of £45,000 in 2018/19. She reinvested £105,000 in a qualifying replacement business asset in 2020/21 (therefore within three years after the disposal).

Show Adeline's CGT position (pre-annual exemption).

Answer

Gain on sale of the old asset which is capable of roll-over is £45,000.

However, £25,000 (130,000 - 105,000) of the sale proceeds from the sale of the old asset have not been reinvested in any new assets.

The amount which was not reinvested of £25,000 will be taxed on Adeline immediately, i.e. in tax year 2018/19.

Only the difference between the original gain and the gain immediately taxed is rolled-over.

The gain eligible for roll-over is, therefore:

Total gain	45,000
Rolled-over gain	(20,000)
Taxed now	25,000 (Proceeds £130,000 less reinvested amount £105,000)

The rolled-over gain is simply the difference between the total gain and the gain taxed now (i.e. the proceeds not reinvested).

Thus, £20,000 will reduce the base cost of the replacement asset to £85,000 (i.e. 105,000 - 20,000).

Notes

The chargeable gain is the lower of the proceeds not reinvested and the full gain.

If the sale proceeds reinvested had been, say, £85,000 (i.e. 45,000 not reinvested) or less, then the whole gain of £45,000 would have been immediately chargeable with no part being eligible for roll-over:

Total gain	45,000
Rolled over gain	(0)
Taxed now	45,000 (Proceeds £130,000 less reinvested amount £85,000)

Non-business use

Where the asset being replaced has not been used entirely for business purposes during its period of ownership the roll-over relief is scaled down.

This can be achieved by assuming the asset is, in fact, two assets one of which is that which was used entirely for business purposes and one asset which was not.

Two separate CGT calculations are then performed normally assuming that the costs and proceeds are pro-rated in the same manner. Alternatively, a single computation may be carried out reducing pro rata according to the amount of business and non-business use.

Example 15.3

Ron purchased a factory in July 2001 for a cost of £500,000. 15% of it was let out as Ron did not need it for his trade. In May 2020 the factory was sold for £800,000 and a replacement factory was bought for £900,000.

Calculate Ron's CGT position (pre annual exemption).

Answer

Original asset

Sale proceeds	800,000
Less	
Cost	(500,000)
Gain	300,000

Taxable element of gain = 15% x 300,000 = 45,000

Thus, 85% of 300,000 is eligible for roll-over = 255,000

Base cost of new asset 900,000 – 255,000 = £645,000

Depreciating assets

Rollover relief is modified where the new asset purchased is a "depreciating asset". A depreciating asset for this purpose is an asset with an expected life of 50 years or less at the time of acquisition (or will become so in the next 10 years).

Unlike rollover relief, the held over gain on sale of the old asset does not reduce the cost of the new asset. This gain is simply "held over" until the earliest of one of the following three occurrences and then at that time is charged as a gain:

- the sale of the 'new' depreciating asset, *or*
- the cessation of its use in the business, *or*
- the 10 anniversary of the acquisition of the depreciating asset.

Leases of 60 years or less and fixed plant and machinery are examples of depreciating assets.

Example 15.4

Maggie bought a factory in June 2010 for £250,000. She then sold it for £600,000 in January 2013. In August 2013 she acquired a 40-year lease on a new factory for £750,000 and subsequently sold it in March 2021 for £1,250,000.

Show Maggie's CGT position.

Answer

The reinvestment of the proceeds from the sale of the factory in 2013 was into a depreciating asset (i.e. a short lease). Only *hold-over* relief is thus available.

Gain on sale of factory = 600,000 – 250,000 = £350,000

This gain is held over until the earliest of the events mentioned above which in this case is the sale of the replacement factory lease in March 2021.

The gain of £350,000 is now taxable in tax year 2020/21 (not 2012/13 when the factory was in fact sold).

In addition, any gain on the assignment of the lease will also be taxable.

Note

If Maggie did not dispose of the lease in March 2021 and continued to trade, the deferred gain would be taxable in August 2023, the 10-year anniversary of the acquisition of the replacement asset.

Gifts relief ("gift relief")

Gifts of assets are deemed to be made at their market value at the date of the gift. In other words, even though no sale proceeds are received, for CGT purposes a disposal is deemed to have been made and therefore a gain or loss will arise. (Remember that this is not a problem for married couples and civil partners where assets are transferred for no gain/no loss).

However, a capital gain deemed to have been made on a gift can be deferred by way of gift relief provided:

- the donor (the person making the gift) and donee (the person receiving the gift) jointly elect within four years from the end of the tax year in which the disposal is made, *and*
- the donee is resident in the UK, *and*
- the asset is a qualifying asset.

Qualifying assets

These are:

- business assets; and
- transfers of assets subject to an immediate charge to inheritance tax (namely lifetime transfers of assets to a trust – see Chapter 24).

Only gifts of business assets are relevant for Gift relief purposes.

Transfers of business assets are transfers of:

- business assets used by the donor in his or her business *or* used by his or her personal trading company;
- shares or securities held in the donor's personal trading company; and
- shares or securities in an unquoted trading company.

A *personal company* is one in which the donor controls at least 5% of the voting rights and can be either quoted or unquoted.

Shares in an unquoted company include shares listed on the Alternative Investment Market (AIM).

Note that unlike the position for roll-over and hold-over relief discussed above for replacement of business assets, in the case of gift relief there is no restriction on the type of assets which qualify other than that they must be used in the business.

Thus, it can be seen that gift relief would not apply to for example a gift by a mother to her daughter of a piece of family jewellery or a painting as neither asset are used in any business.

Effect of gift relief

There are two effects of the donor and donee claiming gift relief:

- the donor will be treated as making neither gain nor loss on the gift, *and*
- the donee will be treated as taking the asset at its market value – the deemed disposal proceeds – but this market value will be reduced by the amount of the gain deferred on the part of the donor.

Example 15.5

Gerald gave a business asset to his son Jim in May 2020 when it's market value was £50,000. Gerald originally bought the asset in January 2000 for £22,000. Gerald and Jim make a joint gift relief claim.

What is the CGT position of both Gerald and Jim?

Answer

Gerald	£	
Deemed sale proceeds	50,000	(Actual proceeds £Nil)
Less:		
Cost	(22,000)	
Gain	28,000	
Less:		
Gift relief	(28,000)	
Chargeable gain	nil	
Jim		
Market value of asset acquired	50,000	
Less:		
Gift relief	(28,000)	
Base cost of asset	22,000	

Note

You will note that in effect Gerald's original base cost becomes Jim's base cost.

Not pure gift – sale at undervalue

Gift relief also applies where the "gift" is, in fact, a sale but at less than its true market value to a connected person.

However, in such cases, only part of the gain can be subject to gift relief with part of the gain becoming immediately chargeable.

The part of the gain which is chargeable immediately is the excess of the proceeds received by the donor over the donor's original cost. The balance of the gain can then be deferred i.e. subject to gift relief.

Example 15.6

Sally purchased shares in an unquoted trading company for £50,000 in December 2009. She then sold them to her son Ben for £80,000 in February 2021 when their market value was £175,000. Sally and Ben intend to claim gift relief on the transaction.

What is the CGT position for Sally and Ben?

Answer

Sally	£
Deemed sale proceeds	175,000
Less:	
Cost	(50,000)
Gain	125,000
Less:	
Gift relief (See Note 2)	(95,000)
Chargeable gain (See Note 2)	30,000

Ben	
Market value of shares acquired	175,000
Less:	
Gift relief	(95,000)
Base cost of shares	80,000

Notes

1. If Sally had simply gifted the shares to Ben gift relief of £125,000 would have been available.

2. However, as Ben paid Sally £80,000 then Sally is immediately chargeable on the actual gain arising of £30,000 (i.e. 80,000 – 50,000). Only £95,000 (i.e. the difference between the full gain and the gain taxed now (125,000 – 30,000)) is available for gift relief.

Assets not used wholly for business purposes

Business assets other than shares

It may be that during an individual's ownership of an asset it qualifies as a business asset for part of the time and as a non-business asset for the rest of the time.

This may occur because the asset was itself used only partly for business purposes throughout its period of ownership or alternatively the asset was used wholly for business purposes but only for a part of its period of ownership.

For individual trading assets (e.g. land and buildings; plant and machinery; goodwill) the overall gain is simply pro-rated accordingly.

Example 15.7

Lionel owns a factory which he purchased in May 2001 for £100,000. In July 2020 Lionel gave the asset to his daughter, Jo, when it's market value was £300,000 and a joint gift relief election was made. 80% of the factory has been used in Lionel's business with the remaining 20% being let out to a third party (i.e. this part is not used in Lionel's business).

Show Lionel and Jo's CGT position.

Answer

Of Lionel's gain of £200,000 (i.e. 300,000 - 100,000) 20% of it (i.e. £40,000) is chargeable immediately (the gain attributable to the part let).

The balancing 80% (i.e. 160,000) is eligible for gift relief.

Jo will, therefore, receive the asset at its market value of 300,000 less gift relief of 160,000 giving a base cost of £140,000.

Shares

In the case of a gift of shares, the above rule is applied differently.

Where a gift of shares in a personal trading company is made and not all of the company's assets are business assets then part of the gain on the sale of the shares is not eligible for gift relief.

Only the gain on the shares attributable to any underlying *chargeable* **business** *assets* as opposed to *chargeable assets* of the company qualifies for gift relief calculated as follows:

Gain on the gift of shares x $\dfrac{\text{Market value of chargeable } \textit{business} \text{ assets}}{\text{Market value of company's } \textit{chargeable} \text{ assets}}$

An example of chargeable assets of a company which are not chargeable *business* assets would be investments held by the company, for example where the company used its surplus cash to invest in shares of another company. These are investments and therefore not business assets (i.e. they are not used in the company's business).

Transfer of a business to a company (Incorporation relief)

It is not unusual for a sole trader to decide to convert their business to a limited company. This gives rise to a disposal of the assets transferred at market value. Subject to satisfying certain conditions so-called incorporation relief may be available when a person transfers their sole trader business to a company (incorporates) as a going concern.

Incorporation relief permits the transfer to take place without any capital gains tax liability arising on the deemed disposal of the chargeable business assets which would otherwise occur. The capital gain which would arise is rolled-over against the cost of the shares issued to the sole trader in exchange for the acquisition of their sole trader business. For the relief to apply, the business and all of its assets, other than cash must be transferred and the relief is automatic without a formal claim.

Example 15.8

Alisha transferred her business to a limited company and in exchange received 1,000 ordinary £1 shares in her new limited company. The business was valued at £90,000 on incorporation. It was agreed that the chargeable gain on the transfer of Alisha's business was £27,000. However, Alisha does not have a capital gains tax liability. Instead, the gain, £27,000 is deducted from the cost of her shares, £90,000, leaving a base cost of f63,000 on any future share disposal.

For complete roll-over relief to apply all of the consideration for the business transferred must be in shares of the acquiring company. If a part of the consideration is in cash a partial roll-over may apply and a CGT liability will immediately arise on the cash element received. In this latter case, the amount of gain eligible for roll-over relief is given by:

Capital gain x $\dfrac{\text{Value of shares received}}{\text{Total consideration received}}$

Example 15.9

Clare a sole trader who set up her business in 2011 has decided to transfer her entire business to a limited company CPT Ltd on 31 December 2020 in exchange for an issue of ordinary shares. The assets and liabilities as at 31 December 2020 are as follows:

	Cost	Market Value
	£	£
Assets		
Cash	4,000	4,000
Freehold property	14,000	30,000
Fixtures and fittings	10,000	2,000
Trading stock	2,000	1,200
Goodwill	nil	3,000
Debtors	nil	1,000
TOTAL	**30,000**	**41,200**
Liabilities		
Trade creditors	nil	1,200
Net assets	30,000	40,000

What is Clare's CGT position for tax year 2020/21 and what difference would it make if Clare received her consideration as shares worth £25,000 and cash of £15,000 (i.e. a total consideration of £40,000 the sole trader's net worth)?

Answer

Chargeable gains on the transfer of chargeable assets are as follows:

Freehold property:	30,000 – (14,000)	=	16,000
Goodwill:	3,000 – (nil)	=	3,000
Total gain			19,000

(Note that the only other chargeable asset for CGT purposes are the fixtures and fittings, which are sold at less than cost, giving rise to an appropriate balancing allowance/charge obtained for capital allowance purposes, but no capital gain/loss).

Gain eligible for roll-over relief = 19,000 as all consideration in the form of shares.

Base cost of new shares = 40,000 – 19,000 = £21,000

Had the consideration been shares plus cash, then of the £19,000 of gain above only:

[25,000/40,000] x 19,000 = £11,875 of gain can be rolled over against the cost of the shares of £25,000.

The balancing gain of £7,125 (i.e. 18,000 – 11,875) is taxable immediately.

It is possible to elect for incorporation relief not to apply.

Business asset disposal relief (previously known as "entrepreneurs' relief
This relief was introduced by Finance Act 2008 to provide individual's disposing of a business interest some element of CGT relief to replace some of the benefits lost previously by the removal of retirement relief and business asset taper relief.

Although it is referred to as a "relief", it does not reduce the amount of the chargeable gain. Its impact is to reduce the rate of CGT charged on qualifying gains to 10%.

There is a lifetime limit on the total value of gains that can qualify for Business asset disposal relief. This limit is currently £1,000,000 (£10,000,000 for disposals before 11 March 2020).

The relief may be available to an individual on:
(a) a disposal of the whole or part of a business;
(b) a disposal of one or more assets in use, at the time at which a business ceases to be carried on; or
(c) a disposal of shares in or securities of a trading company.

In all cases, for the relief to be available, the business or shares must have been owned by the individual for at least 24 months before the date of disposal, or cessation of the business in respect of (b) above (The period of ownership was increased to 24 months from 12 months for disposals made on or after 6 April 2019 by FA2019).

Disposal of whole or part of a business
The disposal must be of the whole business or a clearly identifiable part, for example, a separate branch in its entirety. Therefore, it will not apply to the sale of individual business assets, where the business continues unchanged. Relief is not available for non-business assets. Relief may also not be available where goodwill is sold to a related close company.

Disposal of one or more assets in use, at the time at which a business ceases
The disposal must take place within three years after the date of cessation. In this case, the relief is available on the disposal of individual business assets. Again, relief is not available for non-business assets.

Disposal of shares in a company
Throughout the 24-month period prior to disposal, the individual must be an officer or employee of the company and the shares must be in the

individual's personal company. For this relief "personal company" means a company in which the individual holds at least 5% of the ordinary share capital, at least 5% of the voting rights and at least 5% of the distributable profits and net assets of the company. Therefore, for example, if a husband and wife each hold 4% of the ordinary shares of a trading company, neither would qualify for business asset disposal relief. The shares may be quoted.

Example 15.10

In which of the following three scenarios will business asset disposal relief be available?

Lisa owns and runs two restaurants in neighbouring cities. She closes one of the restaurants and makes a capital gain on the disposal of the property.

Neil has traded for over 10 years and ceases to trade on 7 June 2019. On 1 November 2018, Neil had acquired new business premises which he traded from up until cessation of his trade. This property was sold at a gain on 12 December 2019.

Mel owned 6% of the ordinary shares in her employee and had worked for this company for five years when she decided to sell her entire shareholding. She continues to work for the same employer after the sale.

Answer

Lisa will not be entitled to Business asset disposal relief as she has disposed of a business asset and not the whole or part of her business. If she had sold the restaurant as a going concern, then she would have sold part of her business and may have been eligible for Business asset disposal relief.

Neil will be entitled to business asset disposal relief as the sale occurred within three years of the cessation of treading. The 2-year qualifying period prior to cessation relates to the time that Neil has been trading and not the period of ownership of each individual asset.

Mel will be entitled to Business asset disposal relief assuming that the shares entitled her to 5% of the voting rights and at least 5% of the distributable profits and net assets of the company. She was an employee of the company for more than two years before the date of the sale and there is no requirement for her to leave the company or retire.

As mentioned above there is a lifetime limit on business asset disposal (and entrepreneurs' relief for earlier years) of £1million.

Example 15.11

Lee, a higher rate taxpayer, has owned and run his own business for the last seven years. There are no non-business assets. He sells the entire business in October 2018 for £600,000. The allowable costs are £140,000.

Therefore, Lee has made a taxable gain of £460,000, assuming that Lee has already used his annual exemption.

He can claim Business asset disposal relief, or entrepreneur's relief as it was then known, and as a result, the rate of CGT will be 10% rather than the normal higher rate of 20%.

After the sale, Lee starts up another business, which he sells after five years at a gain of £700,000, again comprising entirely of business assets. Lee's lifetime limit for Business asset disposal relief is £1,000,000. £460,000 was claimed on the earlier disposal. Therefore, relief of £540,000 is available on the later disposal, with the balance chargeable at the normal CGT higher rate.

Where there are both gains and losses during a tax year on assets qualifying for Business asset disposal relief, these must be netted off. Otherwise, CGT losses and the annual exemption can be claimed against qualifying and non-qualifying gains in the most advantageous manner to the taxpayer. In determining the rate of tax applicable where there are qualifying and non-qualifying gains, the qualifying gains are taxed first. This will have no impact on the rate of tax applied to these gains but may increase the rate of tax on the non-qualifying gains.

Business asset disposal relief must be claimed by the first anniversary of 31 January following the end of the tax year of disposal (For 2020/21 by 31 January 2023).

Investors' relief

This relief is very similar to business asset disposal relief.

Investors' relief also reduces the rate of CGT for qualifying gains to 10%, and there is a lifetime limit to qualifying gains totalling £10,000,000. Broadly, the relief applies to gains on the disposal of ordinary shares subscribed for in cash on or after 17 March 2016 in unlisted trading companies or groups that have been held by the individual for at least three years (or three years from 6 April 2016 where the shares were issued between 17 March and 5 April 2016). The individual must not have been an officer or employee of the company during the period from acquisition to the date of disposal of the shares (There are some limited exceptions to this rule, for instance, in respect of unpaid directors).

Investors' relief must be claimed by the first anniversary of 31 January following the end of the tax year in which the disposal was made.

SUMMARY

The CGT liability which arises on a sale of qualifying business assets may be rolled-over where a replacement qualifying business asset is purchased. If the purchased asset is a depreciating asset (e.g. a lease) then hold-over relief applies. The replacement asset must be acquired during the period commencing one year before the disposal to three years after.

The relief is only available where the various conditions are satisfied. The failure to reinvest all of the sale proceeds will give rise to an immediate taxable gain on part of the overall gain.

It should be noted that gift relief (holdover relief):

- only applies to shares in trading companies or business assets, not all assets;
- also applies to gifts that are immediately chargeable to inheritance tax;
- applies not just to gifts but also to sales at below market value; and
- gift relief needs the consent of both donor and donee.

Incorporation relief can be used to roll over the capital gain that would otherwise arise on the transfer of a business and its assets from a sole trader business to a limited company in exchange for shares.

Business asset disposal relief is a valuable relief available on the sale of a business or by an employee of shares in a personal trading company, potentially reducing the rate of CGT from 20% to 10%. Failure to meet all of the qualifying conditions will result in the denial of the relief. The relief is available on gains up to the lifetime limit of £1,000,000. Business asset disposal relief must be claimed. This relief was known as entrepreneur's relief up to 11 March 2020.

Investors' relief works similarly to business asset disposal relief on certain unquoted share disposals.

Questions for students

See Appendix 2 for practice questions relating to Chapters 13 to 15. Answers are available online.

CHAPTER 16

Corporation Tax: General Principles

INTRODUCTION

This chapter looks at the basic rules about the taxation of companies. Companies are not liable to income tax or capital gains tax. Companies pay corporation tax on both profits and capital gains. Other bodies such as clubs and associations may also be subject to corporation tax.

Liability to corporation tax

A company's liability to corporation tax depends upon its fiscal residence. A company which is resident in the UK is liable to corporation tax (CT) on its worldwide profits. Non-resident companies may still be subject to UK tax on profits attributable to a permanent establishment in the UK.

Dividend income from other companies is *not* subject to corporation tax but may impact on the due dates for payment.

Company residence

The basic rule: place of incorporation

If a company is incorporated in the UK then it will be treated as UK resident.

Place of central management and control

If a company is not incorporated in the UK, it may still be UK resident if it is controlled and managed in the UK. In most cases, the control and management of a company are exercised where its board of directors meet and take strategic decisions in relation to the company.

Taxable total profits (TTP)

For each accounting period, it is necessary to calculate a company's TTP, which requires separate computations of income from each source and capital gains. Corporation tax is charged on the TTP of an accounting period.

TTP is equal to the aggregate of the income and chargeable gains made by a company in the accounting period less certain deductions, including losses and qualifying charitable donations.

In computing the TTP for an accounting period the following pro-forma should be followed:

Adjusted trading profit	x
Property business profit	x
Non-trading Loan relationship profits	x
(Deduct if a deficit)	
Chargeable gains	x̲
Total profits	x
Less: Loss claims against TTP	(x)
	x
Less: Qualifying charitable donations	(x)
Taxable Total Profits (TTP)	**X**

See Chapters 17 and 18 for detailed rules regarding chargeable gains and losses respectively.

Qualifying charitable donations

A company may obtain a deduction from its TTP for payments to a qualifying charity.

Such payments are made gross (i.e. tax at source is not deducted from the payment; remember an individual makes a gift aid payment net of basic rate income tax).

Qualifying charitable donations (QCD) are deductible from TTP after any losses are offset against TTP. Therefore, a claim for losses can result in a waste of relief for QCD.

Only QCD which are actually paid in an accounting period are deductible.

Dividends

Companies are not subject to CT on the receipt of dividends and do not obtain tax relief for dividends paid (but see Chapter 22 for the impact of dividends received when considering CT payment dates).

Each of the other items included in the calculation of TTP is explained further later in this chapter.

Example 16.1

The adjusted income and gains of BCL Ltd for the year to 30 June 2020 have been calculated as follows:

Adjusted trading profits	275,100
Rental profits	14,200
Capital gains	94,400
Non-trading loan interest paid	10,500

BCL Ltd paid qualifying charitable donations of £6,000 during the year.

Calculate the TTP of BCL Ltd for the year ended 30 June 2020.

Answer	
Adjusted trading profits	275,100
Rental profits	14,200
Capital gains	94,400
Non-trading loan interest paid	(10,500)
Total profits	373,200
Less: Qualifying charitable donations	(6,000)
TTP	367,200

Rates of corporation tax and financial years

Rates of corporation tax are determined not for income tax years/years of assessment but for *financial years* (FY). For example, the financial year 2020 refers to the period 1 April 2020 to 31 March 2021.

The rate for the financial year 2020 (FY2020) is 19% and the rate for the financial year 2019 was also 19%.

If a company's accounting period straddles more than one financial year, the amount of the profits arising in the accounting period must be apportioned between the financial years in which the accounting period falls to determine the corporation tax liability.

Two separate computations are then carried out and then aggregated to get the company's overall corporation tax liability.

Example 16.2

KRO Ltd has TTP of £1.2 million for its accounting period 1 April 2020 to 31 March 2021.

Calculate the company's corporation tax liability.

Answer

The entire accounting period falls within FY2020.
Corporation tax liability £1,200,000 x 19% = £228,000

Example 16.3

CDO Ltd has TTP of £600,000 for its accounting period 1 July 2016 to 30 June 2017.

Calculate the company's corporation tax liability.

Answer

Part of the accounting period falls within FY2016 and part within FY2017. The CT rate for FY2016 was 20%.

Apportion TTP on a time basis TTP into the two financial years covered by the accounting period.

FY 2016
TTP for the 9 months to 31 March 2017 falls within FY 2016
TTP £600,000 x 9/12 x 20% =   £90,000

FY 2017
TTP for the 3 months to 30 June 2017 falls within FY 2017
TTP £600,000 x 3/12 x 19% =   £28,500

Aggregate the figures from to get the corporation tax liability for the whole 12 month accounting period i.e. 1 July 2016 to 30 June 2017.

Corporation Tax = 90,000 + 28,500 = £118,500

Chargeable accounting period

A company's period of account is any period for which a company may prepare its financial statements. This may be for 12 months, less than or more than 12 months. As noted above, however, corporation tax is levied on TTP for an *accounting period.*

An accounting period for corporation tax, however, cannot be longer than 12 months.

A chargeable accounting period *starts*:

- when a company starts to trade; *or*
- otherwise becomes liable to corporation tax; *or*
- immediately after the previous accounting period ends.

A chargeable accounting period *ends* on the earliest of the following:

- 12 months after its start;
- end of the company's period of account;
- the date that a company ceases to be resident in the UK;
- the date that a company ceases to be liable to corporation tax; *or*
- commencement of the company's winding up.

Short accounting period

Where a company's period of account is less than 12 months long this period of account is also the company's accounting period.

Corporation tax is computed as above.

Example 16.4

EFD Ltd has TTP of £200,000 for the nine month accounting period 1 April 2019 to 31 December 2019.

Answer

The whole of the accounting period falls within FY2019

Corporation tax liability 200,000 @ 19% = £38,000

Long period of account

Where a company's period of account is more than 12 months (referred to as a long period of account) this complete period cannot be an accounting period because the accounting period of a company for corporation tax purposes cannot be longer than 12 months.

In such cases, the period of account must be split into two separate accounting periods, one for the first 12 months; and one for the balance of the period. Two calculations of TTP are then necessary, producing two separate corporate tax liabilities, one for each accounting period, which are *not* then aggregated.

In these cases, before any calculations can be carried out it is necessary to split the individual items of income and gains (e.g. rental income; interest income; etc.) comprising the company's profit for the whole period of account between the two accounting periods created. This split is carried out using the following rules:

- trading income *before* capital allowances is time apportioned;
- capital allowances need to be calculated separately for each accounting period (first 12 months, then a short period for the balance);
- property business profit is usually time apportioned;
- other income is allocated to the accounting period to which it relates (i.e. accruals basis);
- chargeable gains/losses are allocated to the accounting period in which the gains arise based on the date of disposal;
- allocate qualifying charitable donations to the accounting period in which paid; and
- dividends are allocated to the accounting period in which received (only necessary for determining payment dates).

Example 16.5

JSC Ltd has the following results for the 16 months to 31 December 2020:

Trading profit before capital allowances	320,000
Property business profit	160,000
Bank interest received and accrued to 31 December 2020	8,000
Capital gain made on 30 August 2020	89,000
UK dividend received 1 September 2020	36,000

Tax written down value of plant and machinery in the main pool as at 1 September 2019 was £100,000. There are no purchases or sales of plant and machinery during the period of account.

Calculate the TTP for the two accounting periods and the corporation tax liability for each accounting period.

Answer

The period of account 1 September 2019 to 31 December 2020 is divided into an accounting period of 1 September 2019 to 31 August 2020 (the first 12 months) and an accounting period of 1 September 2020 to 31 December 2020.

	1.9.19 to 31.8.20	**1.9.20 to 31.12.20**
	(12 months)	*(4 months)*
Trading profit		
320,000 x 12/16	240,000	
320,000 x 4/16		80,000
Capital allowances (see below)	(18,000)	(4,920)
Property business profit		
160,000 x 12/16	120,000	
160,000 x 4/16		40,000

Interest income		
8,000 x 12/16	6,000	
8,000 x 4/16		2,000
Capital Gain 30 August 2020	89,000	
TTP	**437,000**	**117,080**
Capital allowances		
1.9.19 to 31.8.20 (12 months)		
TWDV as at 1.9.19	100,000	
WDA (18%)	(18,000)	
1.9.20 to 31.12.20 (4 months)		
TWDV as at 1.9.20	82,000	
WDA (18% x 4/12)	(4,920)	
TWDV as at 31.12.20	77,080	

1.9.19 to 31.8.20
Corporation tax liability =

FY2019	437,000 x 7/12 x 19%	=	48,434
FY2020	437,000 x 5/12 x 19%	=	34,596
			83,030

1.9.20 to 31.12.20
Corporation tax liability =

FY2020	117,080 x 19%	=	22,245

Notes
1. Capital allowances are calculated for the first 12 month period and then for the shorter four-month period.
2. There are separate tax liabilities for the two different accounting periods and these are not added together; they are also payable by different dates; see Chapter 22.

Trading profits

Companies are taxed on their trading profit for the accounting period on the normal accruals basis and the normal "wholly and exclusively" rules regarding the deductibility of expenses apply (see Chapter 6).

Unlike the case for sole traders:
- there are no commencement or cessation rules and no overlap profits;
- there is no disallowance for any private proportion of any expenses (i.e. the full amount of the expense is deductible; this is because in the case of companies any private part of an expense (e.g. private fuel costs of a company car) may be taxed as income on the part of the relevant employee as a benefit in kind; see Chapter 10); and
- there is no restriction for the private element of any asset on which capital allowances may be claimed (see Chapter 7).

Capital allowances
Capital allowances are claimed for accounting periods by reference to acquisitions and disposals in that accounting period.

All allowances are in principle calculated as for sole traders (see Chapter 7) using the same rates. As companies cannot have private use of assets, there will never be the requirement to separate assets with private use from the pools.

Groups of companies (see Chapter 19) are only entitled to one AIA.

Period of account exceeds 12 months

As an accounting period cannot exceed 12 months for corporation tax purposes, writing down allowances can never exceed 18%/6% of the relevant tax written down values/costs (compare this with that of the sole trader where a 15 month period of account may produce writing down allowances of 18% x 15/12; see Chapter 6 and 7).

Where the period of account is over 12 months, two separate capital allowance computations are necessary for each of the two accounting periods which are created (see Example 16.5 above).

Period of account less than 12 months

Where the period of account is *less* than 12 months, writing down allowances are reduced proportionately. In addition, the AIA limit will also be time apportioned.

Capital allowances are deductible from trading income.

Property business profit

Property business profit is determined in a very similar manner as applies to individuals (see Chapter 5); however, the accruals basis always applies (e.g. dates of receipt of rent irrelevant). It is, however, assessed for an accounting period (not a year of assessment as for individuals).

Property business profit comprises:

- rents; and
- premiums received on the grant of a short lease (i.e. a lease of 50 years or shorter)

In computing the amount of property business profit the normal rules relating to the calculation of trading profits also apply here (see Chapters 5 and 6), e.g.:

- expenses must have been wholly and exclusively incurred for the purposes of the property business;
- capital expenditure disallowed; and
- general provision for bad debts disallowed etc.

Property business profits from more than one property are aggregated producing a single assessable property business profit figure.

One important point to note here is that where a company pays interest on a loan to purchase or improve investment property such interest is *not* allowed as an expense in computing the property business profit (as is the case for individuals; see Chapter 5). The interest is, in fact, deductible against any interest income of the company under the loan relationship rules. This may give rise to net interest income or loss (see below). In addition, there is no restriction on finance costs paid by a company in respect of residential property as apples to individuals.

Premiums received for grant of a short lease

The rules detailed in Chapter 5 regarding the receipt or payment of a short lease premium also apply to companies. A short lease is one of 50 years or less.

A premium is in effect treated as if it was additional rent in the accounting period in which the lease is granted. However, only part of the premium is chargeable to tax as property business income:

Amount of premium chargeable as property business income =
Premium − [2% x Premium x (duration of the lease in complete years − 1)]

Example 16.6

MNT Ltd received a premium of £10,000 on 1 June 2020 when it let out a property under a 10 year lease to a trading company, PQM Ltd. In addition, a monthly rent of £5,000 is payable on the first day of each month.

Calculate MNT Ltd's property business profit to be included as part of its profit for the accounting period 1 April 2020 to 31 March 2021 and the allowable amounts to be deducted in PQM Ltd's accounting period for the year to 31 December 2020.

Answer

MNT Ltd to 31 March 2021

Both the rent (on an accruals basis) and a proportion of the premium (in the accounting period of granting of the lease) are taxable.

Taxable element of premium = 10,000 − [2% x 10,000 x (10 − 1)] = 8,200

Rents accrued from 1.6.20 to 31.3.21 = £5,000 x 10 months = 50,000

Therefore:
Property business profit = £8,200 + £50,000 = £58,200

PQM Ltd to 31 December 2020

The rent due under the lease should be included in the financial statements of PQM Ltd on the accruals basis.

Rents accrued 1.6.20 to 31.12.20= £5,000 x 7 months = 35,000

PQM Ltd will also be entitled to deduct from its trading profits a proportion of the lease premium. This is calculated as the amount of the lease premium taxable as income on the grantor of the please spread over the life of the lease.

The amount taxable on the grantor (MN Ltd) is £8,200 as calculated above.

For PQM Ltd the deduction is 8,200/ 10 years = £820.

However, as the lease was only in place for seven months in the accounting period to 31.12.20, the deduction will be £820 x 7/12 months = £478.

PQM Ltd would be entitled to a deduction of £820 during the accounting period to 31.12.21 and subsequent years until the full £8,200 is relieved.

Interest income and expenses

Non-trading loan relationships

Non-trading interest income and interest expenses are dealt with under the non-trading loan relationship provisions.

Interest income or loan relationship credits primarily consists of interest income from bank and building society deposits and on loans to other companies. *Interest expenses or loan relationship debits* include the interest payable on a non- trading borrowing such as loans incurred to buy property for renting out (i.e. for a property business) or investments, and any associated costs. The write off of a non-trading loan may also be a loan relationship debit.

In essence, such interest income/expense items are not received/paid as part of the company's trade.

Such income and expenses are taxed on an accruals basis and are aggregated to produce a net interest income/expense figure.

Excess of interest income over interest expense

The net amount is included as interest income in the calculation of TTP.

Excess of interest expense over interest income

Where the aggregate interest expense exceeds the aggregate interest income the excess or deficit may be relieved by:

- setting against TTP of the same accounting period (*after* trading losses brought forward but *before* a trading loss of the same or future periods and *before* qualifying charitable donations);
- surrendered as group relief (See Chapter 19);
- carried back and set against surpluses on non-trading relationships for the previous year; or
- carried forward and set against future non-trading profits (this is the default option if other methods of relief are not claimed).

Trading loan relationships

Trading loan relationships refer to the position where the interest payable or receivable is paid/received as part of the company's trade, for example, interest paid on a bank loan to buy new equipment for use in the company's trade. In such cases interest payable is allowed as a trading expense and trading interest receivable is treated as trading income (normally any interest income will not be treated as trading income but income as part of a non-trading relationship; see above).

Comprehensive example

The following provides a comprehensive example of the calculation of adjusted trading profit and TTP for a limited company.

Example 16.7

BRG Limited's accounts for the year ended 31 March 2021 show profits before tax of £656,870.

Included in this amount are rents of 48,000 that the company received from letting an investment property.

The expenses deducted include when calculating the profit include the following items:

Depreciation of 63,420 has been charged.

Legal expenses have been included of 12,000 in respect of the purchase of new business premises. Accountancy fees of 7,800 were included in connection with the preparation of the annual accounts.

The following items were included under the heading Entertaining:

Meals for customers	860
Christmas gifts of wine for suppliers	600
Staff party	970

Motor expenses include lease fees in respect of two motor cars:

Car 1 CO_2 rating 166 g/km leasing fees	8,000
Car 2 CO_2 rating 100 g/km leasing fees	5,000

Donations were made as follows:

Donation to local charity	100
Donation to national charity	2,000
Political donation	400

The company paid private golf club membership fees for the director of 900.

Capital allowances have been calculated as 288,028.

What is the adjusted trading profit and TTP of BRG Limited to 31 March 2021?

Answer

Profit per accounts		656,870
Less: Rents received		(48,000)
Add:		
Depreciation	63,420	
Legals:		
Property purchase (capital)	12,000	
Accountancy	0	
Entertaining:		
Meals for customers	860	
Christmas wine	600	
Staff Party	0	
Car lease restriction		
8,000 x 15%	1,200	
Charitable donations		
Local charity	0	
National charity	2,000	
Political donation	400	
Golf club membership	0	

		80,480
		689,350
Less: Capital allowances		(288,028)
Adjusted trading profits		401,322

Total taxable profits to 31 March 2021

Adjusted trading profit	401,322
Rental income	48,000
Less	
Qualifying charitable donations	-2,000
TTP	447,322

Notes

1. Rent received is not trading income. It is deducted when calculating the adjusted trading profit but must be included in the calculation of TTP.
2. See Chapter 6 for detailed rules of adjustments to trading profits. Where items of expenses are allowable, such as Accountancy no adjustment is required. Some exam conventions require this to be shown as an adjustment of "0" as included in this example.
3. Donations to the national charity are added back as not allowable in the calculation of adjusted trading profit but are deducted as qualifying charitable donations in the calculation of TTP.
4. The golf club subscription is effectively part of the managing director's remuneration. It is, therefore, an allowable part of the company's employment costs but will create a benefit in kind on the individual.

SUMMARY

Corporation tax is calculated on a company's TTP for an accounting period which cannot be longer than 12 months and not by reference to tax years.

Where an accounting period exceeds 12 months it must be split into two accounting periods of 12 months and the balance of the period with trading profits etc. apportioned as appropriate.

The rate of corporation tax is determined by the Financial Year. The profits of an accounting period may fall into more than one Financial Year.

Company taxable trading profits must be established by adding back any disallowable expenses to the accounting profits before tax and deducting any non-trading income and capital gains. However, no adjustments are required for private use.

Non-trading interest received and paid are aggregated to establish the net non-trade loan relationship result.

Qualifying charitable donations can be deducted when calculating TTP, however, deductions must be made in strict order, which in some circumstances can deny relief for QCD.

Companies pay corporation tax on capital gains (see Chapter 17).

CHAPTER 17

Chargeable Gains for Companies

INTRODUCTION

This chapter looks at the taxation of capital gains made by companies. Companies are not liable to capital gains tax. As detailed in Chapter 16, companies are liable to corporation tax on their profits *and* gains, known as taxable total profits (TTP).

Differences from CGT for individuals

Many of the rules applicable to individuals for calculating capital gains also apply to companies.

However, companies:

- do *not* pay capital gains tax but corporation tax on chargeable gains for an accounting period;
- are *not* entitled to an annual exemption;
- are not entitled to business asset disposal relief, gift relief or main residence relief;
- are entitled to indexation allowance (but frozen at 31 December 2017);
- have different rules for the identification of shares disposed of;
- For pre 31 March 1982 assets, the gain is the lower of the gain calculated using the original cost and the gain using the 31 March 1982 value.

With respect to share sales, the matching rules are similar, but not identical, to those applying to individuals.

The matching rules for companies are as follows:
1. same-day purchases, then
2. previous nine days purchases, then
3. share pool.

On the sale of certain business assets, roll-over relief may be claimed as applies to sole traders (see Chapter 15).

Indexation allowance

Indexation allowance is an attempt to allow for inflation (i.e. the time value of money). Indexation allowance is deducted when calculating any gain arising to a company, with certain restrictions detailed below.

The indexation allowance is computed by multiplying the allowable expenditure of an asset by an indexation factor. The resulting indexation allowance is then deducted, reducing the capital gain on that asset.

The indexation factor is calculated by reference to the Retail Prices Index (RPI):

<u>RPI for the month of disposal - RPI for the month of acquisition</u>
        RPI for the month of acquisition

Indexation allowance is limited to the increase in RPI since March 1982. For earlier acquisitions use March 1982 as the month of acquisition when calculating indexation allowance.

Under Finance Act 2018, indexation allowance has been frozen for disposals after 31 December 2017. Indexation allowance is still given but is only calculated up to 31 December 2017 – for disposals after December 2017, use December 2017 as the month of disposal to calculate indexation allowance.

RPI refers to the Retail Price Index (a monthly figure calculated for the UK government).

The index factor is normally shown as a decimal and is rounded to three decimal places except when applying to a share pool.

Indexation allowance can only reduce any capital gain to nil. Therefore indexation allowance cannot turn a capital gain into a capital loss or increase a capital loss.

No indexation allowance is available for the incidental *disposal* costs. Such costs are simply deducted from gross sale proceeds.

Example 17.1

JKP Ltd sells an asset in December 2020 for £26,000 before selling costs of £400. JKP Ltd acquired the asset in May 2012 for £10,000.

The RPI for May 2012 is 242.4 and for December 2017 is 278.1.

Calculate JKP Ltd's capital gain.

Answer

Gross sale proceeds	26,000
Less:	
Incidental costs of disposal	(400)
Net sale proceeds	25,600
Less: Cost of asset	(10,000)
Unindexed capital gain	15,600
Less: Indexation allowance	(1,470) (See below)
Indexed capital gain	14,130

Indexation allowance
The increase in RPI is calculated as:
(RPI for December 2017- RPI for May 2012)/RPI for May 2012
The RPI for May 2012 is 242.4 and for December 2017 is 278.1
(278.1-242.4)/242.4 = 0.147277 rounded to three decimal places = 0.147
Indexation allowance is cost x increase in RPI
Indexation allowance = 10,000 x 0.147 = £1,470

Example 17.2

LMP Ltd sells an asset in June 2020 for £30,000 before selling costs of £1,000. LMP Ltd acquired the asset in March 2008 for £15,000.

In addition, further capital expenditure of £5,000 was incurred in June 2010, enhancing the value of the asset.

Indexation allowance must be calculated separately for the initial cost from March 2008 and from June 2010 for the enhancement expenditure.

The Indexation factor for the period March 2008 to December 2017 is 0.311 and for the period June 2010 to December 2017 is 0.241

Calculate LMP Ltd's capital gain.

Answer

June 2019 Gross sale proceeds		30,000
Less: Incidental costs of disposal		(1,000)
Net sale proceeds		29,000
Less:		
Cost of asset	15,000	
Enhancement expenditure	5,000	
		(20,000)
Unindexed capital gain		9,000
Less:		
Indexation allowance		
15,000 x 0.311	4,665	
5,000 x 0.241	1,205	
Total indexation allowance		(5,870)
Indexed capital gain		3,130

Notes

1. A calculation of indexation allowance is required separately for each individual item of cost (e.g. original purchase cost and enhancement expenditure).
2. If the indexation allowance was £3,130 or more than calculated, then the gain would be reduced to Nil. Any excess indexation allowance cannot create a loss.
3. Indexation allowance is only calculated to 31 December 2017.

As can be seen, the indexation allowance simply reduces the amount of the unindexed capital gain, it cannot create or increase a loss.

Example 17.3

WXT Limited sold an asset in March 2021 for £26,000 having acquired it in January 2015 for £24,500.

The RPI for January 2015 is 255.4 and for December 2017 is 278.1.

Calculate WXT Ltd's capital gain.

Answer

Gross sale proceeds	26,000
Less:	
Cost of asset	(24,500)
Unindexed capital gain	1,500

Less:
Indexation allowance (Maximum)   2,180
Indexation allowance (Restricted)   (1,500)
Indexed gain   0

Notes

Indexation allowance cannot create or increase a loss. The full indexation allowance would reduce the unindexed gain of £1,500 to a loss. Therefore, indexation allowance is restricted to £1,500, giving an indexed gain of £Nil.

Indexation allowance
The increase in RPI is calculated as:
(RPI for December 2017 - RPI for January 2015)/RPI for January 2015
(278.1-255.4)/255.4 = 0.08888 rounded to three decimal places = 0.089
Indexation allowance is cost x increase in RPI
Indexation allowance = 24,500 x 0.089 = £2,180

Share identification and indexation for share pools

Where share disposals are made by companies rather than individuals the matching rules are slightly different.

Shares in a single company sold by a company are matched as follows:
1. First with acquisitions on the same day
2. Then with acquisitions within the preceding nine days on a first in, first out basis
3. Finally, with shares in the pool.

Companies are entitled to indexation allowance up to the date of a share sale or 31 December 2017 if earlier.

Therefore, it will be necessary to calculate the indexed cost of the share pool at the date of any share disposals. In other words, it may be necessary to work out the amount of any indexation allowances on a "rolling basis".

In calculating the pool it is necessary to index the pool cost (without rounding to three decimal places when working out any indexation factors) between successive operative events (i.e. subsequent purchases and sales) to find the indexed cost before the disposal. The indexed cost of any shares disposed of can then be calculated and deducted from the pool.

Example 17.4

JSD Ltd acquired 1,000 shares in ABC plc in October 2000 for £3,000. In August 2005 a further 2,000 shares in ABC plc were acquired for £7,000 and in October 2010 a further 1,500 shares in ABC plc were acquired for £4,000.

JSD Ltd then sold 3,000 shares in ABC plc on 11 May 2020 for £15,600.

JSD Ltd prepares its accounts to 31 March each year.

RPI was as follows:

October 2000	171.6
August 2005	192.6
October 2010	225.8
December 2017	278.1

What is JSD Ltd's chargeable gain for its accounting period ended 31 March 2021?

Answer

No shares in ABC plc were purchased either on the same day of the sale (i.e. 11 May 2020) or in the nine days prior to it.

Therefore, any matching is with shares forming part of the share pool. Before any matching can be done the indexed value of the pool as at the date of the share sale must be calculated. The indexation allowance("IA") must be calculated between each event, creating a "rolling" indexed cost.

ABC plc shareholding	Number of shares	Cost £	Indexed cost £
October 2000	1,000	3,000	3,000
IA 10/2000 to 8/2005 £3,000 x (192.6-171.6)/171.6 =			367
			3,367
August 2005	2,000	7,000	7,000
	3,000	10,000	10,367
IA 8/2005 to 10/2010 £10,367 x (225.8-192.6)/192.6 =			1,787
			12,154
October 2010	1,500	4,000	4,000
	4,500	14,000	16,154
IA 10/2010 to 12/2017 £16,154 x (278.1-225.8)/225.8 =			3,741
			19,895

Therefore, at May 2019, prior to the sale, 4,500 shares were held with a cost of £14,000 and an indexed cost of £19,895 (the difference between these two amounts being the cumulative indexation allowance)

May 2019 sale	(3,000)	(9,333)	(13,263)
Pool balances	1,500	4,667	6,632

The gain can now be calculated:

May 2019 3,000 shares sold proceeds	15,600
Less: Cost	(9,333)
Indexation allowance (Note 3)	(3,930)
Gain	2,337

Notes

1. The pool is indexed to each successive operative event (i.e. each subsequent purchase and sale) in turn until the pool value as at the date of any sale is known. Indexation factors are not restricted to three decimal places.
2. The cost of the shares sold in May 2019 is calculated as 14,000 x 3,000/4500 and a similar apportionment is used for the indexed cost.
3. The indexation allowance on the sale is the difference between the indexed cost of £13,263 and the cost £9,333. In this case, there seems little point in showing these

amounts separately but this calculation can be useful when ensuring that indexation allowance does not create or increase any loss.

4. A similar share pool calculation will be required for each shareholding.

Scrip and rights issues

The comments made in connection with bonus and rights issues for individuals in Chapter 14 apply equally to companies, subject to the fact that indexation allowance will apply to the cost of rights issues.

Capital losses

A capital loss must be offset against any chargeable gains of the same accounting period and any unrelieved amount of loss may then be carried forward for offset against future chargeable gains.

Capital gains reliefs applying to companies only

Substantial shareholdings exemption

From April 2002, a chargeable gain made by a company on the disposal of the whole or any part of a qualifying substantial shareholding in another trading company is exempt from corporation tax.

A qualifying substantial shareholding is an ordinary shareholding of 10% or more. The shareholding must give a beneficial entitlement of at least 10% of profits available for distribution to shareholders *and* assets available for distribution on a winding up. In addition, the disposing company must have held the qualifying shareholding for a continuous period of 12 months during the six years preceding the disposal. This allows part disposals to continue to qualify for relief for five years after the shareholding has fallen below 10%.

The 12 months rule can also be met where the shares are in a new company, where that company received assets from another 75% group company and the assets transferred were used by another group trading company for the 12 months before transfer. F(2)A2017 has also extended the relief to certain holdings of less than 10% provided it cost at least £20 million.

Similarly, capital losses on such shareholdings are not allowable.

Where the substantial shareholdings exemption applies, it is automatic and does not require an election.

Replacement of business assets or Roll-over relief

Chargeable gains roll-over relief is not available for companies concerning the sale and purchase of intellectual property (e.g. goodwill, patents etc. (Asset classes 4 to 7A detailed in TCGA1992 section 155)).

Chargeable gains roll-over relief continues to be available for other chargeable assets as previously described in Chapter 15.

SUMMARY

A company's capital gains are included in TTP for an accounting period and subject to corporation tax.

Companies are not entitled to an annual exemption but gains are reduced by indexation allowance.

Indexation allowance reduces the gain by the increase in the RPI between acquisition and disposal. Indexation allowance cannot increase or create a loss. Indexation allowance is frozen at 31 December 2017.

Share identification or matching rules for companies are different to the rules for individuals.

Companies can take advantage of the relief for replacement business assets and substantial shareholding exemption.

CHAPTER 18

Company Losses

INTRODUCTION

This chapter examines how a company may claim corporation tax relief for any losses incurred.

The following chapter will look at how a company's trading loss may be used by other companies in the same *group* as the loss-making company.

Types of loss

An ongoing company may incur various types of loss for an accounting period. These losses are:

- trading loss
- property business loss
- net interest loss (or loan relationship deficit)
- capital loss

Trading losses

A company making a trading loss for an accounting period has three options:

1. Make a claim under CTA2010 section 37 to offset the loss against total profits for the same accounting period (current year claim).
2. Once a claim has been made against current year profits, a further claim, under section 37, can be made to offset the loss against total profits for the 12 month period preceding the loss-making period (previous year claim).
3. Carry forward trading losses arising on or after 1 April 2017 against a specified amount of total profits for future accounting periods (CTA2010 section 45A).

A trading loss is computed in the same way as a trading profit for any accounting period. Capital allowances increase any loss claim, so it is possible to claim less than the maximum capital allowances available.

Claim against total profits of the current year (CTA2010 section 37)

Under section 37, a company may make a claim for the losses to be set against total profits of the same accounting period. The loss reduces profits before the deduction of qualifying charitable donations (QCD) as noted in the example below.

The loss must be relieved to the maximum amount possible – the claim will be for the lower of the available loss or the total profits of the year of claim, which may deny relief for QCD.

Loss claims under section 37 must be made within two years after the end of the loss-making period.

Example 18.1

LMC Ltd has the following results for the year to 31 March 2021:

	£
Trading loss	(118,000)
Chargeable gains	40,000
Net interest income	15,000
Qualifying charitable donations	(2,000)

How much section 37 loss relief can be claimed against profits to 31 March 2021?

Answer

	£
Trading profit	0
Chargeable gains	40,000
Net interest income	15,000
Total profits	55,000
S37 Current year loss claim	(55,000)
	0
Qualifying charitable donations	Wasted
TTP	0

Notes

1. Trading profit to 31.3.21 is £Nil. (Do not include the loss in the computation at this point).
2. Losses must be claimed to the full extent of profits and gains.
3. Loss relief is given before relief for qualifying charitable donations (QCD). For the year to 31.3.21, this means that relief for QCD is lost or wasted.
4. A loss memo is a useful way of tracking losses arising and utilisation:

Loss year ended 31 March 2021	118,000
Current year claim	(55,000)
Balance of loss	63,000

Claim against total profits of the previous year (CTA2010 section 37)

After the loss has been claimed against total profits of the accounting period of the loss, a further optional claim may be made to carry back any remaining trading loss to the previous 12 months. (Compare this to the position for sole traders under the equivalent section 64; see Chapter 8). There is, however, no requirement to carry back any unrelieved loss.

The loss must be relieved to the maximum amount possible – the claim will be for the lower of the available loss or the total profits. It is not possible, for example, under section 37 to carry back to the previous 12 months only a selected portion of the unrelieved loss; the maximum possible relievable loss must be carried back.

Loss claims under section 37 must be made within two years after the end of the loss-making period.

Example 18.2

Following on from example 18.1 above, LMC Ltd has the following results for the year to 31 March 2020:

	£
Trading profit	44,000
Chargeable gains	6,000
Net interest income	9,000
Qualifying charitable donations	(1,500)

How much of the balance of loss may be claimed under section 37 against profits to 31 March 2020?

Answer

	£
Trading profit	44,000
Chargeable gains	6,000
Net interest income	9,000
Total profits	59,000
S37 Previous year loss claim	(59,000)
	0
Qualifying charitable donations	Wasted
TTP	0

Notes

1. Losses must be claimed to the full extent of profits and gains.
2. Loss relief is given before relief for qualifying charitable donations (QCD). For the year to 31.3.20, this means that relief for QCD is lost or wasted.
3. The loss claim is optional but cannot be made unless a current year claim has been made.
4. The loss memo can be updated:

	£
Loss year ended 31 March 2021	118,000
Current year claim	(55,000)
	63,000
Previous year claim	(59,000)
Balance of loss	4,000

Accounting periods of different lengths

It may be that a company's accounting year end changes. This would then mean that the length of the accounting period will vary.

For example, a company may make its accounts up to 31 December each year. Following the preparation of the accounts to say 31 December 2018 the company may then decide to change to a 31 March year end. A set of accounts will then be prepared to 31 March 2019 and 31 March each year thereafter. The accounting period to 31 March 2019 will thus be only three months long.

In such case, care is needed in offsetting any trading losses carried back, as detailed in the following example.

Example 18.3

JK Ltd has the following results:

	Year ended 31.12.19	3 months to 31.3.20	Year ended 31.3.21
Trading profit	50,000	150,000	(750,000)
Chargeable gains	50,000	40,000	30,000
Net interest income	25,000	15,000	40,000
QCD	12,000	3,000	15,000

Show how section 37 losses can be claimed.

Answer

The loss strategy set out above requires that the trading loss for the accounting period ended 31.3.21 should be used first against current income and gains; then against those of the previous 12 months. In this case, however, the previous 12 months is the period 1.4.19 to 31.3.20.

This period includes nine months of the accounting period ended 31.12.19 (i.e. 1.4.19 to 31.12.19) and the three months from 1.1.20 to 31.3.20.

Finally, if any surplus loss remains it should be carried forward to the accounting period ending 31.3.22.

	Year ended 31.12.19	3 months to 31.3.20	Year ended 31.3.21
Trading profit	50,000	150,000	nil
Less:			
Chargeable gains	50,000	40,000	30,000
Net interest income	25,000	15,000	40,000
Total profit	125,000	205,000	70,000
Less.			
Section 37 loss current year			(70,000)
Section 37 loss	(93,750)	(205,000)	
Less:			
QCD	(12,000)	(nil)	(nil)
TTP	19,250	nil	nil

Notes

1. The trading loss of £750,000 is first used, under section 37, against "total profit" to 31.3.21 of £70,000 leaving £680,000 loss remaining.
2. The surplus can then be carried back and offset against "total profit" of £205,000 for the three months to 31.03.20. However, under section 37, the £680,000 loss can be carried back 12 months. £205,000 of it has been carried back three months.
3. The balance (i.e. £680,000 less £205,000) can still be carried back a further nine months covering the period 1.4.19 to 31.12.19. The profits available for offset for these nine months are 9/12 x 125,000 = 93,750. The remaining profits arose up to 31.3.19 and are therefore not inside the 12 month carryback period.
4. Of the trading loss of £750,000, some £368,750 has been used under section 37 leaving £381,250 for future carry forward.
5. The QCD for the accounting periods ended 31.3.19 and 31.3.20 are unrelieved. They cannot be carried back or forward for relief.

Carry forward against total profits (CTA2010 section 45A)

Section 45A was introduced by F(No2)A 2017 and extends the scope for claims for losses carried forward. Trading losses arising on or after 1 April 2017 may be carried forward and claimed against total profits of future accounting periods. (see Appendix to this chapter for losses arising before 1 April 2017).

A claim under section 45A may specify the amount of the loss to be claimed and, for example, may be restricted to avoid wasting relief for QCD. If any loss remains, then this will continue to be carried forward. A claim must be made within two years of the end of the accounting period of relief.

There are a number of conditions which must be met for section 45A losses to be set off against total profits. These include:

- the company must continue to carry on the trade in all subsequent accounting periods up to and including the one in which the losses are offset;
- the trade must not have become small or negligible in the loss-making period; and
- the trade must be carried on commercially in both the loss-making period and period of set-off.

Example 18.4

Following on from Example 18.2 above, LMC Ltd has the following results for the year to 31 March 2022:

	£
Trading profit	18,000
Chargeable gains	0
Net interest income	6,000
Qualifying charitable donations	(1,000)

How much of the balance of loss may be claimed under section 45A against profits to 31 March 2022?

Answer

	£
Trading profit	18,000
Chargeable gains	0
Net interest income	6,000
Total profits	24,000
S45A Loss brought forward	(4,000)
	20,000
Qualifying charitable donations paid	(1,000)
TTP	19,000

Notes

1. Loss relief is given before relief for qualifying charitable donations (QCD). For the year to 31.3.22, this leaves sufficient profits so that relief for QCD is not lost. However, the

---

loss claim may be for a specified amount therefore, it is possible to avoid the loss of relief for QCD.

2. The loss memo can be updated:

Loss year ended 31 March 2021	118,000
Current year claim (APE 31.3.21)	(55,000)
	63,000
Previous year claim (APE 31.3.20)	(59,000)
	4,000
Carry forward claim (APE 31.3.22)	(4,000)
Balance of loss	0

The loss has now been claimed in full.

Restriction on carried forward loss claims

For carry forward loss claims after 1 April 2017, there is a cap on the losses that may be relieved, regardless of when the losses arose.

Generally, the loss restriction only limits the amount of losses that can be claimed by carrying forward where profits are above £5 million. The restriction limits the carry forward loss claim to £5 million referred to as the deductions allowance, plus 50% of profits above £5 million. If the accounting period is less than 12 months then the £5 million limit is time apportioned. It is also shared by group companies.

Example 18.5

FGH Ltd has total profits for the year to 30 June 2021 of £12 million and post-1 April 2017 losses brought forward of £20 million. What is the maximum claim under section 45A?

Answer

The section 45A loss claim will be restricted to £5 million plus 50% of the remaining profits of £7m, giving a maximum of £8.5m profits to be relieved by carried-forward losses. The result of this is that FGH Ltd will pay corporation tax on the remaining profits of £3.5m.

Terminal loss relief (CTA2010 section 39)

Where a company ceases to trade, terminal losses may arise, which can no longer be carried forward.

Terminal loss relief is available for the trading loss for the last 12 months of trading.

A company must first claim relief under section 37 against total profits of the loss making accounting period. Then, the remaining loss arising in the last 12 months of trading, or terminal loss, may be carried back (under CTA2010 section 39) against income and gains (before QCD) of the three previous years, giving relief against later years first (LIFO basis).

Example 18.6

YZ Ltd has the following results:

	Year ended 31.12.19	Year ended 31.12.20	3 months to 31.3.21
Trading profit	50,000	50,000	(250,000)
Chargeable gains	50,000	40,000	30,000
Net interest income	25,000	15,000	40,000
Qualifying charitable donations	12,000	3,000	15,000

YZ Ltd ceased to trade on 31 March 2021.

Show how the trading loss to 31.3.21 may be used.

Answer

	Year ended 31.12.19	Year ended 31.12.20	3 months to 31.3.21
Trading profit	50,000	50,000	nil
Chargeable gains	50,000	40,000	30,000
Net interest income	25,000	15,000	40,000
Total profit	125,000	105,000	70,000
Less:			
Section 37 loss			(70,000)
Section 39 losses	(75,000)	(105,000)	
Less:			
QCD	(12,000)	(nil)	(nil)
TTP	38,000	nil	nil

Notes

1. Under section 37, £70,000 of the trading loss for the three months ended 31.3.21 has been offset against other profits to 31.03.21. This leaves £180,000 losses to be relieved.
2. The terminal loss is for the last 12 months (i.e. 1.4.20 to 31.3.21 and is the aggregate of the trading losses for the periods 1.4.20 to 31.12.20 and 1.1.21 to 31.3.21. For the period 1.4.20 to 31.12.20 a trading profit, not a trading loss arose. For the purpose of calculating the terminal loss, this is ignored.
3. £105,000 of the Terminal loss is claimed against the year to 31.12.20 to reduce total profits to £Nil. The remainder of the loss, £75,000 is claimed against total profits to 31.12.19.

Property business losses

A property business loss for an accounting period must be set off against non-property business income and chargeable gains (Total profits) of the same accounting period before QCD. The relief is given before relief for any trading losses and must be for the lower of the available loss or the total profit – a partial claim is not allowed. This current year claim is automatic and a formal claim is not required.

Any unrelieved property business loss may be carried forward and claimed against total profits of future accounting periods before QCD. However, the amount of the claim for brought forward losses may be limited to any specified amount to prevent wasting relief for QCD. Alternatively, any unrelieved property business loss may be surrendered as group relief (see Chapter 19).

Non-trading loan relationship debits

As mentioned in Chapter 16 where the aggregate non-trading loan relationship debits (broadly non-trading loan interest) exceeds the aggregate non-trading-interest income the loss arising may be relieved by:

- claiming against total profits of the same accounting period (*before* the trading losses, property business losses and *before* qualifying charitable donations);
- carried back and set against surpluses on non-trading loan relationships of the previous year; or
- carried forward and set against future total profits;
- surrendered as group relief (see Chapter 19).

Relief is not automatic and may be claimed for a specified amount.

Capital losses

A capital loss must be offset against any chargeable gains of the same accounting period and any unrelieved amount of loss may then be carried forward for offset against future chargeable gains. The limit of brought forward losses that may be relieved is subject to the same restriction on carried forward trading loss claims detailed above.

Capital losses may not be carried back to earlier accounting periods.

Loss strategy

Losses should be used in the most tax efficient manner available. Generally speaking, this will mean using the loss as soon as possible but care should be taken to avoid wasting tax relief for QCD.

Historically, losses would be utilised against profits subject to the highest rate of corporation tax, however, corporation tax rates have remained unchanged for several years now.

SUMMARY

Since April 2017, the rules for companies to claim loss relief have generally become more flexible. However, for some larger companies, there will be a limit on the amount of loss relief that may be claimed.

A company may make a current year claim for relief for trading losses against other income and gains of the loss-making accounting period. After this, the company may optionally claim relief against profits of the previous 12 months.

Alternatively, subject to meeting the qualifying conditions, a claim may be made for loss relief of a specified amount in subsequent accounting periods. This carry forward claim is limited to the deductions limit, usually £5 million plus 50% of the profits above £5 million.

Property losses and excess non-trade loan relationship deficits can be relieved in-year or carried forward.

Additional relief is available for losses in the final year of trading under the terminal loss rules.

Capital losses must first be offset against in-year capital gains and are then carried forward against future capital gains.

Alternative loss claims should be considered to maximise the benefit of the relief.

APPENDIX

Carry forward of losses arising before 1 April 2017 (CTA2010 section 45)

Under section 45, where losses arising prior to 1 April 2017 were brought forward, the loss must be relieved against the first available profits from the same trade only, but otherwise can be carried forward indefinitely until fully utilised. Loss relief under section 45 was automatic against the first available profits of the same trade and a formal claim was not required.

Example 18.7

PQR Ltd has the following results:

	Year ended		
	31.12.14	**31.12.15**	**31.12.16**
Trading profit	(350,000)	250,000	115,000
Chargeable gains	50,000	40,000	30,000
Net interest income	25,000	15,000	40,000

Show how section 45 relief applies. Assume that a section 37 claim is not made.

Answer

	Year ended		
	31.12.14	**31.12.15**	**31.12.16**
Trading profit	0	250,000	115,000
Less:			
Section 45 loss carried forward	0	(250,000)	(100,000)
Chargeable gains	50,000	40,000	30,000
Net interest income	25,000	15,000	40,000
TTP	75,000	55,000	85,000
Loss memo:			
Loss available/ brought forward	(350,000)	(350,000)	(100,000)
Loss claim s45	0	250,000	100,000
Loss carried forward	(350,000)	(100,000)	0

Note

1. The loss is shown as 0 in the computation of TTP for the CAP to 31.12.14.
2. Under section 45 the trading loss of the accounting period ended 31.12.14 is simply carried forward and offset to the maximum extent possible against future trading profits only, of future accounting periods.
3. A loss memo is a useful tool to record losses arising and how they are claimed.

Where pre 1 April 2017 are carried forward after that date, the claim is no longer automatic and the restriction on brought forward loss relief detailed earlier in the chapter also applies.

CHAPTER 19

Groups of Companies

INTRODUCTION

Chapters 16 to 18 examined the corporation tax position of a single company.

This chapter looks at the position where there is more than one company and together the companies form a *group* for corporation tax purposes. There are several advantages for group companies.

Where a group exists four key provisions may arise:

- the trading losses of one group company can be transferred and used by other companies in the same group (referred to as group relief);
- the chargeable assets of one group company can be transferred to another company in the same group without creating an immediate chargeable gain/loss;
- chargeable gains and allowable losses may be transferred to another group company; and
- chargeable gains roll-over relief is available amongst group companies.

Definition of group

There is not one single definition of a group for corporation tax purposes. The definition depends upon whether the objective is to ascertain whether group relief is available or whether tax free intra-group asset transfers and other capital gains aspects are possible.

Group relief

The term group relief refers to the ability of one company in a group, as defined below, (referred to as the *surrendering* company) to give or surrender a trading loss to another company in the same group (referred to as the *claimant* company).

Both the claimant and surrendering company must be within the charge to UK corporation tax (i.e. be resident in the UK or trading in the UK through a permanent establishment). However, an overseas company can be used to link UK based companies, for example where an overseas parent company has two wholly owned UK subsidiaries, a group relief claim would be possible between the UK companies.

In addition to group relief for trading losses, a company can also surrender net non-trade loan relationship debits, excess QCD and property business losses of an accounting period to another group company.

For group relief purposes two companies are members of the same group if one of the companies is a 75% subsidiary of the other *or* both companies are 75% subsidiaries of a third company.

A company is a *75% subsidiary* of another company if:

- 75% or more of its ordinary share capital is owned directly or indirectly by the other company; *and*
- the other company is entitled to at least 75% or more of its profits available for distribution to ordinary shareholders; *and*
- the other company is entitled to at least 75% of the assets in the event of a winding-up of the company.

Example 19.1

A Ltd owns 75% of B Ltd. B Ltd owns 75% C Ltd.

B Ltd is a direct 75% subsidiary of A Ltd. Therefore A Ltd and B Ltd *are* in the same group for group relief.

C Ltd is a direct 75% subsidiary of B Ltd. Therefore B Ltd and C Ltd *are* in the same group for group relief.

What about A and C?

Is C a 75% direct or indirect subsidiary of A? A's indirect shareholding interest in C is 75% x 75% = 56.25%. Therefore, C is not either a direct or indirect 75% subsidiary of A and therefore A and C are *not* in the same group.

There are in effect two separate groups for group relief i.e. A and B; and B and C. Thus, A and B can surrender losses to each other and so can B and C. However, C cannot surrender its loss to B which in turn then surrenders it to A.

Note:

For *group* purposes, it is necessary to multiply percentage share ownership to ascertain whether one company is an indirect subsidiary of another (e.g. A and C above).

Example 19.2

X Ltd owns 75% of both Y Ltd and Z Ltd

X and Y are in the same group for group relief.

X and Z are in the same group for group relief.

In addition, as Y and Z are both 75% subsidiaries of the same third company (i.e. X) then Y and Z are also in the same group (see group definition above).

Therefore, X, Y and Z are all in the same group for group relief.

Example 19.3

A Ltd		
75%	60%	75%
B Ltd	C Ltd	D Ltd

A and B are in a 75% group.
A and D are in a 75% group.
B and D are in the same group as both are 75% subsidiaries of A.

Therefore A, B and D are in the same group for group relief.

A and C are *not* in the same group (C is *not* a 75% subsidiary of A).
B and C are *not* in the same group (as both are not 75% subsidiaries of the same company).
C and D are *not* in the same group (as both are not 75% subsidiaries of the same company).
C is simply not part of any group as it is not a 75% subsidiary of any company.

Briefly, group relief allows one group company to surrender all or part of current year or brought forward losses to other group companies to reduce their taxable profits. Group relief may be used without the company with the trading loss first using the current year loss itself (e.g. under CTA2010 section 37). The option chosen will depend upon where the greatest tax saving can be made.

Current year trading loss surrender

The surrendering company can surrender its current year trading loss for an accounting period either in full or in part to another group company and does not first need to use the trading loss itself (note, however, that in the case of surplus QCD and property business losses the surrendering company must have first tried to itself obtain relief for these two items before they can be surrendered).

The trading loss may be surrendered simply to one other group company or may be split amongst any number of group companies.

Up until 31 March 2017, group relief could only be given for current year losses.

Example 19.4

PRT Limited owns 90% of the ordinary share capital of RTU Limited. For the year to 31 March 2020, PRT Limited has a trading loss of £205,000. For the same accounting period, RTU Limited has trading profits of £180,000 and paid QCD of £6,000.

Show how PRT Limited can surrender losses as group relief to RTU Limited without wasting any relief for QCD.

Answer

PRT Limited should surrender trading losses of £174,000 to RTU Limited by way of group relief:

	PRT Limited	RTU Limited
Trading profits	0	180,000
Less: QCD		(6,000)
Less: Group relief		(174,000)
TTP	nil	nil

PRT Limited has trading losses remaining of £31,000 (£205,000 less £174,000). This loss can be carried forward by PRT Limited.

From 1 April 2017 – Expansion of relief to include losses brought forward

The reformed loss relief rules applying from 1 April 2017 expand claims with the introduction of group relief for carried forward losses. This only applies to losses arising from 1 April 2017.

Before brought forward losses can be surrendered, a company must first maximise the loss against its own profits.

Limitation on loss relief for brought forward losses for groups

When considering relief for brought forward losses after 1 April 2017, the deductions allowance applies of £5 million, as detailed in Chapter 18. This allowance must be shared between members of the same group, broadly following the rules for group relief. Group companies must nominate a company to formally claim the £5 million allowance for the entire group. The nominated company will be required to submit a statement within 12 months of the end of its accounting period setting out how the £5 million group deductions allowance has been allocated within the group.

Change of ownership

Where there is a change of ownership, the surrender of brought forward losses as group relief is not available for pre-acquisition losses in the following five years.

Example 19.5

On 31 May 2019, two companies IJ Limited and KL limited are in the same group and are both eligible to surrender losses brought forward to the other. On 1 June 2019, both companies are acquired by XY Limited.

For the five years from 1 June 2019 IJ Limited and KL Limited will be unable to surrender losses incurred before 1 June 2019 to XY limited.

However, they are still able to surrender losses incurred before the change to each other.

Use by claimant company of group relief

The claimant company deducts the group relief against its own TTP (i.e. after QCD).

This, therefore, means that before the claimant company can use the trading loss claimed from another group company it must deduct any QCD of the current accounting period. If the claimant company has its own current year trading losses these do not need to be claimed under section 37 but an assumed claim must be deducted to calculate the maximum group relief that can be claimed.

Group relief is, however, utilised before deductions of any reliefs from a *subsequent* accounting period (e.g. trading loss carried back under section 37).

A claimant company cannot claim an amount of trading loss from a surrendering company which exceeds its own TTP against which the trading loss is to be offset. In other words, the maximum group relief a claimant company can claim is the *lower* of its own TTP and the loss available for group relief.

Example 19.6

A Ltd has a 100% wholly owned subsidiary B Ltd. Both companies prepare their accounts to 31 March 2021.

For the year ended 31 March 2021, A Ltd has a trading loss of £250,000 and no other profits.

For the same accounting period, B Ltd has a trading profit of £90,000; interest income of £25,000; property business income of £45,000; and chargeable gains of £60,000; and makes a qualifying charitable donation of £30,000. B Ltd also has a trading loss brought forward from an earlier accounting period of £25,000.

Show how A Ltd might use its trading loss under the group relief provisions.

Answer

Adopting the pro-forma from Chapter 16 for B Ltd (the claimant company) for the accounting period to 31 March 2021:

Trading profit	90,000
Property business profit	45,000
Interest income	25,000
Chargeable gains	60,000
Total profits	220,000
Less: Trading loss b/f	(25,000)
Less: QCD	(30,000)
	165,000
Less: Group relief	(165,000)
TTP	nil

Notes

1. Only £165,000 of A Ltd's trading loss of £250,000 should be surrendered by A Ltd to B Ltd as B Ltd only had TTP of £165,000.
2. The balance of the trading loss of (250,000 - 165,000) i.e. £85,000 can be carried forward by A Ltd or claimed by A Ltd under section 37.

Corresponding accounting periods

As indicated above a trading loss of an accounting period can be offset against the TTP of another group company. However, for the whole of the trading loss to be potentially available for surrender and offset against the other group company's TTP for an accounting period both companies accounting periods must coincide exactly (coterminous accounting periods).

In Example 19.4 this occurred as both companies accounting periods ended on 31 March each year.

Where the companies involved in the group relief claim do not have coterminous accounting periods (i.e. their respective accounting periods end on different dates) then any trading loss surrendered may only be used by the claimant company against its TTP for the *corresponding accounting period* i.e. that part of the accounting period of the claimant company which falls in the accounting period of the surrendering company's accounting period.

In fact, both the trading losses surrendered and the corresponding TTP are time apportioned.

Example 19.7

Parent Ltd has a wholly owned subsidiary, Sub Ltd. Parent Ltd makes a trading loss of £24,000 for its year ended 30 June 2020.

Sub Ltd has TTP of £36,000 and £20,000 for its years ended 30 September 2019 and 2020 respectively.

How can the group relief provisions be used?

Answer

Parent Ltd and Sub Ltd do not have coterminous accounting periods. Some apportionment is therefore necessary.

Parent Ltd		1.7.19	(24,000)	30.6.20	
Sub Ltd	1.10.18	36,000	30.9.19	20,000	30.9.20

Sub Ltd year ended 30 September 2019

Only the period of 3 months from 1.7.19 to 30.9.19 falls within Parent Ltd's accounting period ended 30 June 2020.

Therefore, Sub Ltd can potentially claim Parent Ltd trading loss attributable from 1.7.19 to 30.9.19, i.e. 3/12 x (24,000) = (6,000) for offset against its TTP for this corresponding period, i.e. Sub Ltd's TTP for this period is 3/12 x £36,000 = 9,000.

As Sub Ltd's TTP for this corresponding period exceeds the available trading loss of Parent Ltd the whole £6,000 loss may be claimed by Sub Ltd.

Sub Ltd year ended 30 September 2020

Sub Ltd can also potentially claim Parent Ltd's trading loss attributable to 1.10.19 to 30.6.20, i.e. 9/12 x (24,000) = (18,000).

Sub Ltd's TTP for this period is 9/12 x £20,000 = 15,000.

In this case, Sub Ltd's TTP is smaller than the trading loss of Parent Ltd available for relief.

Therefore, for its accounting period ended 30.9.20 Sub Ltd can only claim the lower of the trading loss potentially available i.e. £18,000 and its TTP for the corresponding period i.e. £15,000. The loss claimed is restricted to £15,000.

In total therefore of Parent Ltd's trading loss for the accounting period ended 30 June 2020 of £24,000, some £6,000 + £15,000 = £21,000 is available for group relief as shown above.

The balance of the trading loss of £3,000, which cannot be used for group relief, can be used by Parent Ltd against its current and prior year's profits under section 37 or be carried forward under section 45A.

Optimising group relief

Where a group comprises more than two companies and one company incurs a trading loss then the question arises as to how group relief should be claimed for the loss. In other words, against which of the other companies' TTP in the group should the loss be surrendered.

The amount of the loss surrendered to any company should be the claimant's TTP after deducting any QCD, to prevent the loss of relief for the QCD. Unlike some loss relief claims, the group relief claim is for a specified amount.

As all companies now pay a single rate of corporation tax, there is usually no tax benefit in choosing one company over another. However, this could be used to take a company out of the quarterly CT payments regime. In addition, as noted above, care should be taken where year ends do not correspond.

Example 19.8

A, B and C are three UK resident companies that form a 75% group for group relief purposes. All companies prepare accounts to 31 March annually.

The results for the year ended 31 March 2021 for each company are as follows:

	A	B	C
Trading profit	200,000	(250,000)	80,000
Property business profit	5,000	15,000	20,000
Interest income	20,000	nil	10,000
Chargeable gains	24,000	3,000	2,000
QCD paid	(5,000)	(2,000)	(15,000)

Show how the losses of B may be used.

Answer

First, calculate the position without any section 37 loss or group relief claims

	A	B	C
Trading profit	200,000	nil	80,000
Property business profit	5,000	15,000	20,000
Interest income	20,000	nil	10,000
Chargeable gain	24,000	3,000	2,000
Less:			
Section 37	nil	nil	nil
Less: QCD	(5,000)	(2,000)	(15,000)
TTP	**244,000**	**16,000**	**97,000**

Notes

1. Each of the companies will pay corporation tax at the same rate, so there is no saving by favouring a group relief claim to A over C.
2. We will assume that B would like to reduce its CT liability as far as possible in priority to other group companies, although as a group this will have no impact on the overall CT burden.

---

3. B does not have to make a claim under section 37 before group relief. Therefore, it may make a group relief claim to maximise the section 37 claim. By surrendering losses as group relief, the section 37 relief claim can be restricted to 16,000, B's TTP. Any higher claim by B Ltd will result in the loss of relief for QCD.

4. Therefore, of B's trading loss of 250,000, some 16,000 should be left after any group relief claim for B to claim under section 37.

5. Of the balance of the loss of 234,000, it makes no difference to the overall group liability if the loss is surrendered to A or C Ltd. However care should be taken to maximise relief for QCD.

6. If we assume that group relief is to be claimed by C Ltd first, then this should be for 97,000, C's TTP.

7. The balance of B's loss, 234,000 less 97,000, can be claimed by A Ltd.

8. Both B and C will now have TTP of Nil. However, A is still subject to tax on its post group relief Profit.

9. The actual position is that of B's loss of 250,000, 97,000 is claimed as group relief by C and 137,000 by A. The remaining loss of 16,000 is claimed under section 37 by B.

10. The revised TTP for all group companies can now be computed:

	A	B	C
Trading profit	200,000	nil	80,000
Property business profit	5,000	15,000	20,000
Interest income	20,000	nil	10,000
Chargeable gain	24,000	3,000	2,000
Less:			
Section 37	nil	(16,000)	nil
Less: QCD	(5,000)	(2,000)	(15,000)
TTP before Group relief	**244,000**	**nil**	**97,000**
Group relief	(137,000)		(97,000)
TTP after Group relief	**43,000**	**nil**	**nil**

Notes

Normally a claim under section 37 must be for the full amount of profits before deduction of QCD. However in this example by surrendering losses to other group companies, the loss remaining available for B to claim under section 37 have been reduced to £16,000, therefore preserving tax relief for the QCD in full.

In this example, there are various other options that the group could make. For example, the group relief claim by A could be increased and C would have TTP of £43,000 remaining taxable instead.

As was illustrated in the above example in some cases it may be appropriate for the company incurring the trading loss to use some of the losses itself under section 37 rather than surrendering it fully to other group companies.

In most cases, it will make no difference to the overall CT liability of the group if one company claims group relief in priority to another. However, the claims should be structured to avoid the loss of relief for QCD. Also, group relief may be targeted to remove a company from the requirement to pay CT by instalments.

If the claimant company makes a payment for the group relief, this is ignored for corporation tax purposes by both companies involved in the claim.

Chargeable gains group

For chargeable gains reliefs to apply a group is defined differently to that applicable for group relief.

For this purpose, a chargeable gains group is one with a principal (or top) company plus its 75% subsidiaries plus the subsidiaries' 75% subsidiaries and so on, subject to the principal company itself also possessing an effective interest of more than 50% in each company. A company can only be a member of one chargeable gains group.

Example 19.9

Using the structure of Example 19.1:

A Ltd owns 75% of B Ltd. B Ltd owns 75% of C Ltd.

A is the principal or top company.

B is a direct 75% subsidiary of A. Therefore, A and B *are* in a chargeable gains group.

C is a direct 75% subsidiary of B. Therefore, B and C and indeed A *are* all in the same chargeable gains group if, in addition, A possesses a greater than 50% shareholding in C. In fact A's effective shareholding in C is 75% x 75% = 56.25%.

A, B and C, therefore, form a chargeable gains group even though they do not form a group for group relief purposes (see Example 19.1).

It should, therefore, be noted that a group for group relief purposes may be a different group than one for chargeable gains purposes as shown in the above example.

However, the groups may also be the same (see below).

Example 19.10

A Ltd owns 75% of both B Ltd and C Ltd.

A is the principal or top company.

B and C are 75% subsidiaries of A and therefore A, B and C are in a chargeable gains group and are also in the same group for group relief purposes.

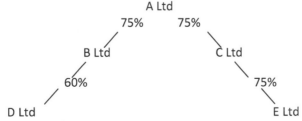

A is the principal company.

B and C are 75% subsidiaries of A and therefore A, B and C form a chargeable gains group.

D is not a 75% subsidiary of B. Therefore D is not a part of a chargeable gains group.

E is a 75% subsidiary of C. In addition A indirectly holds 75% x 75% = 56.25% of E. Therefore, E is also a part of the A, B and C chargeable gains group.

(Note that for group relief purposes A, B and C form a group, and C and E form a separate group).

The relevance of a chargeable gains group

The existence of a chargeable gains group allows three forms of relief to apply:

- assets may be transferred within the group without gains or losses arising;
- chargeable gains and allowable losses may be transferred to another group company; and
- roll-over relief may apply as if all the group companies were a single company.

Intragroup chargeable gains relief

Chargeable gains relief refers to the ability of a chargeable gains group of companies to transfer chargeable assets amongst themselves at no gain and no loss thus avoiding a corporate tax liability on the transfers. Typically this will legally transfer an asset no longer used by one company to another group company that can use the asset. The asset is deemed to have been transferred at original cost plus indexation allowance to the date of the transfer (up to December 2017).

As and when the chargeable asset is eventually sold outside the group a gain or loss will arise at that time and then be subject to corporation tax.

One advantage of this facility is that it enables the capital gains of one group company to be offset against the capital losses of another group company. This is achieved by the transfer of the asset from the one company to the other before sale to a third party so that the same company makes the gain and the loss.

Note, however, that any capital losses carried forward within a company must remain within that company. Therefore if one company is about to sell an asset at a gain then the asset on which the gain arises must be transferred to the company with the capital loss carried forward if these losses are to be used.

Example 19.11

JKL Ltd acquired a chargeable asset in January 2012 for £100,000. It transferred it to ABC Ltd a chargeable gains group company in January 2014 when it's market value was £175,000. ABC Ltd subsequently sold the asset outside the group in May 2019 for £300,000. Both companies prepare their accounts to 31 March each year.

Assume the indexation allowances for Jan 2012 to Jan 2014 and Jan 2014 to May 2019 (frozen at December 2017) are £31,400 and £11,169 respectively.

Show the position of both companies.

Answer

Transfer on January 2014

JKL Ltd is deemed to have transferred the asset to ABC Ltd at no gain and no loss i.e. at its original cost to JKL Ltd plus indexation to January 2014:

Asset transferred at £100,000 + £31,400 = £131,400

Thus the base cost of the asset to ABC Ltd = £131,400

Sale on May 2019

Sale proceeds	300,000
Less: Cost	(131,400)
	168,600
Less: Indexation (Jan 2014 to Dec 2017)	(11,169)
Indexed Gain	157,431

Note

The market value of the asset at the date of the inter-group transfer (i.e. £175,000) is irrelevant.

Election to transfer chargeable gains and allowable losses

Alternatively, members of a capital gains group may make a joint election simply to transfer current year gains and losses to another group company without legally transferring the asset. Therefore, for example, a company with losses brought forward may "receive" gains from another group company to utilise the losses and reduce the overall tax burden of the group. Both companies must be members of the group at the time that the gain or loss is made and the election must be made within two years after the end of the accounting period in which the disposal occurs. This means that the claim can be made retrospectively after the sale. This election can, therefore, reduce the administrative cost of legally transferring assets within a chargeable gains group.

Intragroup chargeable gains replacement of business assets relief (roll-over relief)

On the sale of certain business assets (i.e. land and buildings and fixed plant and machinery) *and* subject to satisfying certain conditions (i.e. reinvestment of the sale proceeds from the sale of the old asset in another new business asset must occur within one year before and three years after the sale of the old asset) a company may claim roll-over relief on the gain on the sale of the old asset (see Chapter 15 for further details).

Roll-over relief applies by allowing the company to defer a gain by reducing the base cost of the replacement asset by the indexed gain on the sale of the old asset.

However, where a chargeable gains group exists it is also possible for the indexed gain on the sale of a business asset by one company to be rolled-over against the acquisition cost of a business asset by another group company subject to satisfying the above conditions.

Example 19.12

HIJ Ltd sells a factory in January 2019 for £250,000 which had cost it £75,000 in March 2012. In March 2021 ABC Ltd a chargeable gains group company purchased another factory for £350,000.

Assume the indexation allowance for March 2012 to December 2017 is £29,475 (Indexation allowance is frozen at 31 December 2017).

What is the position for each of the two companies if roll-over relief is claimed?

Answer

As the replacement asset was acquired by a company within the same chargeable gains group within three years of the disposal, rollover relief is available.

HIJ Ltd

Sale proceeds	250,000
Less: Cost	(75,000)
	175,000
Less:	
Indexation allowance	(29,475)
Indexed gain	145,525
Rolled over gain	(145,525)
Chargeable	Nil

ABC Ltd

The base cost of the factory acquired by ABC Ltd is £350,000 – £145,525 = £204,475 (i.e. the actual cost reduced by the rolled over gain).

Where the full amount of the sale proceeds received by one company on the sale of a business asset are not reinvested by another member of the chargeable gains group, only a partial roll-over of the gain occurs and a balancing chargeable gain immediately occurs.

Example 19.13

If in Example 19.12 above ABC Ltd had bought a business asset for £225,000 then the position for each company would be as follows:

HIJ Ltd

Indexed gain (as above)		145,525
Less:		
Excess of sale proceeds over reinvestment	(250,000 – 225,000)	(25,000)
Gain eligible for roll-over		120,525
Gain immediately chargeable on HIJ Ltd		25,000

(this gain will be subject to corporation tax in the accounting period in which the sale by HIJ Ltd occurred).

ABC Ltd

The base cost of the asset acquired by ABC Ltd is £225,000 – £120,525 = £104,475.

It should be noted that to prevent the use of tax avoidance involving the transfer of assets to a chargeable group company prior to the sale outside of the group, a so-called degrouping charge can apply when a company ceases to be a member of a group owning an asset acquired from another group member within the previous six years.

SUMMARY

Groups of companies may benefit from various tax reliefs:

- group relief allowing relief against TTP for current year losses and brought forward losses surrendered by other group companies;
- tax free transfer of chargeable assets between group companies;
- the transfer of chargeable gains and allowable capital losses between group companies; and
- chargeable gains business asset roll-over relief within a group.

The definition as to what constitutes a group differs according to the relief under consideration.

Questions for students

See Appendix 2 for practice questions relating to Chapters 16 to 19. Answers are available online.

CHAPTER 20

National Insurance Contributions (NICs)

INTRODUCTION

National Insurance Contributions (NICs) may be payable on earned income, in addition to any income tax which may be due. Certain NICs give entitlement to state benefits. In particular, entitlement to full State Retirement Pension requires a minimum number of years NICs.

NICs are paid on employment income and self-employed profits including partnership trading profits. NICs are therefore not payable on income from holding investments. The amount of NICs payable is determined by the Class of NIC applying.

Classes of contributions

There are four classes of NIC applicable to individuals; namely, Classes 1, 2, 3 and 4. In addition, employers are also required to pay Class 1 NIC and Class 1A where appropriate.

Class 1

Employee

NICs under this class are paid by both employees *and* employers.

An employee pays Class 1 *Employees or Primary* NICs on *gross earnings* at the rate of 12% or 2%.

The 12% rate applies to gross earnings above a threshold of £9,500 per annum (£183 per week) up to a maximum of £50,000 per annum (£962 per week). In addition, employees must pay 2% on gross earnings above £50,000 per annum without further limit.

Gross earnings are any remuneration (wages, bonuses etc.) from an employer, paid in money or vouchers readily convertible to cash or goods. (but note also included are certain other readily convertible assets, e.g. wine, gold bars). No deductions are allowed for contributions to an employer's approved pension scheme, charitable donations under the payroll giving scheme or any expenses borne by the employee.

Excluded from gross earnings are mileage allowance payments to an employee who uses their own car on business (see Chapter 10) where such payments are up to 45 pence per mile for business mileage (any payments over this allowable limit are subject to both primary and secondary Class 1). Certain other cash benefits which may be paid to an employee (e.g. relocation expenses within the tax free limit; reimbursement of business expenses) are also excluded as are tips received directly from a customer.

The employee must be 16 years or older to be liable to NICs.

No Class 1 contributions are payable by an employee who reaches pensionable age but an employer is still liable for secondary contributions (see below).

Employer

Employers pay Class 1 Employers or *Secondary* NICs on their employee's *gross earnings* at the rate of 13.8% above the threshold of £8,788 per annum (£169 per week) with no upper limit.

Example 20.1

Mark is an employee and for the tax year, 2020/21 earns £400 per week.

His own (primary) Class 1 NICs = 12% x (£400 − £183) = £26.04 per week.

His employer (secondary) NICs = 13.8% x (£400 − £169) = £31.87 per week

Example 20.2

Tracy is an employee and for the tax year, 2020/21 earns £1,000 per week.

Her own (primary) Class 1 NICs = 12% x (£962* − £183) + 2% x (£1,000 − £962) = £93.48 + £0.76 = £94.24 per week.
*maximum £962 per week for employee

Her employer (secondary) NICs = 13.8% x (£1,000 − £169) = £114.67 per week

---

Contribution periods

Both employer and employee Class 1 NICs are calculated for a contribution period.

A contribution period is a week or a month, or another such period, matching how the employee is regularly paid. Gross earnings for a contribution period then form the amount on which NIC is payable. Throughout the tax year, each contribution period is treated separately i.e. gross earnings are not cumulated throughout the tax year.

In order to avoid potential abuse by directors of companies such individuals are deemed to have an *annual* earnings period (rather than a weekly or monthly period for employees) with:

- an annual earnings threshold of £9,500 and an upper limit of £50,000 for employee's contributions; and
- an annual earnings threshold of £8,788 for employer's contributions.

The object is to stop directors paying themselves a low weekly/monthly salary and a large single bonus in one single week/month.

Example 20.3

Kevin is paid a monthly salary of £3,000. In March 2021 a bonus is paid to Kevin of £10,000.

What are the primary Class 1 NICs payable by Kevin in 2020/21 if
(a) Kevin is an employee?
(b) Kevin is a director?

Answer

a) As an employee

Kevin, therefore, receives 11 monthly payments of £3,000 and one monthly payment of £3,000 plus the one-off bonus payment of £10,000.

For all months up to March 2021, Kevin's primary NIC will be

12% x (£3,000 – £792*) = £264.96 per month

*£9,500/12 = £792 per month

For March 2020 Kevin's primary NIC will be based on his pay and bonus, totalling £13,000 (£3,000 + £10,000 bonus)

12% x (£4,167*-£792) + 2% x (£13,000-£4,167) = £405.00 + £176.66 = £581.66

Kevin's total primary NIC liability will therefore be

(11 x £264.96) + (1 x £581.66) = £3,496.22

*£50,000/12 = £4,167 per month

b) As a director

In this case, the NICs must be calculated on an annual basis. Kevin's total pay and bonus for the year is 12 months at £3,000 plus a bonus of £10,000 giving total pay of £46,000. Kevin's primary NIC will be

12% x (£46,000 - £9,500) = £4,380.00

Class 1A

Class 1A NICs are only paid by employers (i.e. not employees) and are payable at the rate of 13.8% on the taxable value of any benefits in kind provided to employees (e.g. company cars; car fuel; etc.; see Chapter 10).

Example 20.4

For the tax year 2020/21, Adam receives, in addition to his salary, the use of a company car which has a taxable benefit of £4,050 and private fuel paid for by his employer which has a taxable benefit of £3,675.

Answer

No employee's NICs are payable by Adam on the benefits (Adam will, of course, pay the normal Class 1 NICs on his salary and income tax on the salary plus benefits in kind).

However, his employer is required to pay Class 1A NICs of

13.8% x (£4,050 + £3,675) = £1,066.05

Also, from 6 April 2020, Class 1 A NIC will apply to any taxable termination payments in excess of £30,000. The Class 1A NIC liability at 13.8% will apply to the balance above £30,000.

Class 2

Class 2 NICs are paid by the self-employed at a flat rate of £3.05 per week.

However, where the assessable tax adjusted profits for 2020/21 are below £6,475 no Class 2 NICs are payable.

A sole trader or partner must be 16 years or older to be liable to Class 2 NICs. Class 2 NICs are not payable after reaching pensionable age.

Class 4

Class 4 NICs are also paid by the self-employed at the rate of 9% on *taxable profits* assessed to income tax for the tax year above £9,500 up to profits of £50,000 and at 2% on *taxable profits* above £50,000.

Class 4 NICs are payable in addition to Class 2.

Taxable profits are arrived at for NIC purposes after allowing for a deduction for trading losses.

Example 20.5

Annie is self-employed and prepares her accounts to 31 March each year. For the tax year 2020/21 Annie's adjusted trading profit is £65,000. What are Annie's NIC liabilities for 2020/21?

Answer

Annie's Class 2 NICs = 52 weeks x £3.05 = £158.60 per annum.

Annie's Class 4 NICs = 9% x (£50,000 - £9,500) + 2% x (£65,000 - £50,000) = £3,645 + £300 = £3,945.

Class 3

These are voluntary payments of NIC and are made at the weekly rate of £15.30.

Such payments may be made voluntarily where an individual's NIC contribution record is insufficient in order to provide for full State benefits.

Tax deductibility of NICs

The self-employed may *not* deduct either Class 2 or 4 NICs in arriving at taxable trading profits.

Similarly, an employee cannot deduct Class 1 NICs in arriving at net taxable employment income.

However, employers (sole trading or company) may deduct their Class 1 and 1A employer contributions made in respect of employees in arriving at taxable trading profits.

Administration

An employee's Class 1 NICs are collected by the employer by deducting the appropriate amounts from the employee's salary each week or month as appropriate.

The employer is responsible for paying both the employee's and employer's contributions to HMRC no later than 14 days (i.e. by 19) after the end of each PAYE month (ending on day 5 of every month).

Employers can claim an employment allowance of up to £4,000 per tax year (£3,000 for 2019/20). This amount is deducted from the total employer's Class 1 NICs only. If the employer's NIC liability is £4,000 or less, then no employer's NICs are payable. The allowance is only available to employers whose employers NIC liability was £100,000 or less in the previous tax year.

In addition, this allowance is not available where a director is the sole employee. The employment allowance cannot be used against employee's NIC or Class 1A NIC.

In the case of Class 1A, the employer pays over the relevant amount to HMRC in one lump sum by the 19 July (22 July if paid online) after the end of the tax year.

Class 4 NICs are paid by the self-employed at the same time as their income tax payments are due (see Chapter 21) which, generally, means that Class 4 NICs due for a tax year are paid by way of two equal payments on account on 31 January within the tax year and on 31 July after the end of the tax year with a balancing payment due on the 31 January following the end of the tax year.

Class 2 NICs are paid with the balancing payment, therefore by 31 January following the end of the tax year.

SUMMARY

NICs are payments made by employees, employers and the self-employed to HMRC. In return employees and the self-employed receive entitlement to certain state benefits including a state retirement pension on reaching pensionable age.

NICs are not tax deductible either by employees or the self-employed; however, NICs payable by employers on behalf of their employees are tax deductible in computing the trading profits of employers.

The rates of NIC are higher for an employee than for the self-employed.

Questions for students

See Appendix 2 for practice questions relating to Chapter 20. Answers are available online.

CHAPTER 21

Tax Administration for Individuals

INTRODUCTION

This chapter explains the administrative provisions relating to individuals and the penalties that HMRC may charge for failure to comply with the requirements of the current tax legislation. In particular, it should be noted that HMRC may charge penalties for failure to notify liability, failure to make a return on time and failure to make a payment of tax on time.

HM Revenue and Customs

The UK tax system is managed by HM Revenue and Customs (HMRC).

HMRC is responsible for the administration and collection of both direct and indirect taxes in the UK. HMRC has additional duties including the collection of student loan repayments and enforcement of the National Living Wage.

UK tax law

The UK tax legislation is comprised of a number of specific taxes acts, for example, the Corporation Tax Act 2010, supported by annual Finance Acts. The Finance Acts put into law the announcements made by the Chancellor of the Exchequer in their annual Budget statement to the House of Commons.

In addition to the statute law, there is a large body of tax case law which can be useful to expand upon or clarify the meaning of the legislation. All case law originates from a disagreement between HMRC and a taxpayer.

Finally, HMRC provide technical guidance via their website, although it must be considered that this only represents HMRC's view of the law!

Individuals – income tax and capital gains tax

Notifying chargeability

An individual, who has not received a notice to complete a tax return, must notify HMRC that they are chargeable to income tax or capital gains tax within six months of the end of the tax year, therefore by 5 October 2021 in respect of the tax year to 5 April 2021. This will typically apply when an individual commences a business, has a one-off capital gain or expects to have an underpayment of tax for example due to higher rate tax on savings and dividends. Failure to meet this deadline will result in a tax geared penalty as detailed later in this chapter.

Self-assessment tax return

Around early April each year, HMRC issues a notice to complete a self-assessment tax return to those taxpayers who are likely to need one (i.e. taxpayers who receive income which has not been taxed at source e.g. sole traders; those receiving rental income and/or capital gains). Most taxpayers will have had their tax correctly deducted under PAYE and are not required to complete a tax return.

The information requested in the return relates to the tax year just ended (e.g. tax return notices issued in April 2021 require information concerning the taxpayer's income and gains for the tax year 2020/21 and in addition, the return enables the taxpayer to claim allowances and reliefs for the same year i.e. 2020/21).

Tax return filing date

The Self-assessment tax return needs to be filed electronically online by 31 January following the tax year to which the return relates. Therefore, for the tax year ending 5 April 2021 the annual filing date is 31 January 2022. If the taxpayer wishes to complete a paper return, then this must be submitted by 31 October following the end of the tax year. In either case, the deadline may be later if, having been notified of liability to tax on time, HMRC is late issuing a notice to complete a return. In this case, the deadline is three months from the date of issue of the notification, if later than the normal deadline.

Where any tax return is filed late automatic penalties apply.

Late filing penalties

If a tax return is filed after the dates stated above, then an initial penalty of £100 will be imposed, regardless of the tax liability or even if a refund is due.

Additional penalties apply if there are further delays as follows:
- 3 months late – daily penalties of £10 per day for a maximum of 90 days
- 6 months late – 5% of the tax outstanding with a minimum of £300
- 12 months late – 5% of the tax outstanding with a minimum of £300

In the case of returns that are 12 months late additional tax geared penalties may be charged if the delay is considered deliberate or is concealing a tax liability.

Example 21.1

Andy, having received a notice to submit a tax return in good time, submitted his tax return for the year ended 5 April 2021 to HMRC on 16 October 2022. His return shows an outstanding tax liability of £1,100. What is the total penalty that HMRC may impose for late filing?

Answer

Normal due date for submission 31 January 2022

Initial Penalty	£100
Daily penalty (£10 x 90 days)	£900
Penalty for 6 months late	£300 (Minimum penalty)
Total penalties	£1,300

HMRC has the discretion to reduce a penalty if there are reasonable grounds for so doing.

Amendments and corrections to tax returns

Normally an individual has 12 months from 31 January following the end of the tax year to make amendments to their tax return. HMRC may correct any obvious errors or omissions on a tax return up to nine months after they receive a return. An individual has 30 days to reject any such correction.

Record keeping

HMRC may impose a penalty of up to £3,000 for failure to meet the Self-assessment recordkeeping requirements. These rules require an individual to keep all records relating to the preparation of their tax return for 22 months from the end of the tax year concerned (for the tax year to 5 April 2021 this would be 31 January 2023). If the tax return includes trading or property income this is extended to five years and 10 months.

Tax return enquiries

Under the Self-assessment system, HMRC may issue a notice (under TMA 1970 section 9A) that they are to make an enquiry (or compliance check) into a tax return. Such an enquiry may be limited to a single item on the return or may cover all entries. HMRC has until 12 months from the date that the tax return is submitted to open such an enquiry. Where the return is submitted late HMRC has 12 months after the end of the quarter in which the return is submitted to make enquiries. If as a result of the enquiry it is discovered by HMRC that the individual has underpaid tax, then in addition to interest for late payment, additional penalties may apply to the additional tax charged (see **Tax geared penalties** below).

If the individual does not agree with the findings of HMRC then they may, within 30 days of the decision, appeal the case to the independent First-tier Tribunal (or direct to the Upper Tribunal for some complex appeals) or request that the case is reviewed by another HMRC officer (and then if not satisfied appeal to the First-tier tribunal). If the decision is not resolved then it may be appealed, by either party, to the Upper Tribunal and ultimately if not resolved at this point, on a point of law, to the Court of Appeal. The decisions of such cases make up the case law that supplements and supports UK tax statute law.

Discovery assessments

Although the time limit for a compliance check may have passed, HMRC has the power to re-examine earlier years tax returns if they "discover" the non-disclosure of items leading to the loss of tax. The normal time limit for such a discovery assessment is four years, extending to six years if the taxpayer is considered careless and 20 years in the case of a deliberate error.

Equally, if a taxpayer "discovers" that they have omitted a claim for tax relief, whether on a return or not, they can make such a claim for repayment up to four years after the end of the tax year involved.

Payment of income tax, CGT, Class 2 and Class 4 NIC
Payments on account
Under Self-assessment, two payments on account ("POA") of a tax year's income tax liability are required to be made by *31 January in the tax year, and 31 July following the tax year.*

Example 21.2

Samantha is self-employed and submits an annual Self-assessment tax return. When are her payments on account for 2020/21 due for payment?

Answer

She will be required to make POA on 31 January 2021 and 31 July 2021 in respect of the tax year 2020/21.

Relevant amount
As the first POA falls due before the end of the tax year that it relates to, the actual liability will not be known. Therefore, POA are estimated based on the liability of the previous tax year.

Each POA is calculated as an amount equal to 50% of the aggregate of the income tax and Class 4 NIC liabilities of the *previous* tax year less any tax deducted at source, for example under PAYE.

The income tax liability for the previous tax year plus Class 4 NIC liability less tax deducted at source is referred to as the "relevant amount". Thus, each POA is equal to 50% of the relevant amount.

However, no POAs are required where:
- the relevant amount is less than £1,000; *or*
- if more than 80% of the taxpayer's income tax liability plus Class 4 NIC for the previous tax year is satisfied by deduction of tax at source; *or*
- if no relevant amount exists for the previous tax year (for example the taxpayer was not required to file a return for the previous tax year).

It is possible to submit a claim to reduce POA if information is held to suggest that they will be excessive, for example when self-employment has ceased.

Balancing payment
When the actual income tax payable for the tax year is finally known, a balancing payment (or repayment) may be due on the 31 January following the tax year end equal to the income tax, capital gains tax, Class 4 NIC and

INDIVIDUALS

Class 2 NIC payable for the tax year less the total POAs which have been made. Therefore for 2020/21, any balancing payment is due by 31 January 2022.

Where any balancing payment and/or POA are paid late and/or are insufficient interest will be levied and penalties may also apply if the balancing payment is late.

Example 21.3

For the tax year 2019/20 Suki's total income tax and Class 4 NIC liability was £38,000. She also has a Class 2 NIC liability of £156. Income tax of £8,000 was deducted under PAYE.

For 2020/21 Suki's income tax and Class 4 NIC liability is £42,000 of which £5,000 is paid at source, under PAYE. Suki is also required to pay Class 2 NIC of £158.

State the dates on which Suki is required to pay her 2020/21 income tax and NIC liabilities and the amounts payable.

Answer

Suki's income tax and Class 4 NIC liability for 2019/20 was £38,000. Suki paid income tax of £8,000 at source.

Relevant amount = (£38,000 - £8,000) = £30,000

2020/21

POA on 31 January 2021: £15,000 (i.e. 50% of 2019/20 relevant amount)
POA on 31 July 2021: £15,000 (i.e. 50% of 2019/20 relevant amount)
Note that Class 2 NIC is not included in the calculation of POA.

The balancing payment due by 31 January 2022 is £7,158

This represents the total income tax, class 4 NIC and Class 2 NIC for 2020/21 less tax deducted at source and the payments on account already made (i.e. £42,000+ £158 - £5,000 - £15,000 - £15,000).

Note: It should be noted that the first payment on account for 2021/22, in the sum of £18,500, will also fall due by 31 January 2022 and the whole process commences again!

Example 21.4

Duncan's income tax liability and Class 4 NICs for 2019/20 was £20,500 of which £19,500 was paid at source.

For 2020/21 his income tax and Class 4 NIC liability is £20,000 of which £16,000 was paid at source.

What amount of tax is Duncan to pay and on what dates in respect of the 2020/21 tax year?

Answer

More than 80% of Duncan's income tax and Class 4 NIC liability for 2019/20 was paid by way of tax deducted at source, i.e. 19,500/20,500 = 95.1%.

Therefore no POAs are required for 2020/21.

Duncan's remaining tax and NIC liability of £4,000 (£20,000 - £16,000) for 2020/21 is payable on 31 January 2022 in one single amount.

Interest

Interest is charged on all late payments of income tax and NIC due under Self assessment.

Interest is also charged where a claim to reduce POAs has been made and the POAs which in the event should have been paid are greater than those actually made following the claim.

The interest charge is calculated as simple interest at the rate prescribed by HMRC from the due date until the date of payment. This will apply to both POA and the balancing payment. Where an excessive claim has been made to reduce POA, interest will run from the normal due date on any underpayment.

Example 21.5

Patrick paid his POA on 20 March 2021 and 15 September 2021 in respect of the tax year 2020/21 with a balancing payment on 15 February 2022.

From and to what dates will interest be charged?

Answer

Interest will be charged for the following periods:

First POA	31 January 2021 to 20 March 2021
Second POA	31 July 2021 to 15 September 2021
Balancing payment	31 January 2022 to 15 February 2022

Late payment penalties

Late payment penalties are payable *in addition* to any interest which may be charged.

Penalties do not apply to POA dates; only to balances outstanding after the due date of the balancing payment.

Where all or part of a tax and NIC liability for a year remains unpaid for more than 30 days after the balancing payment due date an initial penalty of 5% of the unpaid amount will be charged.

Any tax that remains unpaid more than six months after the due date (i.e. by 31 July) is subject to a further 5% penalty and a further 5% penalty will apply after 12 months (i.e. by the following 31 January).

In every case, the penalty is in addition to the tax itself and to any interest charged in relation to that tax.

Example 21.6

Greg has a balancing payment of £7,000 due on 31 January 2022 for 2020/21 but only £4,250 is actually paid on time. The balance is eventually paid on 14 June 2022.

What penalties will arise?

Answer

A balance of £2,750 is outstanding on 2 February 2022, 30 days after the normal due date. Therefore, a penalty of (5% x £2,750) = £137.50 will also be due in addition to the tax liability and interest.

As the balance was paid before 31 July 2022 a second 5% penalty was avoided.

Interest on overpaid income tax

Repayments to a taxpayer of overpaid income tax attract interest calculated at a lower rate than the interest rate charged on overdue income tax.

Interest on any repayment runs from the later of the date that the tax was due or the date HMRC received the payment, until the date of repayment.

Interest paid on tax repayments is exempt from income tax.

Deductibility of interest payments and late payment penalties

Any interest and penalties payable by an individual in respect of late payments of income tax etc. are not tax deductible.

Mitigation of penalties

HMRC may, in their discretion, mitigate any penalty where they are satisfied that an individual is able to prove that they had a reasonable excuse for not meeting a tax obligation. For example, the death of a spouse shortly before a deadline may be considered reasonable. However, simply having insufficient funds available at a payment date would not be considered to be a reasonable excuse.

Capital gains tax (CGT)

As mentioned above CGT is normally payable with the balancing payment on the 31 January following the end of the tax year to which the tax relates (e.g. 31 January 2022 for tax year 2020/21).

POAs are never required for CGT. However, as mentioned in Chapter 13, CGT on residential property sales is payable within 30 days of the completion of the sale.

Interest on late payments and any repayment supplement are the same as those for income tax (see above).

National insurance contributions

As indicated in Chapter 20, Class 4 NICs which are payable by the self-employed are to be paid at the same time and in the same manner as an individual's income tax liability.

As a consequence, in any tax year, POAs are required, these can include Class 4 NIC.

Class 2 NIC is paid with the balancing payment on the 31 January following the end of the tax year to which the tax relates (e.g. 31 January 2022 for tax year 2020/21).

POAs are not required for Class 2 NIC.

Example 21.7

Joe is self-employed and his tax and NIC liabilities for 2019/20 were as follows:

Income tax	£3,700
Class 4 NIC	£1,966
Class 2 NIC	£156
CGT	£4,800

Calculate Joe's payments on account for 2020/21?

Answer

Income tax and class 4 NIC

Income tax liability for 2019/20	3,700
Class 4 NIC liability for 2019/20	1,966
Relevant amount	5,666

Payments on account for 2020/21:

31 January 2021	5,666 x 50%	2,833
31 July 2021	5,666 x 50%	2,833

Note: Class 2 NIC and CGT are not included in the calculation of the "relevant" amount (i.e. are not included in POA).

Joe's balancing payment will be due on 31 January 2022.

There is no requirement to make POA for the CGT and Class 2 NIC liability. These are due on 31 January following the end of the tax year as part of any balancing payment.

Tax geared penalties

As mentioned above, in certain circumstances, such as failure to notify or where a tax underpayment is identified following an enquiry, a tax geared penalty may be imposed on an individual. The maximum penalties that can be charged and the minimum that HMRC may reduce them to, in the particular circumstances for each case are as follows:

Type of behaviour	Unprompted disclosure	Prompted disclosure
Reasonable care	No penalty	No penalty
Careless	0% to 30%	15% to 30%
Deliberate error	20% to 70%	35% to 70%
Deliberate and concealed	30% to 100%	50% to 100%

As can been seen, the penalties are set based on the behaviour of the taxpayer. An unprompted disclosure would, for example, be a case where the taxpayer voluntarily discloses an undeclared source of income.

INDIVIDUALS

SUMMARY

The self-assessment system requires individuals to meet specific deadlines for filing tax returns and making tax payments.

Under the self-assessment system, individuals may be required to make two payments on account of their income tax and Class 4 NIC liability plus a balancing payment which will also include any capital gains tax and Class 2 NIC.

There are separate penalty regimes that apply for late filing and late payment.

HMRC have the power to make enquiries into a tax return for up to 12 months from the date a return is submitted.

Penalties may apply if a tax liability increases as a result of HMRC enquiries.

CHAPTER 22

Tax Administration for Corporation Tax and Employers

INTRODUCTION

Companies, like individuals, must self-assess their tax liability in respect of each accounting period and submit a tax return.

This chapter examines the administrative provisions relating to corporation tax and the penalties that HMRC may charge for failure to comply with the regulations. Again it should be noted that HMRC may charge penalties for failure to notify liability, failure to make a return on time and failure to make a payment of tax on time.

In addition, this chapter also looks at the obligations of employers under PAYE, whether incorporated or not.

Notifying chargeability

A company may be charged a tax geared penalty (see Chapter 21) based on the amount of tax paid late if it fails to notify HMRC that it is chargeable to corporation tax within three months of starting any business activity or receiving taxable income.

Corporation tax return

The corporation tax return must be submitted within 12 months of the end of the period of account to which it relates. Where accounts are prepared for more than 12 months two tax returns will be required but both will be due by the same date, 12 months after the end of the period of account.

HMRC requires companies to submit returns online using the iXBRL format. A complete corporation tax return must include the tax return with accompanying financial statements and tax computations.

Tax return enquiries

As for individuals, HMRC has the right to make an enquiry into a corporation tax return. HMRC has until 12 months from the date that the tax return is submitted to open such an enquiry. Where the return is submitted late HMRC has 12 months after the end of the quarter in which the return is submitted to make enquiries.

Interest and penalties

Failure to submit the return by the due date gives rise to a penalty of £100 with an increase to £200 if the return is three months or more late. Where the return is more than six months late an additional tax geared penalty equal to 10% of the corporation tax unpaid is charged which rises to 20% if the return is more than 12 months late. The fixed penalties increase to £500 and £1,000 respectively if the two preceding returns were also late.

In addition, HMRC may charge a penalty of up to £3,000 for failure to keep the required records. All records required for the preparation of a CT return are required to be retained for six years after the end of the accounting period.

Payment of corporation tax

Any corporation tax liability for a chargeable accounting period must be paid within nine months and one day after the end of the accounting period unless the company is large. Where accounts are prepared for more than 12 months each chargeable accounting period will have a separate payment date.

Example 22.1

FGH Limited prepares its accounts for the 12 months ended 31 March 2021. FGH Ltd is not a large company. What are the filing and payment deadlines for FGH Ltd for the accounting period to 31 March 2021?

Answer

The corporation tax liability is due for payment on 1 January 2022 (nine months and one day after the end of the accounting period).

The corporation tax return must be filed online by 31 March 2022 to prevent a filing penalty.

Instalment basis

As indicated above most companies are required to pay their corporation tax liability nine months after the end of the accounting period. However, where a company is considered to be large, then an alternative, instalment based payment system applies.

A company is considered to be large if it has augmented profits of £1,500,000 or more for an accounting period. Augmented profits are calculated as TTP plus non-group dividends received.

If the accounting period is less than 12 months the limit mentioned above is time apportioned.

For a 12 month accounting period, the instalment basis requires a company to pay four equal instalments of CT payable on the 14 of months 7, 10, 13 and 16 following the start of the accounting period.

Unlike the position of individuals, the corporation tax instalments for an accounting period are based upon estimates of the corporation tax liability for the accounting period and not on the liability for the previous accounting period.

Example 22.2

JS Ltd a large company prepares its accounts to 31 March 2021.

Its corporation tax liability will, therefore, need to be settled in four equal instalments due on 14 October 2020, 14 January 2021, 14 April 2021 and 14 July 2021.

If the accounting period is for less than 12 months, there may be insufficient time to fit in all four instalments. In this case, the rule for setting the first instalment date remains the same, with the next following after three months. However, the last instalment is due three months and 14 days after the end of the accounting period. In addition, the instalments are calculated based on the length of the accounting period.

Example 22.3

FG Ltd is a large company and prepares its accounts for the eight months to 31 August 2020. When are its instalments payments of CT due?

Answer

The accounting period commences on 1 January 2020. Therefore, the first instalment will be due on 14 July 2020, the next instalment will be due by 14 October 2020 and the final will be due on 14 December 2020, three months and 14 days after the end of the accounting period.

As the accounting period is for eight months, the first two instalments will be for 3/8th of the CT liability with the final payment being the remaining 2/8th.

In the case of an accounting period of three months or less the CT is due in a single payment three months and 14 days after the end of the period.

The instalment basis does not apply for an accounting period if the company was not a large company for the previous accounting period *and* the profits for the current period do not exceed £10 million (or pro rata reduced if associated companies exist). In addition, the instalment basis does not apply where the CT liability does not exceed £10,000.

It should be appreciated that the requirement to pay by instalments can have a huge impact on the cash flow of a company.

For accounting periods beginning on or after 1 April 2019, very large companies (profits exceeding £20 million) will be required to make instalment payments four months earlier, on the 14th day of months 3, 6, 9 and 12 of their accounting period.

Interest is chargeable where corporation tax is paid late, running from the date that the liability was due to the date of actual payment and unlike the position for individuals, any such interest is a deductible expense in arriving at the net interest income under the loan relationship rules. Similarly, HMRC will pay interest on tax overpaid and this will similarly be treated as taxable interest income (see Chapter 16).

51% Group companies

The various thresholds for determining instalment payments must be divided equally between companies within a 51% group. For this purpose, control requires ownership or more than 50% of the ordinary share capital directly or indirectly. Therefore two companies can be associated if one owns more than 50% of the shares of the other or where both companies are controlled by a third company (but not an individual – companies can only be grouped by another company).

Dormant companies are excluded but overseas companies are included. Where a controlling interest is acquired in a company, it is not included until the beginning of the next accounting period. Where a controlling interest in a company is lost, it will only be excluded from the start of its next accounting period.

Example 22.4

Rainbow Ltd owns 75% of the ordinary share capital of Red Ltd, Blue Ltd and Green Inc. Red Ltd owns 100% of the ordinary shares of Pink Ltd. All of the group companies are active except for Blue Ltd which is dormant. Green Inc is incorporated in the USA.

What is the augmented profits threshold for Rainbow Ltd?

Answer

The augmented profits limit is normally £1,500,000 but this must be divided equally between 51% group companies.

Rainbow Ltd has three 51% associated companies – Red Ltd, Pink Ltd and Green Inc. Therefore, the threshold is divided by 4 and is reduced to £375,000 (£1.5 million/4). Blue Ltd is ignored as it is dormant.

Tax geared penalties

If as a result of an enquiry by HMRC additional CT liabilities arise, tax geared penalties may arise. These will be calculated on the same basis applicable to individuals as detailed in Chapter 21.

PAYE and Real Time Information

Pay As You Earn (PAYE) is designed to enable employers to deduct income tax and NIC from their employees' salary over a tax year and pay it to HMRC. In effect, every employer acts as a tax collector!

PAYE applies to wages and salaries, round sum allowances and readily convertible assets (i.e. assets readily convertible into cash). It does not, however, apply to reimbursed business expenses.

PAYE does not normally apply to benefits in kind. Benefits will, however, usually restrict the amount of the PAYE code.

PAYE Code

If an employee's sole source of income in a tax year is a salary, by applying the correct PAYE code (see below) to the employee's salary, the employer by the end of the tax year will have deducted an amount of income tax from the salary which equals the employee's income tax liability. In principle, the employee will then have no further income tax liability for that tax year.

An individual's PAYE code is issued by HMRC and takes into account various factors. It will depend upon the level of personal allowances to which the individual may be entitled (e.g. personal allowance; marriage allowance; etc.); whether any further deductions are due (e.g. a deduction for allowable professional subscriptions); whether that individual receives any benefits (e.g. a company car); whether that individual receives any minor amounts of untaxed income and whether the individual has any unpaid income tax from prior tax years. The PAYE code provides an employer with the information to determine an employee's net tax free allowance, without divulging any confidential personal information.

Example 22.5

John, an employee, earns a salary of £30,000, paid monthly, for 2020/21. His taxable company car benefit is £6,200. He pays allowable professional subscriptions of £480.

John is single, aged 35, and a basic rate taxpayer.

Show John's PAYE code for 2020/21.

Answer

Personal allowance	12,500
Benefits	(6,200)
Professional subscriptions	480
	6,780

John's PAYE code is thus 678L.

John 's employer will be notified by HMRC that his code is 678L without any detail of its calculation. A detailed calculation will be provided to John by HMRC.

Note

To create an individual's PAYE code, HMRC simply removes the last digit and replaces it with a specific letter. Thus to get John's code requires that the '0' be removed to get 678 and replaced with a letter, usually "L".

An employer is notified of an employee's PAYE code for a tax year but the employer does not know the breakdown of the code; just the final amount, maintaining the confidentiality of the employee's specific details.

The employer then, each week or month (depending upon how an employee is paid), applies 1/52 or 1/12 of the employee's allowances (against the weekly or monthly salary). In this manner, over the tax year, the employee will have discharged their income tax liability for that tax year. Similarly, the rate bands will be divided by 1/52 or 1/12 etc.

The application of the code is on a cumulative basis. Thus, after the first three tax months of the tax year, an individual would have received one quarter of their annual personal allowance entitlement. For an individual who starts to work for the first time, say from 6 September in 2019, when they are paid on, say 30 September, they will receive six months' worth of annual personal allowances as they had not prior to September used any of them. Thereafter, they will simply receive as normal one month's allowance per month. If at after the end of the tax year, it is established that the tax code number was insufficient and an underpayment of tax has arisen, this will be a matter between the individual and HMRC.

NIC will be calculated by the employer as detailed in Chapter 20.

Any tax and NIC deducted by an employer must be paid to HMRC by 19th of the following month (22nd if paid online).

Forms/returns

A variety of information is required to be supplied by an employer to their employees each tax year. This information is supplied on various forms as follows:

- *Form P60* (deadline 31 May after the end of the tax year). This form shows the employee's total taxable earnings for the tax year, total tax deducted, code number, national insurance number, and employer's name and address.
- *Form P11D* (deadline 6 July after the end of the tax year). This form shows the taxable equivalent of all benefits and expenses provided to the employee.
- *Form P45* (given to an employee who leaves employment). This form shows the employee's PAYE code, the income of the employee to date of leaving and income tax paid to the date of leaving.

RTI (Real Time Information)

Since 6 April 2013, the PAYE reporting system has undergone significant changes. This information must now be reported in "real time". It is not possible to operate PAYE manually, details about employees pay and deductions must be reported to HMRC using payroll software **on or before the day** employees are paid.

The payroll software must provide the following information:

- The amount paid to each employee – (including lower-paid employees below the NIC limit, e.g. students).
- Deductions, e.g. income tax and national insurance contributions (NICs)
- Starter and leaver dates if applicable

The PAYE system itself has not changed; it is only the reporting that has changed.

SUMMARY

Companies must not only file an annual tax return containing information about profits, income and chargeable gains arising but also provide their financial statements and calculation of corporation tax liabilities. The return must be filed by 12 months from the end of the period of account.

If a company fails to meet its submission deadlines penalties will apply.

Large companies are required to pay CT by instalments, with other companies making a single payment nine months and one day after the end of the accounting period.

Interest may be charged where tax liabilities are settled late and/or are of an insufficient amount.

PAYE codes are used by employers to calculate the income tax liability arising on an employee's monthly or weekly salary.

Employers are required to provide HMRC with their payroll details under RTI at or before the date any wages etc. are paid and pay any PAYE tax and NIC deductions to HMRC monthly.

Questions for students

See Appendix 2 for practice questions relating to Chapters 21 to 22. Answers are available online.

CHAPTER 23

Value Added Tax

INTRODUCTION

VAT is a tax on consumer expenditure. It is an indirect tax and its calculation is very different to income tax, capital gains tax and corporation tax. VAT is not a tax on profits or gains and generally, there is no distinction between revenue and capital items. It is administered by HM Revenue & Customs (HMRC). VAT can apply equally to sole traders, partnerships and limited companies.

How it works

VAT is charged on the supply of *taxable goods or services* when made in the UK by a *VAT registered trader* in the course of a business carried on by them.

At its simplest, a VAT registered trader must pay to HMRC the difference between the VAT that they charge on sales to their customers (output tax) and the VAT that they pay to their suppliers on purchases and expenses (Input tax).

Output tax

The VAT charged *by* a taxable person on supplies made *by* them to another person is called output tax. This output tax less any input tax must be paid over to HMRC by the trader periodically.

Input tax

Input tax is the VAT charged *on* a taxable person on goods and services supplied *to* them by a taxable VAT registered business. Input tax charged can be recovered by a VAT registered business from HMRC, usually by deduction from any output tax payable.

Example 23.1

Over a three month period, Nigel, a VAT-registered trader, charges VAT of £3,500 on services supplied by him and pays to his suppliers VAT of £1,500 on purchases.

Nigel will owe £2,000 VAT to HMRC calculated as £3,500 (output) - £1,500 (input) = £2,000.

Example 23.2

During the quarter to 30 September 2019, BCD Ltd, a VAT-registered trader, charges VAT of £1,500 on goods supplied and pays to their suppliers' VAT of £2,500 on purchases.

BCD Ltd will therefore obtain a VAT refund from HMRC for:
£1,500 (output) - £2,500 (input) = £1,000.

Supplies of goods

Goods are supplied in the UK if they are located in the UK and the ownership of the goods passes to another elsewhere in the UK (i.e. sold to a UK based customer).

In addition to a simple sale of goods, a supply of goods also includes, for example, a supply of power or heat, or the application of a treatment or process to another person's goods. A supply of goods also arises where a gift of goods is made or where goods are taken out of the business for private use. Finally, the sale of capital items, for example, a machine no longer required by the business, will also be subject to the normal rules for charging output tax.

Supplies of services

Services are supplied in the country where the service provider belongs; where they are performed is irrelevant. Thus a UK based accountant makes supplies in the UK as they are based in the UK even if providing services to an overseas based client. Supplies of services include anything done for consideration which is not a supply of goods.

Value of supply

VAT is charged on the value of the supply of goods or services which is generally the money paid, after any discounts.

In the case of gifts, replacement cost (usually market value) is used. However, small gifts to the same person up to £50, excluding VAT, in a 12 month period are exempt. Where services are provided for no consideration no supply for VAT is assumed to have been made and thus no VAT is chargeable.

Where goods are taken by a trader for their own use, VAT must be charged on the replacement value of the goods at the time that they are taken.

Standard rated, reduced rated, zero rated and exempt supplies

The type of supply will determine the applicable VAT rate. Although generally speaking a taxable person will tend to make only one type of supply in many cases a mixture of the different rated supplies may be made.

Standard rated

The general rule is that supplies are subject to VAT at the standard rate; currently 20%. Input tax attributable to standard rate supplies is recoverable.

Reduced rated

A lower rate of 5% applies to a small number of supplies including supplies of domestic fuel and power.

Zero rated

Zero rated supplies are subject to VAT but at the zero rate (i.e. 0%). Examples of zero rated supplies are supplies of most food, books (including

VALUE ADDED TAX

digital downloads from 2020) and newspapers and children's clothing and footwear (purchases that could be considered essential).

Exempt

An exempt supply is one where no VAT is charged as the supply is not a taxable supply.

Input tax cannot be recovered where the input tax relates to an exempt supply.

Examples of exempt supplies include supplies of land, insurance, education and health.

Rates of VAT

VAT is charged at 20% on the VAT exclusive value of standard rated goods/supplies.

A supply taxed at the zero rate is still a taxable supply albeit at the rate of 0%.

VAT fraction

VAT is normally calculated at the appropriate percentage of the sale price. But sometimes VAT has to be calculated from a price in which it is already included, the VAT inclusive amount. Where the total value of the supply includes VAT then to calculate the amount of VAT, the VAT inclusive amount is multiplied by the VAT fraction, currently, 20/120, which can be simplified to 1/6.

Example 23.3

Julie charges a customer £300 for a supply of goods including VAT charged at the standard rate.

How much VAT is charged on the sale?

Answer

The VAT included in this amount is = 300 x 1/6 = £50

(Reconciliation: £250 + (20% x £250) = £300)

Care should always be taken to carefully note if outputs and inputs are *exclusive* of VAT (20% for standard rate) or *inclusive* of VAT (1/6 for standard rate) to ensure that the VAT element is correctly calculated.

Taxable supplies

Standard, reduced and zero rated (but not exempt) supplies are referred to as taxable supplies.

Example 23.4

Greg makes the following supplies of goods, exclusive of VAT :

Standard rated	£30,000
Zero rated	£20,000
Exempt	£10,000

Calculate Greg's total taxable supplies and output tax

Answer

Greg's standard rated and zero rated supplies are taxable supplies. He therefore has taxable supplies of 30,000 + 20,000 = 30,000

Greg's total output VAT is charged on his *taxable* supplies as follows

Standard rated	30,000 x 20%	6,000
Zero rated	20,000 x 0%	0
Total output tax		6,000

Mixture of supplies/Partial exemption

If a business makes taxable supplies (i.e. standard and zero rated) and exempt supplies it is referred to as a partially exempt supplier. In this case, the input VAT which is directly attributable to taxable supplies is recoverable (i.e. off-settable) whereas that directly attributable to the exempt supplies is irrecoverable. If any input VAT cannot be directly attributable to a particular type of supply then it may be apportioned between taxable and exempt supplies and partially recovered. If the total unrecoverable input tax is below a *de minimis* level, it will also be recoverable and an annual adjustment may be required.

Registration

VAT must be charged on sales by a VAT registered business. There are two types of registration: compulsory and voluntary.

Compulsory registration

There are two circumstances when a trader must register for VAT.

The Historic Test

Where a trader makes taxable supplies such that at the end of any month the total value of taxable supplies of the previous 12 months (or shorter period since the commencement of trading) exceeds £85,000 (exclusive of VAT) then compulsory registration is required (the "historic" test).

Under the historic test, the trader must notify HMRC within 30 days of the end of the month in which turnover exceeds the annual registration limit. In this case, registration is then effective from the start of the month following this 30 day period.

The Future Test

If at any time there are reasonable grounds for believing that in the next thirty days alone the value of supplies will exceed £85,000 (exclusive of VAT), then compulsory registration is also required (the "future" test).

Under the future test, HMRC must be notified by the end of the 30 day period from the date on which the grounds for registration arose. Registration is effective from the start of the 30 day period.

Example 23.5

Des commenced trading in November 2019. All of his sales are of standard rated goods. His monthly turnover was as follows

November 2019	5,500
December 2019	6,200
January 2020	5,800
February 2020	5,500
March 2020	6,300
April 2020	7,000
May 2020	7,100
June 2020	6,900
July 2020	8,600
August 2020	7,500
September 2020	8,600
October 2020	9,300
November 2020	10,100

In which month does Des' turnover exceed the registration limit and by what date must he notify HMRC?

Answer

Des' cumulative turnover must be checked at the end of each month against the registration limit of £85,000 throughout his first year of trading. His total turnover for the first 12 months, to October 2020 is 84,300 and at this point, he is not required to register.

He must then review his total turnover for the previous 12 months at the end of each subsequent month.

Des' total turnover for the 12 months ending 30 November 2020 is 88,900 calculated as follows:

12 months sales to October 2020	84,300
Less Sales November 2019	-5,500
Add Sales November 2020	10,100
12 months to 30 November 2020	88,900

Therefore, Des' turnover exceeds the registration limit in November 2020 and he must notify HMRC by 30 December 2020 (within 30 days of the end of the month). His registration will be effective from 1 January 2021.

Example 23.6

Tracy started her business on 1 August 2019. She has noted that her total taxable supplies since the start of her business have exceeded £85,000 by the end of April 2020.

By what date should she notify HMRC and when will registration be effective from?

Answer

She will need to notify HMRC of her requirement to register by 30 May 2020. Her registration will then be effective from 1 June 2020.

> **Example 23.7**
>
> Jeff started trading on 1 August 2019. In his first three months of trading, turnover of taxable supplies was £9,000 per month. On 5 November 2019, he received an order for £95,000 for delivery by 30 November 2019.
>
> By what date should Jeff notify HMRC of his need to register for VAT?
>
> **Answer**
>
> Under the future test, on 5 November, Jeff expects to exceed the registration limit in the next 30 days. Therefore, he must notify HMRC within 30 days of knowing this, so by 5 December 2019. Registration will be effective from 5 November 2019.

Disposals of capital assets should be ignored in calculating the value of taxable supplies for registration purposes.

It is the *person* who is liable to be registered, not the business, and therefore in ascertaining if the registration limits are exceeded by any person all taxable supplies made by the person in all of their businesses must be aggregated.

It is important to note that a person making only exempt supplies cannot be registered because such a person is not making taxable supplies.

If a supply is made before liability to registration arises but payment is made after registration, no VAT is due.

Voluntary registration

Where a person is not required to compulsorily register they may still register voluntarily if they are making taxable supplies in the course of a business or are carrying on activities with a view to then making taxable supplies.

Voluntary registration enables any input VAT to be recovered which otherwise would not be the case i.e. unless registration is effected no input VAT can be recovered because in this situation the person will not be making taxable supplies. However, of course, from registration, VAT will need to be charged on sales.

Voluntary registration may be helpful where a trader is worried that they may miss the compulsory registration deadlines and may also help to disguise the size of a small business.

Consequences of registration

Once registration is effective, VAT, at the appropriate rate, must be charged on all taxable supplies. If the business only supplies other VAT registered businesses, this is likely to have very little impact on the trader. However, if the majority of sales are to the general public, this will create an immediate 20% increase in the total sales price of standard rated supplies. The trader may, therefore, decide to reduce their pre VAT prices, reducing their gross profit. However, the trader will benefit from the recovery of input tax on purchases.

After registration, the trader must comply with all of the administrative requirements of the VAT legislation, for example, providing VAT invoices, quarterly VAT returns etc. as detailed later in this chapter.

Deregistration

Where a person ceases to make taxable supplies, HMRC must be notified within 30 days of cessation. Also, where a person expects taxable turnover to fall below £83,000 (the deregistration threshold) in the next 12 months voluntary deregistration may be made.

The effect of deregistration is that no further input VAT may be recovered and no further output VAT may be charged.

On deregistration, the trader must charge output VAT on the value of any trading stock and current assets held at that date, although this is waived if the VAT due is £1,000 or less.

Penalties for late registration

Where a person has failed to notify HMRC of the need to compulsorily register a penalty may be charged, based on the amount of VAT that should have been paid had the registration been made at the correct time.

The penalty will be tax geared based on the taxpayer's behaviour as detailed in Chapter 21. The penalty will be between 30% to 100% of the VAT outstanding but may be reduced for unprompted disclosure.

Example 23.8

Josh started to trade on 1 February 2019 and over the first few months his supplies are as follows:

February	£23,000	June	£30,000
March	£26,000	July	£16,000
April	£20,000	August	£10,000
May	£18,000		

He realises in late August that he should have notified HMRC of the requirement to register by 30 June as the £85,000 limit was exceeded during May (23,000 + 26,000 + 20,000 + 18,000= 87,000) and notifies them on 27 August.

Josh is, therefore, two months late in notifying HMRC. He should have notified by 30 June.

A penalty is thus chargeable based on the net VAT which should have been paid, which is VAT on the July and August supplies (as 1 July is the date from which his VAT registration should have been effective) less any input tax for these months.

The level of penalty will be determined based on the reason for late notification and whether Josh notifies HMRC before they discover his error. In addition to the penalty, any outstanding VAT for the two months (Output tax less input tax) would also be payable.

Transfer of a Business as a Going Concern

If a business is sold as a going concern, the transfer is not a taxable supply and no VAT is charged.

For this to occur:

- the transferor and transferee must be VAT registered and the business concerned must continue to be carried on as a going concern;
- the assets transferred must be used by the transferee in the same kind of business as that of the transferor; and
- there must be no significant break in business activities.

If the transferee takes over the VAT number of the transferor they also take over any outstanding VAT compliance regulations and VAT liabilities of the previous owner.

Where the above conditions are not satisfied then VAT is due on the transfer (i.e. the sale of business assets).

Pre-Registration VAT

Where, prior to registration, VAT is incurred on the purchase of goods and/or services this VAT may be recoverable once the person registers. VAT is recoverable:

- on *goods* including capital goods and trading stock provided:
  - they are still owned at the date of registration, *and*
  - they were purchased within the four years before registration;
- on *services*, if they were supplied within six months before registration,

and the goods or services must have been used for business purposes and invoices must be available to support the claim for VAT recovery.

Time of the supply: tax point

The time of supply whether of goods or services referred to as the tax point determines the period into which the supply falls (important for accounting for VAT purposes; or the rate of VAT to be charged if there is a change of rate).

The basic tax point for goods is when they are removed by the customer or made available to them.

The basic tax point for services is the time when the services are performed.

The above general rules are overridden in the following situations:

1. if an invoice is issued or payment received *before* the basic tax point; the tax point becomes the earlier of the date of invoice and receipt of payment.
2. if an invoice is issued within 14 days after the basic tax point date, the invoice date becomes the tax point unless payment has already been received in which case the payment date remains the tax point.

Therefore, to determine the tax point for any supply or receipt it is necessary to work through the steps. First, establish the basic tax point. Then consider if it can be moved to an earlier date (1. above) in which case that becomes the actual tax point. If it cannot be moved earlier then consider if it can be moved later (2. above), in which case that becomes the actual tax point. If it cannot be moved then the basic tax point applies.

If goods are taken on sale or return, the tax point is the earlier of when the customer accepts them or 12 months after the date of despatch.

On a continuous supply of services (e.g. electricity; tax advice) paid for periodically the tax point is the earlier of receipt of such payments and the date of issue of the invoice.

Separate tax points can apply to a deposit and final payment.

Example 23.9

In the course of his VAT quarter to 30 June, Stuart sold goods to the total value of £24,000, exclusive of VAT, to one of his customers. The goods were not in stock and Stuart had to place an order with his suppliers. The customer was asked to pay a deposit of £6,000 on 25 June.

The goods were delivered to the customer on 2 September. Stuart raised an invoice on 30 September and the balance of the monies owed was paid on 10 October.

Show the tax points for this transaction.

Answer

The basic tax point for both parts of the transaction is 2 September.

Deposit monies

The deposit monies were received on 25 June. This date becomes the tax point for the deposit as it was prior to the basic tax point.

The deposit monies are assumed to include VAT.

Therefore Stuart needs to account for output VAT for the quarter ended 30 June of 1/6 x 6,000 = 1,000.

Balance of payment

The goods were made available to the customer on 2 September.

Stuart issued an invoice on 30 September with payment by the customer on 10 October.

As the invoice was not issued within 14 days after the basic tax point (i.e. 2 September) and payment was not made before 2 September then 2 September remains as the tax point.

Stuart will therefore need to account for output VAT in the quarter ended 30 September of 20% x 24,000 = 4,800 less VAT on deposit (1,000)] = £3,800

Miscellaneous matters

Discounts

Where a trade discount is offered VAT is chargeable on the discounted amount.

Where a settlement discount is offered VAT is initially chargeable on the full amount. If the customer takes advantage of the discount then the VAT is calculated on the discounted price. It may be necessary to raise a credit note to balance this in the trader's records.

Assets for personal use

If goods or services are purchased specifically for private use, no VAT can be recovered (i.e. the VAT payable cannot be treated as input VAT). If, however, there is both business and private use of goods purchased then the input tax can be apportioned (i.e. only the business element is deducted).

As detailed above if goods are withdrawn from a business for personal use, output tax must be accounted for on the replacement value of the goods at the time that they are taken.

Motor cars

No recovery of input tax can be made on the purchase of a motor car unless the car is used wholly for business purposes (which generally is most unlikely).

As a consequence, no VAT is chargeable on the sale of a used car on which input tax was not recovered.

Leased cars

The recovery of input tax on car lease charges is restricted by 50% where the car has any private use.

Accessories

VAT cannot be recovered on the cost of accessories fitted when the car is bought unless there is 100% business use. It is, however, normally possible to recover VAT on accessories fitted subsequently despite potential private use.

Repairs/maintenance

Provided that there is some business use, a taxable trader can recover *all* the VAT on repair and maintenance costs even if the car is used partly for private use.

Car fuel

If fuel is provided for a car which includes private use by an individual (i.e. proprietor, employee or director) at less than the cost of that fuel to the business providing the fuel (not applicable to a van; see below) then the business may recover the input VAT on the total cost of the fuel but it must also account by way of *output* VAT an amount calculated according to the scale rate provided by HMRC.

This fuel scale charge is based on the cars CO_2 emissions with the lowest rate band covering cars with emissions up to 120g/km or less, working up through various bands until the highest band for cars with emissions of 225 g/km or greater.

The amount of output VAT will be determined by taking 1/6 of the appropriate fuel scale charge.

Example 23.10

Jackie, a sole trader, has purchased a motor car, with emissions of 200g/km, which she uses partly for business and partly for private purposes. The scale charge for a car with this level of emissions is £436 per quarter. Her car fuel bills for the quarter totalled £750 (VAT inclusive).

What is the net VAT recoverable for the quarter?

Answer

Jackie can recover VAT on the inclusive cost of the fuel £750 x 1/6 = £125

However, she must also account for output tax on the scale charge calculated as £436 x 1/6 = £72.

Jackie's net position will be £53 input tax increase (£125 - £72).

Note

Strictly, there is an increase in output tax of £72 and recoverable input tax of £125, which gives a net position of £53 recoverable.

A business can opt not to recover any input VAT on any fuel for any of its vehicles. This would be advantageous if the additional output tax would create an overall increase in VAT payable. Alternatively, the scale charge will not apply if only fuel used for business mileage is recovered, supported by accurate mileage records.

Vans

VAT can normally be recovered on the purchase of vans and lorries.

If the trader who sells a used van has recovered input VAT on the cost price, VAT must be charged on the full selling price when it is disposed of.

Accommodation

No VAT can be recovered on the costs of providing residential accommodation for a director or a person connected with him or her.

VAT on staff removal expenses is normally recoverable.

Bad debts

Output tax is usually charged based on the invoiced amount and not the receipt of payment. If a debt becomes bad or irrecoverable, a claim for repayment of output VAT can be made if the following conditions are satisfied:

- the debt has been written off as a bad debt, *and*
  at least six months have elapsed since the debt was due and payable, *and*
- the VAT charged on the supply has been paid to HMRC, *and*
- the appropriate accounting records have been maintained by the supplier.

If a payment on account of the debt has been made it will be allocated on a FIFO basis unless the debtor has attributed it to a specific debt or debts.

The claim for bad debt relief must be made within four years and six months from the due date of payment.

Entertainment

VAT on business entertainment of suppliers or UK customers cannot be recovered whereas VAT on entertaining staff or overseas customers is recoverable. All VAT can be recovered on the costs of hotels and subsistence incurred by a taxable trader or its staff for business purposes.

Calculation of VAT liability

VAT is usually calculated for a three-month period. The following example illustrates how the VAT due for a quarter would be calculated by deducting recoverable input tax from the output tax due.

Example 23.11

Luke is a VAT registered trader and is preparing his VAT return for the quarter to 31 October 2020. During the quarter he made the supply of standard rated services of £36,500, exclusive of VAT.

Luke purchased goods costing £5,040 inclusive of VAT during the quarter. In addition, he incurred various other expenses and has identified the following amounts of input tax:

VAT on petrol	£150
VAT on entertaining suppliers	£30
VAT on mobile phone	£10

It has been established that the scale charge for the car is £296 and that 50% of the use of the mobile phone is for private purposes. Calculate Luke's VAT payable for the quarter.

Answer

Output tax:			
Sales	36,500 x 20% =		7,300
Fuel scale charge	296 x 1/6 =		49
Input tax:			
Purchases	5,040 x 1/6	840	
Petrol		150	
Entertaining – Blocked		0	
Mobile phone – 50%		_5_	
			(995)
VAT Payable			6,354

Administration and penalties

VAT returns

VAT on the supply of goods and services must be accounted for on a quarterly basis. However, the relevant quarters are determined by HMRC. Thus some traders will have quarterly return periods of, say, 31 March, 30 June, 30 September and 31 December; others may have 28 February, 31 May, 31 August and 30 November etc.

The return, which is completed online by the trader, shows the total input and output VAT for the period and the net VAT that needs to be accounted for. HMRC must receive the completed return and the VAT due within one month and seven days following the relevant quarter period.

Where a trader is likely to receive VAT refunds rather than having to make VAT payments, as may occur where a registered trader is making primarily zero rated supplies, monthly returns may be submitted.

Since April 2019, under Making Tax Digital, most VAT registered businesses are required to maintain digital accounting records and submit their VAT return generated directly from within their own functionally compatible accounting software. The accounting software will be required to record details of individual sales and purchases and preserve digital records. It is hoped that this digital process will prevent many common errors that arise in VAT returns.

VAT invoices

If a taxable person makes a taxable supply, a VAT invoice must be issued to the purchaser. This enables the recovery of any input VAT by the purchaser. Without a valid VAT invoice, input tax cannot be recovered. The invoice must show all of the following:

- the supplier's name, address and VAT registration number;
- the name and address of the customer;
- the invoice number, its date of issue and the tax point;
- the type of supply and a description of the goods supplied; and
- the VAT exclusive amount, the rate of VAT, the amount of VAT payable and any cash discount offered.

Less detailed invoices can be issued where the VAT inclusive amount does not exceed £250. There is no requirement to issue a VAT invoice for retail supplies to unregistered businesses or individuals. A retailer may assume that no VAT invoice is required unless the customer asks for one when an invoice should be issued using the rules detailed above.

Late returns or payments – Default surcharge

If either a VAT return is not submitted by the due date or the tax due with the return is paid late, it will trigger a surcharge liability notice.

On the occasion of the first default, a surcharge liability notice is issued covering a period of 12 months from the end of the quarter in respect of which the default has arisen. If any further default occurs during these 12 months, a penalty surcharge of 2% of the VAT outstanding for the quarter is charged. In addition, the surcharge notice period is extended by a further 12 months from the end of the quarter in respect of which the latest default occurred.

Further defaults will similarly lead to additional surcharges and further extensions of the notice period. For the second default within a notice period, the surcharge rises to 5%; 10% for the third; and a maximum of 15% for the fourth and subsequent defaults within the period of the notice.

Surcharge penalties at the rate of 2% and 5% are not made for less than £400. Where the surcharge penalty is at 10% or 15% there is a minimum penalty of £30.

There will be no surcharge levied where the return is late but the VAT is paid on time or a nil return is submitted late. This default will, however, extend the period that a surcharge liability notice is in force and increase the potential percentage surcharge for the next default.

Where the VAT returns and VAT payments are completed satisfactorily for four subsequent VAT quarters, the surcharge regime recommences i.e. any subsequent failure to file a return on time and/or pay the VAT due late will constitute the first default giving rise to a new surcharge liability notice but no default surcharge unless and until a further default arises within the surcharge notice period.

A default surcharge will not apply if the trader can show that the return or payment was submitted on time or that there was a reasonable excuse as to why the failure arose.

Example 23.12

Kira has always submitted her VAT returns on time. However, three returns and accompanying payments were submitted late as follows:
Quarter to 31 March 2020 - submitted on 10 May 2020
Quarter to 30 June 2020 - submitted on 31 July 2020
Quarter to 30 September 2020 - submitted on 10 December 2020
Quarter to 31 December 2020 - submitted on 10 February 2021
What is the position concerning any VAT surcharges?

Answer

Quarter to 31 March 2020 – due by 7 May 2020
This was Kira's first late submission. No penalty will arise but a surcharge notice will be issued covering the period 1 April 2020 to 31 March 2021.

Quarter to 30 June 2020 – due by 7 August 2020
Submissions made on time.

Quarter to 30 September 2020 – due by 7 November 2020
This is Kira's *first* default *within* the surcharge notice period. A penalty surcharge of 2% of the late paid VAT due for the quarter will be charged.
In addition, the surcharge notice period will be extended until 30 September 2021.

Quarter to 31 December 2020 – due by 7 February 2021
This is Kira's *second* default *within* the surcharge notice period. A penalty surcharge of 5% of the VAT paid late for the quarter will be charged.
In addition, the surcharge notice period will be extended until 31 December 2021.

Minor errors and corrections

If a trader discovers an error on a previous VAT return, they may simply adjust the next return to account for this within certain limits. This only applies if the net adjustment is within the greater of £10,000 and 1% of the quarter's turnover, subject to a maximum adjustment of £50,000.

HMRC may impose a penalty if they believe that the error is deliberate or careless.

Larger errors must be notified to HMRC and interest will be charged on the late paid VAT. Again HMRC may also impose a tax geared penalty.

VAT visits and inspections

HMRC has the right to request to visit a business' trading premises and inspect its business records.

If as a result of an inspection an underpayment of VAT is discovered, HMRC may raise an assessment to collect this, together with interest. In addition, a tax geared penalty may be imposed as detailed in Chapter 21.

VAT Records

Records used to prepare a VAT return must be retained for six years. In particular, this must include copies of all VAT invoices issued and invoices used to support the claim for input tax.

Special Schemes

Many small businesses find VAT administration very time-consuming. Three optional special schemes have been introduced to help businesses by reducing the administrative burden.

The three schemes are:
* annual accounting;
* cash accounting; and
* flat rate scheme.

Annual accounting

Where a business has an anticipated annual taxable turnover (i.e. standard plus zero rated supplies excluding the VAT) not exceeding £1,350,000 (excluding VAT) then instead of being required to complete four quarterly returns such a business may make a single annual return for the previous 12 months.

The business must be up to date with all of its VAT returns and must not have committed a VAT offence in the previous 12 months.

Although only one return is necessary, the business is required to make nine equal monthly payments of VAT based upon the net VAT liability for the previous year (i.e. each payment equals 10% of the previous year's net VAT liability). These payments are due in months 4 to 12 inclusive.

A final balancing payment for the year must be made within two months of the end of the year at which time the annual return must also be lodged.

A trader must leave the scheme where taxable turnover for the last annual accounting period exceeds £1,600,000. The trader must notify HMRC with a view to leaving the scheme where they anticipate that their turnover will exceed these limits in the current accounting period.

Cash accounting

As discussed above VAT is calculated for each quarter based on invoices issued and received; basically the accruals basis.

However, where annual taxable turnover does not exceed £1,350,000, a trader may elect to prepare VAT returns on the cash basis, again provided that their VAT position is up to date. This basis simply requires that output and input VAT for a quarter is calculated on a cash received and cash paid basis.

This basis has the advantage that any output VAT which is normally accounted for in the quarter in which an invoice has been raised need not be accounted for until the trader actually receives settlement of the invoice. Therefore, this means that automatic relief for bad debts is obtained.

On the other hand, until the trader settles invoices raised on purchases no input VAT can be recovered.

A trader must leave the scheme if annual taxable turnover has exceeded £1,600,000 at the end of a VAT period.

Flat rate scheme

Under the flat rate scheme, small businesses may calculate their VAT liability as a flat rate percentage of total turnover (i.e. inclusive of VAT, and including standard, zero rated and exempt supplies) thus avoiding the need to keep detailed records of input and output tax.

The scheme is available to small businesses with a taxable turnover which is not anticipated to exceed £150,000 in the next 12 months. A trader must leave the scheme if their annual total VAT inclusive turnover exceeds £230,000.

Under the scheme, a trader charges the customer the normal amount of VAT (i.e. output VAT) on sales and is charged on purchases normal amounts of VAT (i.e. input VAT). However, the output VAT is not paid over to HMRC nor is the input VAT recoverable. Instead, in each VAT period, a flat rate is charged on the VAT inclusive turnover plus any exempt supplies and this amount of VAT is then payable to HMRC as normal.

The flat rate varies according to the type of business or trade sector. Rates vary, and by way of example the flat rate percentage for accounting is 14.5%;

for advertising 11%; estate agency 12%; legal services 14.5%; food manufacturing 9%; and tobacco or newspaper retailing 4%.

This scheme, however, cannot be used in conjunction with the cash accounting scheme (see above) but can be used with the annual return scheme (see above).

Example 23.13

Connor uses the flat rate scheme (applying the appropriate flat rate of 13%) and makes annual standard rated sales (VAT excluded) of £90,000 and exempt sales of £2,000. Connor's purchases amount to £8,800 (all relating to standard rate supplies, VAT inclusive).

Calculate VAT payable under the normal and flat rate methods.

Answer

Under the normal basis Connor would account for

Output tax	Standard rate sales	90,000 x 20% =	18,000
	Input tax	8,800 x 1/6　=	(1,467)
			16,533

Under the flat rate scheme Connor would account for:

Output VAT = 13% x (90,000 + (90,000 x 20%) + 2,000)　　= 　14,300

HMRC became aware that many traders were using the scheme as a way to reduce their VAT liability, as illustrated by the above example, rather than the intended reason of reducing administration. Therefore a flat rate of 16.5% will apply to all 'limited cost business' rather than the normal business specific rates. A limited cost business is one with total purchases less than either 2% of turnover or £1,000 a year.

Substantial traders

If a trader has an annual VAT liability exceeding £2,300,000 then monthly payments on account of each quarter's liability must be paid over to HMRC thereafter.

These monthly payments on account are taken into account when calculating the net VAT payable for the quarter. Each monthly payment is based on the previous year's VAT liability and equals 1/24 of this annual amount.

Interaction of VAT and the other taxes

Generally speaking, VAT is excluded from income tax and corporation tax calculations.

Thus, all calculations are performed net of VAT if the business is VAT registered. The simple reason is that in the majority of cases VAT charged as output VAT on sales and input VAT payable on purchases is offset giving rise to a VAT net payment or net recovery. In other words, VAT does not impact upon the business other than from a cash flow perspective.

However, sometimes VAT may be irrecoverable by a trader (e.g. on the purchase of motor cars or if only exempt supplies are made). In such cases some form of relief is in principle available as follows:

Income and corporation tax

Irrecoverable VAT may be deducted as a business expense in computing trading profit.

However, if such VAT relates to the purchase of a capital item and is irrecoverable it may form part of the cost of the item for capital allowance purposes instead.

Capital gains tax

VAT paid on the purchase of a chargeable asset is excluded from any subsequent capital gain computation if the VAT is recoverable. However, where the VAT is irrecoverable the purchase price will be the VAT inclusive price.

Note, however, that on a future sale any VAT that may be charged on the sale price should be excluded in computing any capital gain.

SUMMARY

VAT is a tax on consumption. Other than from a cash flow perspective VAT is generally neutral for a VAT registered business except if the business makes exempt supplies.

VAT charged on sales (output VAT) is offset by VAT paid on purchases (input VAT) normally, over a three months period and VAT either paid over to or recovered from HMRC who are responsible for administering VAT.

There are some restrictions on the input VAT that may be recovered.

Failure to file a VAT return and/or make the appropriate payment on time may lead to default surcharges.

For small businesses, certain schemes are available to make the administration of VAT easier, including annual rather than quarterly returns, cash accounting and the flat rate scheme. Various conditions need to be satisfied before any of these options may be adopted.

Questions for students

See Appendix 2 for practice questions relating to Chapter 23. Answers are available online.

CHAPTER 24

Inheritance Tax an introduction

INTRODUCTION

The calculation of Inheritance Tax (IHT) is very different from the other taxes detailed in this book.

The chapter will look at the basics of how an individual's IHT liabilities are calculated both during their lifetime and on death.

Basic principles:

IHT is a tax on the transfer of value, most commonly on the death of an individual. Only individuals and trusts are liable to IHT. This book will not consider the IHT charges that can apply to a trust.

Technically speaking, liability to IHT arises when a chargeable person (e.g. an individual or trust) makes a chargeable transfer (e.g. a gift) of chargeable property (e.g. cash, shares etc.). For IHT to be applicable there must be an element of gift (gratuitous benefit). Therefore, a genuine arm's length commercial transaction would not give rise to an IHT liability.

An individual domiciled in the UK is a chargeable person in respect of all of their chargeable property (See Chapter 11 for additional details of domicile). An individual will be deemed to have UK domicile for IHT purposes if they have been resident in the UK for 15 out of the last 20 tax years. In addition, an individual born in the UK with a UK domicile of origin who has acquired a non-UK domicile of choice will be deemed domiciled if they are resident in the UK and were resident in the UK in at least one of the two previous tax years. A non-UK domiciled individual is still liable to IHT on assets located in the UK.

As regards chargeable property this includes almost all property of any type with few exempt items. An ISA, for example, is exempt from income tax and capital gains tax but is chargeable for IHT. A very generous relief, known as business property relief can apply to business interests held for at least two years but again a detailed consideration of this relief is outside of the scope of this introductory chapter.

Lifetime transfers:

For gifts to other individuals, there is no immediate charge to IHT. However, if the individual making the gift dies within the following seven years, then potentially the gift is subject to IHT and must be considered when reviewing the IHT position on death. Therefore, such gifts are referred to as potentially exempt transfers or PETs.

Gifts to most trusts can create an immediate IHT charge and in these cases are referred to as chargeable lifetime transfers (CLT). In addition, where a CLT is made within seven years of death, the CLT will also be reviewed on death with potentially additional IHT payable.

A number of reliefs can apply to lifetime transfers.

First, and perhaps most importantly, any transfers between, UK domiciled, spouses or civil partners are exempt from IHT, whether during lifetime or on death. Gifts to registered charities are similarly exempt.

During each tax year, an individual may make gifts totalling £3,000 completely exempt from IHT. If this annual exemption is not fully used, it may be carried forward and utilized in the following tax year only, after the current year exemption has been used in full. If there are multiple transfers during a year, whether PETs or chargeable, the annual exemption must be used against the earliest transfer first in a tax year and in chronological order against further transfers.

In addition, small gifts totalling no more than £250 per individual recipient each tax year are also exempt.

Example 24.1

Albert made no gifts during the tax year to 5 April 2020. During the year to 5 April 2021, he gave £8,000 to his son and £200 to each of his five grandchildren on their birthdays. All of the gifts were made in cash.

What is the value of the potentially exempt transfers?

Answer

The gifts to each of his grandchildren were below £250 per individual in total during 2020/21 and are therefore exempt.

As Albert did not make any gifts in the previous tax year, he has the annual exempt amount of £3,000 for the current year 2020/21 and the unused allowance of the previous year 2019/20. The gift to his son for IHT is £8,000 - £3,000 - £3,000 = £2,000. This is a potentially exempt transfer or PET.

Therefore, if Albert dies within seven years of making the gift to his son, the PET of £2,000 is potentially subject to IHT.

Gifts made in consideration of marriage are exempt up to specific limits. For gifts from a parent, the exemption is £5,000, reducing to £2,500 for gifts from grandparents and remoter ancestors or from a party to the marriage. Finally, a gift of up to £1,000 by anyone else on marriage is also exempt. This exemption also applies to civil partnerships.

As IHT is charged on capital, a further exemption applies to gifts that constitute normal expenditure out of income. There is no financial limit on this exemption but it must be able to be demonstrated that the gifts are habitual, are made from excess income and do not affect the donor's standard of living.

Value Transferred – Loss to the donor

In the above example, simple cash gifts were referred to. However, a gift could be of property or shares. For IHT purposes the value transferred is based on the reduction in the donor's estate and not the value received by the recipient.

Example 24.2

Reisha owns 70% of the shares in her family company and decides to give a 25% shareholding to her daughter. The gift will reduce Reisha's shareholding to 45%.

It has been established that a 70% shareholding is valued at £500,000, a 45% shareholding £225,000 and a 25% shareholding £100,000. What is the value of the shares gifted for IHT purposes?

Answer

Before the gift, Reisha's 70% shareholding was valued at £500,000 and after the gift, her remaining 45% shareholding has a value of £225,000. The value of the 25% transfer for IHT is the loss to Reisha's estate calculated as £500,000 - £225,000 = £275,000.

Notes

The transfer will be a PET and will fall out of any IHT charge if Reisha survives seven years from the date of the gift.

If the £3,000 annual exemption has not already been used, this will be available to reduce the gift.

IHT on the death estate:

On death, IHT is charged on the basis that the deceased made a transfer of all of their assets immediately before death. This calculation will require all assets to be valued and any liabilities at death to be deducted to arrive at the total estate. Also, any reasonable funeral costs, including the provision of a headstone, may be deducted.

The annual exemption and small gifts exemptions do not apply on death. However, any legacies to a surviving spouse or civil partner, or to charity are exempt.

Example 24.3

John died on 24 August 2019. John had never married and lived in a rented property. On his death, he had the following assets and liabilities:

Quoted shares	150,000
Bank deposits	185,000
ISA	18,000
Household items	3,500
Motor car	6,000
Outstanding gas bill	120

John's funeral cost £3,900.

John had not made any lifetime gifts and under his will, all assets are left to his daughter.

Calculate the value of John's death estate for IHT.

Answer

Quoted shares	150,000
Bank deposits	185,000
ISA	18,000
Household items	3,500
Motor car	6,000
Less:	
Outstanding gas bill	(120)
John's funeral cost	(3,900)
Gross chargeable estate	358,480

Note

Note that the ISA, although exempt from income tax and capital gains tax, is subject to IHT. Similarly, the motor car would be exempt from capital gains tax but again is charge.

The rate of IHT on the death estate:

IHT is charged at a flat rate of 40% on the death estate above the nil rate band of £325,000. However, where there are chargeable lifetime transfers or PETs within the seven years before death, the full nil rate band may not be available.

In addition, a residence nil rate band: (RNRB) of up to £175,000 is also available if the estate at death leaves a residence (for example a house) of the deceased to their direct descendants. The available RNRB is limited to the value of the residence less any outstanding repayment mortgage if lower.

Example 24.4

Continuing from Example 24.3 above, calculate the IHT payable on John's death.

Answer

As John had not made any lifetime gifts, the full IHT nil rate band will be available. John's estate did not include a residence; therefore, the residence nil rate band is not available.

IIT payable

325,000 @ 0%	0
33,480 @ 40%	£13,392
358,480	£13,392

If the deceased was married or in a civil partnership, any unused nil rate band and/or residence nil rate band may be claimed on the death of the survivor. This is based on the proportion of the unused rate band rather than the actual amount. The transferred unused nil rate band may be used against the death estate and any lifetime gifts taxable as a result of death. The transferred residence nil rate band may only be used against the death estate.

Example 24.5

Hilda died in May 2007 leaving £120,000 to her children and the remainder of her estate to her husband, Stan. Stan died on 14 May 2020 leaving his entire estate to his children. The estate comprised his house (i.e. his residence) valued at £280,000 and other assets of £550,000 giving a total estate value of £830,000. The IHT Nil rate band available at May 2007 was £300,000. Stan and Hilda made no lifetime gifts. Calculate the IHT liability on Stan's death.

Answer

Hilda's estate used £120,000 of the £300,000 IHT nil rate band in 2007. This represents 40% (120,000/300,000) of the band, leaving 60% to be claimed on the death of Stan.

Stan's estate at death may, therefore, claim Stan's IHT nil rate band of £325,000 plus 60% of £325,000 transferred from Hilda, giving a total of £520,000.

Stan's estate will also benefit from the residence nil rate band of £175,000 and can claim Hilda's unused RNRB, for a total of £350,000. As this is higher than the value of the residence, £280,000, it is restricted.

The IHT on Stan's estate is therefore calculated as follows:

Nil rate band	325,000 @ 0%	
Transferred Nil rate band	195,000 @ 0%	
RNRB	280,000 @ 0%	
Balance	30,000 @ 40% =	£12,000
	830,000	

The amount of RNRB is reduced for estates in excess of £2 million. The reduction is £1 for every £2 exceeding £2 million before deducting certain reliefs and exemptions.

Reduced rate of IHT:

A reduced rate of inheritance tax was introduced in 2012 to encourage charitable giving. The IHT rate is reduced from 40% to 36% for estates of individuals who die on or after 6 April 2012, where at least 10% of the taxable estate is left to charity. For this relief, taxable estate means the value of the deceased's net assets after deducting the available nil-rate band, and any reliefs or exemptions other than the value of the gift to charity.

IHT on chargeable lifetime transfers :

A lifetime transfer to a trust is referred to as a chargeable lifetime transfer (CLT) as it may create a lifetime IHT charge. The nil rate band of £325,000 still applies but IHT is charged at the lifetime rate of 20%. If the donor agrees to meet the IHT charge then this creates a further loss to the estate. In these cases, the chargeable transfer is effectively grossed up. IHT is charged at 20/80 or 25% and the gross transfer includes both the transfer and associated IHT.

Example 24.6

Erica transfers £400,000 into a trust on 1 December 2020. She has not previously made any lifetime gifts. What is the IHT liability and loss to Erica's estate if:

a) Erica bears the cost of the IHT liability, or

b) the IHT is paid from the trust?

Answer

Erica will be entitled to deduct the Annual exemption for both the current year 2020/21 and the previous year 2019/20. The chargeable transfer is therefore £400,000 – 3,000 – 3,000 = £394,000.

a) If Erica pays the IHT the liability will be:

   325,000 @ 0%

   69,000 @ 25% (20/80)   <u>17,250</u>

The loss to the estate is the net transfer of £394,000 plus the IHT of £17,250, giving a total of £411,250.

b) If the trust bears the IHT liability:

   325,000 @ 0%

   69,000 @ 20%   <u>13,800</u>

The loss to the estate is the net transfer of £394,000 only.

If further chargeable lifetime transfers are made within seven years, then only the balance of the nil rate band will be available.

Example 24.7

Following on from Example 24.6 above, Erica transfers £100,000 into another trust on 1 June 2025 and again agrees to bear the IHT cost. She had made no other lifetime transfers since 1 December 2020. What is the IHT liability and loss to Erica's estate?

Answer

Erica will be entitled to deduct the Annual exemption for both 2025/26 and 2024/25. The chargeable transfer is therefore £100,000 – 3,000 – 3,000 = £94,000.

Next, we must look at the available nil rate band. This will be £325,000 less any chargeable lifetime transfers made within the previous seven years, at this point PETs are ignored.

As Erica made a chargeable lifetime transfer on 1 December 2020 in excess of £325,000, there is no remaining nil rate band available. The IHT liability on the chargeable lifetime transfer on 1 June 2025 will, therefore, be £94,000 @ 25% (20/80) = £23,500, with the loss to the estate of £117,500.

Note

If Erica had waited until after 30 November 2027 to make the second chargeable lifetime transfer, then the transfer on 1 December 2020, would be ignored as it would be more than seven years ago, and the full nil rate band would again be available.

Lifetime transfers – additional IHT on death

As mentioned above where a lifetime transfer, whether a PET or CLT is made within seven years of death, the transfer will come in to charge to IHT at death rates.

Each transfer must be considered in chronological order and may utilise the IHT nil rate band before the death estate. Credit is given for any lifetime IHT paid. If the IHT liability on death is less than the lifetime charge, the excess cannot be refunded.

Example 24.8

Henry made a gift of £120,000 to his daughter in May 2014 and a subsequent gift into a trust of £50,000 in June 2016. Henry died on 12 August 2020 leaving an estate of £300,000. Henry was unmarried, did not make any other lifetime transfers and his death estate did not include a residence. Calculate the lifetime IHT payable by Henry. Calculate any IHT liabilities arising as a result of Henry's death.

Answer

Lifetime transfers

May 2014 Transfer to daughter	120,000
Annual exemption CY 2014/15	(3,000)
Annual exemption PY 2013/14	(3,000)
PET	114,000 – PET No lifetime IHT liability
June 2016 Transfer to trust	50,000
Annual exemption CY 2016/17	(3,000)
Annual exemption PY 2015/16	(3,000)
CLT	44,000
IHT 44,000 @ 0%	0

IHT on death 12 August 2020

Nil rate band available	325,000
PET May 2014	(114,000)
CLT June 2016	(44,000)
Balance of Nil rate band	167,000
Estate on death	300,000
IHT 167,000 @ 0%	
133,000 @ 40%	£53,200

Notes

The IHT position of each lifetime transfer is calculated first in chronological order. The IHT position of each gift within seven years before death is then reviewed to consider any additional IHT payable.

In this case, as the lifetime transfers are below £325,000 there is no IHT payable on the lifetime transfers. However, the lifetime transfers utilise part of the IHT Nil rate band increasing the IHT payable on the death estate.

If as a result of death any IHT is payable on lifetime transfers, the resulting tax liability may be reduced by taper relief. The taper relief increases as the time from the date of the gift to date of death increases according to the following table:

Years before death	Taper relief
0-3	0%
3-4	20%
4-5	40%
5-6	60%
6-7	80%

It should be noted that it is the IHT liability that is tapered and not the transfer. In effect, this means that taper relief can only apply where lifetime transfers are in excess of the nil rate band.

Example 24.9

Dorothy made a gift of £100,000 to her son on 17 January 2010. She then made a transfer of £400,000 to a trust on 1 May 2017 agreeing to pay any IHT arising. Dorothy died on 10 June 2020 with a taxable estate of £600,000. Dorothy had 10% of her late husband's nil rate band available and her estate did not include a residence. Calculate any IHT liabilities arising in Dorothy's lifetime and as a result of her death.

Answer

IHT on Lifetime transfers

17 January 2010 Transfer to son	100,000	
Annual exemption CY 2009/10	(3,000)	
Annual exemption PY 2008/09	(3,000)	
PET	94,000	PET – No lifetime IHT liability
1 May 2017 Transfer to trust	400,000	
Annual exemption CY 2017/18	(3,000)	
Annual exemption PY 2016/17	(3,000)	
CLT	394,000	
IHT 325,000 @ 0%	0	
69,000 @ 25% (20/80)	17,250	

As Dorothy agreed to pay the IHT, the gross transfer (or loss to Dorothy's estate) is:

CLT	394,000
IHT	17,250
Gross transfer	411,250

IHT on death 10 June 2020

Nil rate band available	325,000
Transferred nil rate band (10%)	32,500
Nil rate band	357,500

PET 17 January 2010 (more than seven years before death) no additional IHT liability

CLT 1 May 2017	411,250
IHT 357,500 @ 0%	0
53,750 @ 40%	21,500

Less: taper relief @ 20%	(4,300)	
	17,200	
Less IHT paid on CLT	(17,200) (Actually paid £17,250)	
Additional IHT payable	0	
Balance of Nil rate band	0	
Estate on death	600,000	

All available nil rate band has been fully utilised by the CLT on 1 May 2017. Therefore, the entire death estate is subject to IHT at 40%.

IHT   600,000 @ 40%   240,000

Notes

1. The IHT position of each lifetime transfer is calculated first in chronological order.
2. The IHT position of each transfer within seven years before death is then reviewed to consider any additional IHT payable.
3. The gift to Dorothy's daughter in May 2010 occurred more than seven years before death and is completely exempt.
4. The gift into trust occurred between three and four years before death. Therefore, the additional IHT liability on death is reduced by 20% taper relief.
5. The IHT paid during the lifetime on the transfer into the trust in May 2017 is deducted from the additional liability arising on death. As the lifetime tax exceeds the additional tax on death, no further IHT is payable. However, there can be no repayment of lifetime tax.
6. As the IHT nil rate band has been fully utilised by the lifetime transfer into trust, the estate on death is fully charged at 40%.

When considering the additional IHT on transfers in the seven years before death, any chargeable lifetime transfers or PETs that have become chargeable in the seven years before each transfer must also be taken into account. Although in the case of a chargeable lifetime transfer this may be more than seven years before the date of death, it can still impact the IHT liability.

Example 24.10

Peter died on 12 May 2020 leaving a death estate of £510,000 including a residence valued at £300,000. His entire estate is left to his daughter. Peter was unmarried. In his lifetime Peter had made the following transfers, after deducting any available allowances:

16 July 2011	Transfer to trust	150,000
5 September 2015	Gift to daughter	200,000

The trust agreed to pay any IHT arising on the transfer on 16 July 2011.

Calculate the IHT payable as a result of Peter's death.

Answer

Chargeable transfer July 2011– more than seven years before death – no further IHT liability on death.

PET 5 September 2015		200,000
Nil rate band	325,000	
Less CLT 16 July 2011	(150,000) (within seven years of PET)	

Balance available	175,000
IHT payable 175,000 @ 0%	0
25,000 @ 40%	10,000
Taper relief (4 -5 years) @ 40%	(4,000)
IHT payable	6,000 (Payable by daughter)
Estate on death 12 May 2020	510,000
Nil rate band	325,000
Less PET 5 September 2015	(200,000)
Balance available	125,000
NRB 125,000 @ 0%	0
RNRB 175,000 @ 0%	0
210,000 @ 40%	84,000 (payable from the estate)
510,000	

Notes

1. Although the transfer to a trust in July 2010 is more than seven years before death, when considering the IHT of the PET on 5 September 2015 any CLT in the seven years before that date must be considered.
2. As the PET was to Peter's daughter, she will be responsible for the payment of the IHT liability arising as a result of Peter's death.
3. The available nil rate band on the death estate is reduced by any transfers within the seven years prior to death, both chargeable lifetime transfers and PETs. In addition, the RNRB is available.
4. If Peter had lived until 5 September 2022 the PET would have become fully exempt.

SUMMARY

Inheritance tax (IHT) is charged on transfers of value.

The value of the transfer is based on the principle of the loss to the estate.

IHT can apply in lifetime for transfers to trusts but more commonly applies on death.

Lifetime gifts to another individual are potentially exempt, assuming that the donor survives seven years from the date of the gift.

Transfers to trusts can give rise to a lifetime IHT charge at 20% (or 20/80 if the transferor bears the tax). If the transferor pays the IHT liability arising, then this increases the loss to the estate.

Any lifetime transfers within seven years before death may come into charge to IHT at death rates but credit is given for any lifetime IHT paid.

IHT on death is charged at 40% on the estate above the available nil rate band.

Transfers between UK domiciled spouses and civil partners are exempt from IHT whether in lifetime or on death.

INHERITANCE TAX

An additional residence nil rate band applies where a residence is left on death to descendants.

Questions for students

See Appendix 2 for practice questions relating to Chapter 24. Answers are available online.

APPENDIX 1

How to Study Taxation: Some suggestions

INTRODUCTION

Taxation is something of a "Marmite" topic for many accountants – they either love it or hate it! Tax is a dynamic subject with rules, rates and allowances changing every year. However, this book attempts to simplify the tax rules as much as possible to help you to find studying tax interesting and enjoyable.

The rules of UK taxation can be logical but often they are not! Don't worry therefore if you have difficulty understanding a particular issue because it doesn't seem logical; it probably isn't!

For example, the UK's income tax year runs from the 6 April to the next 5 April (e.g. 6 April 2019 to 5 April 2020). It does *not* operate on a calendar year i.e. 1 January to 31 December basis.[1]

The taxes which you will generally study as part of your course are:

- income tax;
- capital gains tax;
- corporation tax
- national insurance contributions;
- value added tax; and
- inheritance tax.

*Income tax is **very important*** and an understanding of income tax (the tax paid by individuals) is recommended before moving on to corporation tax (the tax paid by companies).

Computational approach

The tax syllabus, whether for undergraduates, ACCA or AAT, primarily involves the ability to perform computations i.e. working out an individual's taxable income and income tax liability or a company's corporation tax liability.

No detailed understanding of the UK's tax case law or its legislation is needed (although reading some tax cases can be surprisingly entertaining!). Students do not, therefore, need to be able to recite details of tax cases heard by the courts or section numbers from the tax legislation (i.e. the various Acts of Parliament) until studying for ATT or CIOT.

---

[1] Well, there is a logic but we need to go into the difference between Julian and Gregorian calendars and understand why the new year was celebrated on Lady Day (25 March).

As the approach is usually computational without doubt one of the keys to passing the examinations is to understand and be able to reproduce the various proforma layouts adopted throughout this book in preparing the various computations.

Proformas

A proforma is simply a standard layout of how a particular computation should be carried out.

The proforma layout not only reflects the order in which a computation needs to be performed but can also effectively be used as a revision aid with the simple addition of your detailed notes.

One approach to studying tax is, therefore, to ensure that you know the proforma for a particular purpose and to make your own notes for each proforma highlighting associated key points. For example, let us look at calculating an individual's income tax liability; one of the first things you are likely to be taught on your course (Chapters 1 to 4):

The proforma is as follows:

	Non-Savings Income	**Savings Income**	**Dividend Income**	**Total Income**
Income by source				
Less: Loan interest paid/losses				
Net Income				
Less: Personal allowance				
Taxable income				

Having then worked out the **Taxable Income** for each category of income (i.e. Non-savings, Savings and Dividend income) the individual's income tax liability can then be worked out as follows:

Income tax liability on:
Non-savings income
Savings income
Dividends
Total income tax on all income
Less: Tax reducers
Income tax liability
Less: Income tax suffered-PAYE on salary
Income tax payable

Don't worry if at this stage you do not follow or understand the above.

I have included it simply to try and illustrate what a proforma looks like and how you can eventually use it together with your own notes as a revision aid. Key proformas include the calculation of adjusted trading profits, computation of capital allowances and TTP for companies, in addition to the personal income tax computation above.

Because of the volume of material covered in a taxation course, there is often little time to revise all of the elements of the course as you go along which is, of course, the ideal way to study. A proforma should help in this regard.

Doing questions

When starting to study a new tax (e.g. capital gains tax) or aspect of it (e.g. use of capital losses) the starting point should be for you to try to understand the theory i.e. an explanation of the underlying concepts. Simply doing questions is *not* the answer.

Try to understand the underlying concepts *before* turning to try any questions yourself. In this book, I have included worked examples in the text which illustrate the points under discussion. Read the text and together with the examples try to understand what is happening. Do not simply try to follow the example without having first tried to understand the theory.

Only when you think you have understood the theory and any related examples does it make sense to try some questions in Appendix 2 for yourself.

In trying questions the more you can try the better. If you find difficulty in answering a particular question then *before* looking at the answer, reread the theory and try the question again. Do not simply and immediately look at the answer; this should only be done as a last resort when you have really tried to answer the question.

When looking at an answer, do not simply check the numbers; note, in particular, the layout and order in which the various issues are tackled.

Make up your own questions!

In theory, the tax rules laid out in this text would apply to any individual or company regardless of any wealth or profit level. Usually, tax questions consist of unrelated amounts of income and gains and your task is to accurately calculate the income, gains or tax liability. Try taking an existing question and simply change all of the numbers and attempt to recalculate the correct answer. Hopefully, you are studying with other students and can challenge one of your colleagues to calculate the answer as well and together you can discuss any differences in your answers.

Common parts of the syllabus

Some tax topics are inevitably relevant to more than one type of tax and certainly, some are, relatively speaking, more important than others.

For example, capital allowances (basically tax depreciation) are relevant to both income and corporation taxes. Therefore studying this particular topic means that you may be able to attempt more questions in your exam than where a particular topic can only appear once (e.g. VAT cash accounting scheme).

Similarly, the adjustment of accounts profits (i.e. converting accounts profits into taxable profits) is highly relevant to both income and corporation taxes. It is, therefore, a good idea when you see that a topic appears relevant to more than one type of tax or situation to make sure you fully understand it. This will enhance your ability to pass your exams.

SUMMARY

The most important point is to understand the underlying concepts.

Simply doing lots and lots of questions without attempting to understand the underlying theory is not a good idea.

Only when you feel you have a reasonable understanding of an area should you then attempt a variety of questions.

When looking at model answers to questions take note of how the answer is laid out and the order in which it's presented.

When you have finished a particular tax, e.g. income tax, it is a good idea to try to find time to look through the material again before starting the next tax. Your proforma plus attaching notes should be of immense help in this regard.

Don't be frightened to look at other tax sources which may also help.

If you are completely stuck, then looking at an alternative text or website may be the key to unlocking the solution. Each learner has their own particular style and sometimes reading an alternative text may instantly make the "penny drop". However, always ensure that any text matches the Finance Act that you are studying. A FA2015 tax text may not look very different from this FA2020 text, but a huge amount of tax legislation will have changed in that period as well as all of the tax rates and allowances!

Although not the easiest of websites for the newcomer to UK tax, the official HM Revenue & Customs website on www. Gov.uk may also sometimes be of help.

Identify in particular those areas which are relevant to more than one type of tax or situation.

Finally, try to enjoy your studies. Tax can be challenging but could hold the key to your future career. Before my first day of work at HMRC, my only previous contact with tax had been in a game of Monopoly! Even if you do not pursue a career in this field, at least you will be equipped to check your payslip!

Good luck with your exams!

APPENDIX 2

Questions for Students

Answers can be found at:
spiramus.com/uk-taxation-a-simplified-guide-for-students-1

CHAPTERS 1 TO 4

Question 1
For the year to 5 April 2021, James has the following income:
Employment income 18,000
Bank interest   800
Dividends   900

Income tax of £1,050 was deducted under the Pay As You Earn (PAYE) regulations from James' employment earnings.

Calculate the income tax payable for 2020/21.

Question 2
For the year to 5 April 2021, Carol has the following income:
Employment income 26,000
Bank interest   1,600
Dividends   5,500

Income tax of £2,600 was deducted under PAYE from Carol's employment income.

Calculate the income tax payable for 2020/21.

Question 3
For the year to 5 April 2021, Harry has the following income:
Self-employment profits 48,500
Bank interest   1,600
Dividends   6,800

Calculate the income tax payable for 2020/21.

Question 4
For the year to 5 April 2021, Helen has the following income:
Employment income 35,000
Rental income   5,000
Bank interest   2,600
Dividends   5,200

Income tax of £4,625 was deducted under PAYE from Helen's employment income.

APPENDIX 2

In addition, Helen paid interest of £2,400 on a qualifying loan.

Calculate the income tax payable for 2020/21.

Question 5

For the year to 5 April 2021, Ed has the following income:

Employment income	95,000
Rental income	15,000
Bank interest	1,800
Dividends	5,900

Income tax of £35,100 was deducted under PAYE from Ed's employment income.

Calculate the income tax payable for 2020/21.

Question 6

For the year to 5 April 2021, Ann has the following income:

Rental income	85,000
Bank interest	2,600
Dividends	7,100

Ann made donations to charity, under gift aid, of £4,800 during the year.

Calculate the income tax payable for 2020/21.

Question 7

For the year to 5 April 2021, Sid has the following income:

State retirement pension	8,500
Occupational pension	4,800
Bank interest	5,500
Dividends	1,600

Calculate the income tax payable for 2020/21.

Question 8

Give two examples of qualifying interest payment.

Question 9

For the year to 5 April 2021, Tom has the following income:

Employment income	205,000
Rental income	15,000
Bank interest	1,600
Dividends	1,800

Income tax of £82,100 was deducted under PAYE from Tom's employment income.

In addition, Tom paid interest of £5,000 on a qualifying loan.

Calculate the income tax payable for 2020/21.

Question 10

For the year to 5 April 2021, Sofie has the following income:

Trading profits	70,000
Rental income	25,000
Bank interest	11,600
Dividends	8,000

In addition, Sofie paid personal pension contributions of £2,400 and a donation to charity under gift aid of £800.

Calculate the income tax payable for 2020/21.

CHAPTER 5
Question 11

Roger owns two properties which he lets.

Property 1

This property was purchased by Roger on 1 May 2020. Immediate repair work costing £2,300 was carried out on the property before it could be let, the damage to the property had been reflected in a reduced purchase price of the property.

The property was let from 1 July 2020 at an annual rental of £6,300, payable monthly on the last day of each month.

Property 2

The property is let furnished for the entire tax year. The rent received was £8,000. Expenditure comprises property repairs of £300, rent collection fees of £700 and new furniture costing £2,000. The new furniture replaced a similar old item, which was sold for £75.

Other general expenditure:

Other costs relating to the property letting business for the tax year ended 5 April 2021 include loan interest of £2,800 and insurance premiums of £900.

All rent was received on the due date and all expenses mentioned were paid during the tax year.

Calculate Roger's property business income for the year to 5 April 2021.

CHAPTERS 6 TO 7
Question 12

Jenny carries on her trade as a sole trader. She prepares her accounts to 30 September each year having started to trade on 1 October 2017.

APPENDIX 2

Her tax adjusted profits were:
Year ended 30 September 2018 12,000
Year ended 30 September 2019 25,000
Year ended 30 September 2020 33,000

Calculate Jenny's assessable profits for each of the first four tax years of trading, identifying the appropriate basis periods for each tax year and identify any overlap profits.

Question 13

Nicholae carries on his trade as a sole trader. He prepares his accounts to 30 June each year having started to trade on 1 September 2018.

His tax adjusted profits were:
10 months to 30 June 2019   18,000
Year ended 30 June 2020   26,000
Year ended 30 June 2021   35,000

Calculate Nicholae's assessable profits for each of the first three tax years of trade identifying the appropriate basis periods for each tax year and identify any overlap profits.

Question 14

Linda carries on her trade as a sole trader. She prepares her accounts to 30 June each year having started to trade on 1 May 2018.

Her tax adjusted profits were:
14 months to 30 June 2019   30,000
Year ended   30 June 2020   27,000
Year ended   30 June 2021   36,000

Calculate Linda's assessable profits for each of the first three tax years of trade identifying the appropriate basis periods for each tax year and identify any overlap profits.

Question 15

Aamil carries on his trade as a sole trader. He prepares his accounts to 30 April each year having started to trade on 1 December 2018.

His tax adjusted profits were:
Period ended 30 April 2020   30,000
Year ended   30 April 2021   27,000

Calculate Aamil's assessments for each of the first three tax years of trade identifying the appropriate basis periods for each tax year and identify any overlap profits.

Question 16

Noah a sole trader started carrying on his trade as a sports retailer (under the trading name of "Sports for All") on 1 May 2019 and his first set of accounts were prepared to 30 April 2020. His accounts prepared by his accountant for the year ended 30 April 2020 showed the following:

Income

Gross profit	115,300
Rental income	15,000
Building society interest received	1,600
	131,900

Expenses

Telephone	1,200	
Depreciation	3,500	
Salaries	39,000	
Rent and rates	9,000	
Light and heat	5,000	
Repairs and maintenance	2,500	
Advertising	25,000	
Motor expenses	10,000	
Sundry expenses	8,000	
		(103,200)
Net profit		28,700

Notes

1. The figure for telephone comprises £800 of the landline for the shop used exclusively for business and £400 for Noah's mobile, 40% of the use of which has been agreed as private.
2. Salaries included a salary to Noah's wife of £15,000 as she works in the shop as a sales assistant. The other sales assistants doing the same job receive a salary of £12,000.
3. Noah and his wife live in a flat above the shop. The figures for "rent and rates" and "light and heat" are for both the shop and the flat. The accountant has agreed with the tax authorities that 30% of these expenses relate to the flat.
4. Of the "repairs and maintenance" £250 related to the decoration of the flat and £2,250 related to repairs to the shop.
5. Included in the figure of £25,000 for advertising was £5,000 which related to Christmas presents to his customers of various wines and spirits, and £4,000 which related to diaries sent out to customers which had cost Noah £10 each and had on the front of them Noah's logo and the name of his business "Sports for All". The rest of the expenditure related to advertisements which Noah had placed in newspapers and trade magazines.

6. Noah decided to lease a new car (rather than buy it outright). The car had an annual leasing charge of £6,000. The balance of the expenditure related to normal running costs (e.g. petrol, repairs etc.). The tax authorities have agreed that 60% of Noah's usage relates to private usage with 40% representing business usage. The car has CO_2 emissions of 140 g/km.

7. Sundry expenses included client entertaining of £2,000; staff entertaining of £450 on a day out in London; a fine of £500 for breach of health and safety regulations; a car park fine of £50 incurred by one of the sales assistants when on business for Noah; a donation to a local charity of £75 and a donation of £50 to his local political party; a subscription of £80 to the Sports Retailers Association; legal fees of £375 in connection with the granting of a brand new lease on the shop; and accountancy fees for accounts preparation of £500.

8. Noah's son wanted a pair of trainers for Christmas. Noah, therefore, took a pair from the shop for his son but did not pay for them. The trainers, if they had been sold to a member of the public, would have a retail price of £135 but their cost to Noah had been £100.

Calculate Noah's adjusted trading profit for tax purposes.

Question 17

Andrew has operated as a self employed consultant for many years. His profit and loss account to 31 March 2021 is as follows:

Fees receivable		120,000
Add: Bank interest received		55
Less: Expenses		
Depreciation	3,200	
Motor expenses	6,600	
Donation to a national charity	1,000	
New photocopier	1,500	
Legal fees for grant of a 5-year lease	900	
Other allowable expenses	43,500	
		(56,700)
Profit for the year		63,355

45% of Andrew's motoring was private.

Andrew's capital allowances pools brought forward are as follows

Main pool	3,600
Car used by Andrew (CO_2 emissions 155 g/km)	15,400

During the year Andrew also acquired two new items of plant and machinery as follows

New van (CO_2 emissions 130 g/km)	14,000
New computer	2,200

Calculate Andrew's adjusted trading profits, after capital allowances for the year to 31 March 2021.

Question 18

Jane a sole trader bought various capital items all of which qualified for capital allowances.

Jane prepares her accounts to 31 December each year. As at 31 December 2019, there is a tax written down value of £2,400 on her main pool.

Her purchases were as follows:

Purchases

1 September 2020	Equipment	16,000
1 August 2020	Motor car	15,000 (emissions 145g/km. Jane uses this car privately 30% of the time)
30 January 2021	Van	8,000

Calculate Jane's capital allowances for the years ended 31 December 2020 and 2021.

Question 19

Ian commenced trading on 1 November 2019 and bought various capital items all of which qualify for capital allowances.

He prepares his first accounts for the 10 months to 31 August 2020. His purchases were as follows:

Purchases

Plant and equipment	96,000 on 14 December 2019
Motor car	18,600 on 20 August 2020 (for an employee; CO_2 emissions 145g/km)
Motor car:	10,400 on 3 June 2020 (for an employee; CO_2 emissions 85g/km)

Calculate Ian's capital allowances for the 10 months to 31 August 2020.

Question 20

Ellie has been in business for several years preparing accounts annually to 31 March. As at 31 March 2020 she has the following tax written down values:

Main pool	6,400
Private use asset	14,016

The private use asset is a motor car (CO_2 95 g/km) originally purchased for £20,000. The private use of the car by Ellie has been agreed at 30%.

During the year to 31 March 2021, Ellie made the following transactions

APPENDIX 2

Purchases

Plant and machinery   24,000

Motor car: 15,500 (for an Ellie, C02 emissions 105g/km)

Sales

Equipment Proceeds   3,000 (all at below original cost)

Car   Proceeds   17,000 (This is Ellie's car at the start of the year)

Calculate Ellie's capital allowances for the year ended 31 March 2021.

Question 21

Phil ceased trading on 16 October 2020 having traded for many years, preparing accounts annually to 31 December.

The balances brought forward at 31 December 2019 were as follows

Main pool   16,700

Special rate pool   2,400

Car with private use   14,405 (CO_2 emissions 160g/km)

During the period to 16 October 2020, Phil purchased new equipment for £1,200.

On cessation, all assets were sold for the following amounts

Main pool assets   10,000

Special rate pool assets   2,600

Car   12,500

All assets were sold for less than their original cost.

Phil has agreed with the tax authorities that his private use of his cars is 25%.

Calculate Phil's capital allowances for the period to 16 October 2020.

CHAPTER 8

Question 22

Kellie a sole trader has been trading for many years and prepares her accounts to 30 April each year.

Her adjusted trading results for the past few years are as follows.

Year ended 30 April 2018	70,000
Year ended 30 April 2019	(50,000)
Year ended 30 April 2020	125,000

Calculate Kellie's assessments for each relevant tax year assuming she makes a claim only under ITA2017 section 83.

Question 23

Karim a sole trader has been trading for many years and prepares his accounts to 31 January each year.

His adjusted trading results for the past few years are as follows.

Year ended 31 January 2019	15,000
Year ended 31 January 2020	(65,000)
Year ended 31 January 2021	12,500

His other income for the tax years 2018/19, 2019/20 and 2020/21 is £18,000, £30,000 and £14,000 respectively.

Calculate Karim's net income for each relevant tax year assuming he makes the maximum claim under section 64 and identify the amount of the trading loss of £65,000 (if any) which remains available for carry forward under section 83.

Question 24

Julie started to trade on 1 July 2018 as a self employed designer and prepared her accounts to 30 June. Her results were as follows:

Year ended 30 June 2019	(24,000)
Year ended 30 June 2020	36,000
Year ended 30 June 2021	48,000

Calculate Julie's assessable profits for the tax years 2018/19, 2019/20 and 2020/21 and identify any overlap profits. Assume she carries forward any losses under section 83.

Question 25

Jimmy started in business on 1 June 2018 and prepares his accounts to 31 May each year.

His results were as follows:

Year ended 31 May 2019	(34,000)
Year ended 31 May 2020	15,000

Before he set up in business Jimmy was an employee and received the following employment income:

2015/16	25,000
2016/17	26,500
2017/18	28,000

Calculate Jimmy's net income for the tax years 2015/16 to 2020/21 assuming that he makes a claim under section 72.

Question 26

For the tax year 2020/21 Martha, a sole trader, made a trading loss of £40,000.

She also had chargeable gains of £45,000 and a capital loss of £14,000. Martha also had a capital loss available for carry forward from prior tax years of £12,000.

Before any loss claim, Martha's net income for 2020/21 was £25,000.

Calculate the amount of Martha's chargeable gains after the annual exemption and after electing to also use section 71. Quantify the amount of capital loss (if any) available for carry forward to future tax years.

Question 27

Hetta is a self employed property developer and made a substantial loss for the year to 31 July 2020. Her results for the last two years were as follows:

Year ended 31 July 2020   Loss (92,000)

Year ended 31 July 2019   Profit 25,000

Also, Hetta received income from Property lettings of £72,000 for the year to 5 April 2021 and £30,000 to 5 April 2020.

Calculate Hetta's taxable income for each of the two years to 5 April 2021 maximising any loss claims. Assume that 2020/21 tax allowances apply to all years.

CHAPTER 10
Question 28

Howard is an employee of ABC Ltd. His salary for the tax year 2020/21 was £100,000. Howard was also provided with a petrol engine company car with a list price of £35,000 and CO_2 emissions of 142 grams/km. The car cost ABC Ltd £29,750. The car was however first provided from the 6 December 2020 and was registered on that date.

Calculate Howard's employment income for 2020/21.

Question 29

Penny is employed as a sales director. She is provided with a petrol engine company car with a list price of £25,800 and CO_2 emissions of 122 grams/km. The car was provided from the 6 April 2020 until 6 December 2020 when it was replaced with a new diesel engine (Not RDE2) car with a list price £30,000 and CO_2 emissions of 167 grams/km. Penny made a capital contribution of £6,000 towards the cost of the new car. Both cars were registered before 6 April 2020.

Calculate the assessable benefit in respect of the cars for 2020/21.

Question 30

Martin is an employee of PQR Ltd receiving a salary for the tax year 2020/21 of £45,000. He was also provided with a company car with a list price of £22,500 and CO_2 emissions of 152 grams/km. The car was registered before 6

April 2020. Martin's employer pays for all the petrol for the car. Martin made a contribution to the car's running costs of £50/month.

Calculate Martin's employment income for 2020/21

Question 31

Michelle accepted a job with XYZ Ltd starting on 6 April 2020. Her salary was £40,000 but her employer did not provide her with a company car. Instead, Michelle was expected to use her own car and the company agreed to pay her expenses when on business at 40p per mile for the first 5,000 business miles and 20p per mile thereafter. In the tax year 2020/21, Michelle did 30,000 business miles.

Michelle contributes 5% of her salary to the XYZ Ltd occupational pension scheme.

Calculate Michelle's employment income for 2020/21.

Question 32

Rob accepted a job with AB Ltd from 6 April 2020. His annual salary is £42,600. He will also be covered by the company's private medical insurance cover. This will cost AB Ltd £360 per annum.

Rob is expected to use his own car and AB Ltd has agreed to pay to him expenses when on business of 50p per mile for the first 5,000 business miles and 30p per mile thereafter. In the tax year 2020/21, James drove 20,000 business miles.

Calculate Rob's employment income for 2020/21.

Question 33

Rachel is employed by XY Ltd and as part of her remuneration package is provided with accommodation. The house in which she lives was purchased by her employer in January 2019 for £450,000. The annual value of the house is £1,500. Rachel pays rent of £100 per month for the provision of the property.

Calculate Rachel's assessable benefit for 2020/21.

Question 34

Malcolm is employed by QR Ltd and as part of his remuneration package is provided with accommodation. The house in which he lives was purchased by his employer in January 2017 for £300,000. Further expenditure was incurred by QR Ltd in improving the house including £50,000 in March 2017, £15,000 in July 2019 and £34,000 in May 2020. The annual value of the house is £1,100. The house was first made available to James on 6 April 2020. John contributes £75 per month to his employer in respect of the provision of the accommodation.

Calculate the assessable benefit for 2020/21.

Question 35

If the accommodation referred to in Question 33 above was job-related accommodation what would then be the benefit taxable on James for 2020/21?

Question 36

Assuming the same circumstances as set out in Question 33, if in addition, QR Ltd paid various running expenses of the house as set out below, calculate the benefit on which Malcolm will be taxed for 2020/21:

Heating	1,550
Cleaning and maintenance	1,000
Telephone	675*
Structural repairs	7,500
Council tax	1,100

*the telephone costs are made up of £250 for the line rental, business calls £350 and private calls of £75.

Question 37

How would your answer differ if in Question 35 if the accommodation was job-related?

Question 38

Martin is employed by DE Ltd who has allowed him the private use of some recording equipment which had a market value of £3,500 at the date it was first provided to James on 6 July 2020.

Calculate the benefit on which James will be taxed for the tax year 2020/21.

Question 39

Emma is employed by FG Ltd who has provided her with some photographic equipment for her private use which had a market value of £3,000 at the date it was first provided to her on 6 April 2018.

On 6 January 2021, Emma's employer gave the equipment to her which at that time had a market value of £500.

Calculate the total taxable benefit on which Emma will be taxed for the tax year 2020/21 in respect of the photographic equipment.

Question 40
How would your answer differ to Question 38 if instead, Emma had paid £500 for the photographic equipment in January 2021?

Question 41
Calculate the taxable value of the following benefits in kind provided to Jim by his employer in the course of his employment throughout 2020/21:
1. removal expenses on relocation of £8,500
2. a car park space near to where Jim works, cost to employer £1,040
3. use of a mobile telephone, cost to employer £480
4. an interest free loan of £6,000
5. job-related accommodation with an annual value of £2,400
6. a company van available for unlimited private use, costing £14,000

Question 42
Eric received an interest free loan of £18,000 from his employer on 6 July 2020. On 6 December he repaid £5,000 to his employer.
Calculate Eric's benefit in kind for 2020/21 in respect of the loan under both the average and strict methods.

Question 43
How would the answers to Question 41 differ if Eric was required to pay interest at 1% per annum on the loan?

CHAPTER 12
Question 44
Tessa is a sole trader. Her trading profit for the tax year 2020/21 was £98,000 and Tessa also received dividends of £10,000 during the year. She paid personal pension contributions during 2020/21 of £50,000.

Tessa has paid personal pension contributions of £30,000 net during each of the three previous tax years.

Calculate Tessa's income tax liability for 2020/21.

Question 45
Explain the difference in the manner in which an employee obtains tax relief for pension contributions that they may make to a company pensions scheme as compared to how a sole trader obtains relief for personal pension contributions. Confirm also whether or not an employee who is a member of a company pension scheme may also make contributions to a personal pension scheme.

CHAPTERS 13 TO 15

Question 46

Diane acquired an investment property in February 2010 for £75,000. She improved the property in May 2012 at a cost of £14,000. The property was sold in September 2020 for £190,000. Diane paid legal fees of £2,000 and agents fees of £750 on the sale.

Calculate Diane's capital gain.

Question 47

Rita acquired an investment property in May 2012 for £105,000. In addition, she paid legal fees of £1,500 in connection with the purchase. In November 2014, when the property was valued at £180,000, Rita transferred the property to her husband Bill. Bill subsequently sold the property in June 2020 for £275,000, incurring legal fees of £2,500.

Calculate Bill's capital gain in 2020/21 on the sale of the property.

Question 48

How would your answer for Question 46 be different (if at all) if Rita and Bill were not married?

Question 49

Tara acquired 8 hectares of land at a cost of £62,000 in July 2009. In October 2020 she sold five hectares of land for £99,800. The market value of the remaining land was valued at £120,000 in October 2020. Calculate the capital gain arising on the sale of the five hectares.

Question 50

Harry sold a painting in May 2020 for £5,000. He had purchased the painting in October 2015 for £3,750. Calculate Harry's capital gain on the sale of the painting.

Question 51

Gwen sold an antique necklace in August 2020 for £8,700, incurring sales commission of £100. She had purchased the necklace for £3,600 in May 2008, Calculate Gwen's capital gain on the sale of the necklace.

Question 52

During 2020/21 Sally sold three paintings. The purchase price and sale proceeds of each were as follows:

Painting 1	Cost	3,000	Sale proceeds	7,000
Painting 2	Cost	7,000	Sale proceeds	12,400
Painting 3	Cost	8,200	Sale proceeds	4,800

Calculate Sally's capital gains for 2020/21 in respect of the sale of the three paintings.

Question 53

James has capital gains of £9,000 and capital losses of £2,500 for 2020/21, before deducting his annual exemption. Calculate James' net capital gains for 2020/21. How much, if any, of his loss and /or annual exemption is available to carry forward?

Question 54

Sarah bought a flat in Birmingham on 1 April 2004 for £75,000 and lived there as her main residence until 30 September 2007 when she moved to Edinburgh in connection with her job. She returned to her flat on 1 October 2010 and lived there until 31 March 2012 when she decided to go overseas backpacking with a friend for two years. She returned on 1 April 2014 and lived in her flat until 30 September 2015, when she moved into her partner's house. Sarah's flat remained unoccupied until it was sold on 31 March 2021 for £185,000, a gain of £110,000.

Calculate Sarah's chargeable gain on the sale of the flat.

Question 55

For 2020/21 Peter has capital gains of £22,400 and losses of £8,200. Peter has capital losses brought forward as at 6 April 2020 of £27,600.

Calculate Peter's net capital gains tax position for 2020/21 and the amount, if any, of capital losses available to carry forward at 5 April 2021.

Question 56

Heather sold a residential property during 2020/21 making a capital gain of £43,000. She also made capital gains of £8,400 on the sale of other assets in 2020/21. Heather had capital losses brought forward of £6,000 and is a higher rate income taxpayer.

Calculate Heather capital gains tax liability for 2020/21.

Question 57

Mary sold a factory unit, held as an investment property, in September 2020 for £202,000. She had acquired the building for £78,000 in May 2010 and had extended it at a cost of £25,000 in July 2014. Mary also disposed of a painting in October 2020 for £18,220, incurring auctioneer's fees of 2%. She had acquired the painting for £40,000 in February 2006. Mary had capital losses brought forward of £5,400 at 6 April 2020. Mary's taxable income in 2020/21 was £33,000.

APPENDIX 2

Calculate Mary's capital gains tax liability for 2020/21 and state the due date for payment.

Question 58

Lilly made the following disposals of capital assets during 2020/21.

(a) In September 2020, she disposed of her classic vintage car for £30,000, which she had bought in 1986 for £10,000.
(b) In May 2020, she sold an antique vase for £8,500. She had bought it in September 1988 for £4,000.
(c) On 13 January 2021, she sold some antique furniture for £9,000. This was purchased at auction in February 2011 for £6,700. Acquisition costs of £300 were incurred.
(d) In September 2020, she sold a painting at an auction for £5,200. The painting cost £8,100 in September 1995.

Calculate the total net gains and losses arising from the above disposals for 2020/21.

Question 59

Helen made the following acquisitions of ordinary shares in AB plc:

Date	Number of shares	Cost £
September 1999	600	1,200
May 2003	400	1,000
September 2007	400	1,200
January 2010	1,200	4,800

During September 2012, Helen acquired further shares in AB plc when the company issued a 1 for 4 rights issue at £5 per share.

Helen disposed of 900 shares in July 2020 for £7 per share.

Calculate Helen's chargeable gain in 2020/21 following her disposal of shares in July 2020, assuming that she made no further acquisitions within the next 30 days.

Question 60

John acquired shares in LM plc as follows:

Date	Number of shares	Cost £
1 July 2006	2,600	2,000
11 April 2009	900	7,500
17 July 2020	200	800
10 August 2020	600	2,000

John sold 4,100 shares for £18,000 on 17 July 2020.

Calculate John's capital gain on the sale in July 2020.

Question 61

Chris bought a business in September 2004 for £120,000. There are no non-business assets. He gave it to his daughter Mary in July 2020 when it was worth £400,000. Gift relief was claimed.

Calculate for the tax year 2020/21:
1. the capital gain assessable on Chris, and
2. Mary's base cost for capital gains tax purposes.

Question 62

Susan bought a business in September 1994 for £10,000. She sold the business to her daughter Jo in July 2020 for £28,000 when it was valued at £50,000. Gift relief was claimed. There are no non-business assets. Jo subsequently sold the business for £95,000 in March 2021.

Calculate for the tax year 2020/21:
1. the amount assessable on Susan
2. Jo's base cost for capital gains tax purposes and
3. Jo's capital gains tax on the sale in March 2021.

Question 63

James decided that his business needed a new factory. He sold his existing factory for £900,000 in June 2020 having acquired it in February 2005 for £250,000. His new factory, acquired in March 2021, cost £1.2 million.

Calculate James' chargeable gain on the sale of the factory. What is the base cost of the new factory if rollover relief is claimed?

Question 64

Assume that in Question 63 James had purchased his new factory in August 2019.

How would your answer be different (if at all)?

Question 65

Heather decided to expand her business and needed new premises. She sold her existing showroom for £90,000 in October 2020 having acquired it in May 2010 for £50,000. Heather purchased a new showroom for £80,000 in March 2021.

Calculate Heather's chargeable gains, if any for 2020/21, assuming that she claims the maximum rollover relief.

Question 66

Les decided that it was time to transfer his company to his son Mark who unfortunately did not have sufficient monies to make the purchase. Les, therefore, decided to simply give all the shares in his company, JK Ltd, to Mark.

The gift comprised 100,000 ordinary shares (100% of the company) worth £750,000 and the gift was made in October 2020. The shares had cost Les £25,000 in July 1994.

The company's net value at the date of the gift was as follows:

Freehold factory	500,000
Motor cars	50,000
Investments (shares)	150,000
Current assets	100,000
	800,000
Current liabilities	(50,000)
Net value	750,000

Calculate Les' chargeable gain and identify how much (if any) of the gain may be rolled-over if gift relief is claimed. Assuming gift relief to have been claimed as appropriate identify the base cost of the shares for Mark.

Question 67

Rupinder is a director of PR Ltd a trading company and has worked for the company since 2017. Rupinder owns 10,000 shares in PR Ltd that she acquired at £1 per share in May 2016, representing 10% of the ordinary share capital. Rupinder sold her entire shareholding in June 2020 for £1,200,000. PR Ltd owns no non-trading assets. Rupinder has never previously made a chargeable gain and has no other gains during 2020/21. Rupinder is a higher rate taxpayer for 2020/21.

Calculate Rupinder's capital gains tax liability for 2020/21.

Question 68

How would the answer to Question 67 differ if Rupinder's shares only represented a 4% shareholding in PR Ltd?

Question 69

Tim, a higher rate taxpayer sold shares qualifying for Business asset disposal relief in September 2020 making a gain of £650,000. Tim had previously claimed Business asset disposal relief of £400,000 in respect of another gain in 2014/15.

Calculate Tim's capital gains tax liability for 2020/21.

Question 70

During 2020/21 Claire made the following capital gains and losses

Qualifying for Business asset disposal relief

Gains	150,0000
Losses	(25,000)

Other gains

Residential property	75,000
Shares	22,000

Claire has never previously claimed business asset relief and has capital gains losses brought forward of £16,000. Claire's Taxable income for 2020/21 was £30,000.

Calculate Claire's capital gains tax liability for 2020/21.

CHAPTERS 16 TO 19

Question 71

JB Ltd's accounting period for the year ended 31 March 2021 shows the following items:

Adjusted trading profit	45,000
Interest income	4,000
Rental income	6,000
Chargeable gain	5,000
Dividends received	10,000
Non trade loan interest paid	1,000
Charitable donations paid	15,000

Calculate JB Ltd's TTP and corporation tax liability for the accounting period ended 31 March 2021.

Question 72

If in Question 71 JB Ltd also paid dividends of £5,000 how would this affect your answer (if at all)?

Question 73

If in Question 71 JB Ltd's accounting period is for the year to 31 December 2020 how would this affect your answer (if at all)?

Question 74

KL Ltd prepares its accounts to 31 March each year.

For the year ended 31 March 2021, the company's net profit was £3 million.

This figure of £3 million was arrived at after the following items:

Other income and gains:

Dividends received	12,000
Interest received	40,000
Profit on sale of an office block	350,000

Expenses:

Entertaining (clients)	15,000
Accountants fees for preparing accounts	9,000
Health and safety fine	5,000
Depreciation	300,000
Interest payable (trading loan)	400,000
Donation to national charity	20,000

Capital allowances of £120,000 may be claimed (not included in the above) and whilst the office block sale produced a capital profit of £350,000 computed on accounting principles for tax purposes it produced a chargeable gain of £570,000.

Calculate KL Ltd's adjusted trading profit, TTP and corporation tax liability for the year ended 31 March 2021.

Question 75

MN Ltd's accounting period for the year ended 31 March 2021 shows the following results before taking into account the implications of a lease payment and capital allowances:

Trading profit	45,000
Chargeable gain	12,000
	57,000
Less: Charitable donations	(5,000)
TTP	52,000

On the 1 December 2020 MN Ltd was granted a 40-year lease of a commercial property by a third party for a premium of £50,000.

As at 1 April 2020, the plant and machinery pool had a tax written down value of £60,000. On 3 May 2020, an item of plant was sold for £16,000 (original cost £25,000) and on 1 November 2020 a motor car was purchased for £30,000, CO_2 emissions 105 g/km, and was used by MN Ltd's managing director. 20% of the use of this car was for private purposes.

Calculate MN Ltd's corporation tax liability for the accounting period ended 31 March 2021.

Question 76

Identify the accounting periods of GH Ltd in respect of which corporation tax will be charged given that it has prepared a set of accounts for the period 1 January 2019 to 30 April 2020.

When will the corporation tax liabilities have to be settled and when will the relevant returns need to be filed. GH Ltd is not a large company.

Confirm whether each of the following statements is true or false:

(1) Rental income is apportioned on a time basis.
(2) Trading income is apportioned on a time basis.
(3) Interest income is apportioned on a time basis.
(4) Dividend income is taxable when received.

Question 77

EF Ltd's results for the accounting period ended 31 December 2020 were as follows:

Trading profit	410,000
Rental income	60,000
Chargeable gain	150,000
Donation to charity	25,000

For the accounting periods ended 31 December 2018 and 31 December 2019, trading losses of £185,000 and £425,000 respectively arose.

Calculate EF Ltd's corporation tax liability for the period ended 31 December 2020 after the relief for any losses has been claimed and identify any losses remaining to carry forward.

Question 78

LK Ltd's results were as follows:

	Year ended 31/12/19	3 months ended 31/03/20	Year ended 31/03/21
Trading profit	150,000	60,000	(650,000)
Rental income	60,000	35,000	150,000
Interest income	8,000	40,000	90,000
Charitable donations	12,000	10,000	15,000

Calculate LK Ltd's TTP for each of the above periods utilising the trading loss of £850,000 in the most tax efficient manner and identify (if any) the amount of trading loss remaining to carry forward.

Question 79

JB Ltd, MB Ltd and NB Ltd form a group for group relief purposes. Their results were as follows for the accounting period ended 31 March 2021:

	JB Ltd	MB Ltd	NB Ltd
Trading profit	150,000	(250,000)	13,000
Rental income	5,000	15,000	10,000
Interest	20,000	2,500	5,000
Chargeable gains	30,000	4,000	2,000
Charitable donations	5,000	-	15,000

Calculate the TTP for each company assuming that MB Ltd claims any loss relief available and the balance of the loss is surrendered as group relief.

APPENDIX 2

Question 80

During the year to 31 March 2020 GH Ltd made a trading loss of £25 million. During the year to 31 March 2021 GH Ltd has taxable profits before losses brought forward of £18 million, comprised entirely of trading profits.

Calculate the TTP for GH Ltd to 31 March 2021 after claiming the maximum relief for losses brought forward and the balance of the loss, if any.

Question 81

For the year to 31 December 2019 JK Ltd made a trading loss of £40,000. JK Ltd's taxable profits to 31 December 2020 as follows:

Trading profits	38,000
Chargeable gains	5,000
Interest received	1,000
Qualifying charitable donations paid	8,000

Calculate the TTP for JK Ltd to 31 December 2020 assuming the optimum claim for losses brought forward.

Question 82

CD Ltd and HD Ltd form a group for chargeable gain purposes. Each company prepares its accounts to 31 March 2021.

CD Ltd transferred a factory which it no longer wished to use to HD Ltd in November 2017 – when it's market value was £750,000. CD Ltd had originally paid £350,000 for the factory in August 1997.

HD Ltd subsequently sold the factory for £900,000 in July 2020.

Indexation allowances:

August 1997 to November 2017	9,100
November 2017 to December 2017	100

Calculate the chargeable gains (if any) arising on the transfer of the factory to HD Ltd and the chargeable gain arising on the sale of the factory by HD Ltd in July 2020.

CHAPTER 20

Question 83

Sandy is a sole trader and his accounts are prepared to 30 June each year. For the tax year 2020/21 Sandy's trading profit is £57,500. Sandy also received rental income of £8,500.

Calculate the total amount of National Insurance Contributions (NIC) payable by Sandy for 2020/21.

Question 84

James is an employee and received a salary of £52,000 during 2020/21.

Calculate the employees and employers NIC payable in respect of James' salary.

Question 85

Steph is an employee of CD Ltd. The company prepares its accounts to 30 June each year. For the tax year 2020/21 Steph's salary is £25,000 and her taxable benefits (including a company car and an interest free loan) amount to a £7,200.

Identify which classes of National Insurance Contributions (NIC) apply to Steph and CD Ltd and calculate the amount(s) payable for 2020/21.

Question 86

How would the answer to Question 85 differ if Steph informed you that she was a member of the CD Ltd approved occupational pension scheme and her personal contributions during 2020/21 were £1,250?

Question 87

Identify the dates on which Classes 1, 1A, 2 and 4 are payable.

CHAPTERS 21 AND 22

Question 88

In the tax year 2019/20 Ben's income tax liability amounted to £10,300. £2,500 of his income tax liability had been deducted under PAYE. In the tax year 2020/21, the corresponding figures were £15,600 and £3,000 respectively.

Calculate the payments on account (if any) Ben would have been required to make on behalf of his income tax liability for the tax year 2020/21 and the amount of any balancing payment. State the dates on which these payments were due to be paid.

Question 89

In the tax year 2019/20 Gill's income tax liability amounted to £12,800. £11,900 of her income tax liability had been satisfied by way of tax deducted under PAYE. In the tax year 2020/21, the corresponding figures were £15,600 and £2,100 respectively.

Calculate the payments on account (if any) Gill would have been required to make on behalf of her income tax liability for the tax year 2020/21 and the amount of any balancing payment. State the dates on which these payments were due to be paid.

APPENDIX 2

Question 90

Brian's total tax and national insurance liabilities for 2019/20 were as follows

Income tax	8,400
Capital gains tax	2,100
Class 2 NIC	148
Class 4 NIC	1,500

What will his payments on account be for 2020/21 and what are the due dates?

Question 91

Hannah is due to make her balancing payment for the tax year 2020/21 of £8,500. She made the payments on 21 June 2022.

Explain the additional charges that Hannah may have incurred as a result of this late payment.

Question 92

Colin submitted his tax return for the tax year ended 5 April 2020 on 31 March 2021. What penalty (if any) may be charged? If Colin had submitted the return on 31 July 2021 would any additional penalty be due and if so how much?

Question 93

UV Ltd prepares its annual accounts each year to 31 December. For the year ending 31 December 2020 state the payment date on which its corporation tax liability has to be settled and the deadline for filing the corporation tax return. UV Ltd is not a large company.

Question 94

In Question 93 if the accounts were prepared for the 15 months to 31 March 2021 what (if any) difference to your answer would this make.

Question 95

PM Ltd has TTP of £1,480,000 for the year to 31 March 2021. During the accounting period, PM Ltd received dividends of £150,000. PM Ltd is not a member of a group and was considered a large company in the previous accounting period.

State corporation tax liability of PM Ltd for the year to 31 March 2021, the payment date for the corporation tax liability and the filing date for the Corporation tax return.

CHAPTER 23

Question 96

Tony charged a customer £475 inclusive of standard rate VAT. The customer asked Tony how much of this amount represented VAT.

Advise Tony of the amount of VAT.

Question 97

Julia sells a sculpture to the value of £1,000 plus VAT. She receives a payment on account of £250 on 25 March 2020. The sculpture is delivered on 28 April 2020. Julia's VAT returns are made up to calendar quarters. She issues a VAT invoice on 4 May 2020 and receives payment of the balance outstanding on 27 May 2020.

State the tax point(s) and amounts(s) due.

Question 98

Alan prepared his VAT returns to 31 March, 30 June and, 30 September 2020. The submission and payment dates for each of the quarters were as follows:

	Date of payment/ submission	VAT due
31 March 2020	10 May 2020	7,000
30 June 2020	12 August 2020	15,000
31 September 2020	18 December 2020	12,000

Explain the consequences for Alan.

Question 99

Victoria commenced trading on 1 May 2020. For the first six months of trading, Victoria made standard rated supplies of £8,000 per month and zero rated supplied of £3,500 per month.

For subsequent months Victoria's turnover was as follows

	Standard rate	Zero rate
November 2020	8,500	4,000
December 2020	9,100	5,300
January 2021	10,500	6,100

In which month did Victoria's turnover exceed the registration limit?

By what date should she notify HMRC and from what date will she be registered?

Question 100

Graham is a sole trader and is registered for VAT. During the quarter to 30 June 2020 the following transactions occurred:

Standard rated sales	60,000
Zero rated sales	35,000

APPENDIX 2

Standard rated purchases   28,000
(This includes £1,500 client entertaining)
Zero rated purchases   20,000
Purchase of new car   22,500
Purchase of new computer   1,000

All of the above amounts are exclusive of VAT and are standard rated unless otherwise specified.

In addition, Graham has reviewed his outstanding credit sales and has written off as bad debts the following sales:

18 October 2019   1,200
5 March 2020   600
2 April 2020   1,500

All of these amounts were payable 30 days after the date of sale and are shown inclusive of VAT.

Calculate the VAT payable by Graham for the quarter to 30 June 2020.

CHAPTER 24
Question 101

Helen died on 14 June 2020. On that date, she held the following assets:

House and contents (Helen's residence)   495,000
Quoted shares   150,000
ISA investments   95,000
Cash at bank   78,000
Car   6,000

Helen's funeral cost £5,000. Helen's husband had died two years earlier, leaving £195,000 to their daughter and the balance of his estate to Helen. At the time of Helen's husband's death the IHT nil rate band was £325,000. Helen's estate has been left in her will to her daughter. Helen did not make any lifetime gifts.

Calculate the IHT liability arising on Helen's death.

Question 102

Robert died on 6 May 2020, leaving an estate at the date of death of £600,000 including his main residence, valued at £350,000. The entire estate was left equally to his son and daughter.

In June 2014 Robert had made a gift of £50,000 to his son. In September 2018, Robert had made a gift of £400,000 into a trust, with Robert paying any IHT arising.

Calculate the IHT arising on the two gifts, both in lifetime and as a result of Robert's death. Calculate the IHT liability on Robert's estate on death. There is no transferable nil rate band available.

APPENDIX 3
True or False Questions

This Appendix is intended to be a bit of fun whilst at the same time testing your basic knowledge.

I would suggest that you answer, say, 10 questions at a time before checking the answers. If having checked an answer you are still not sure then re-read the relevant section of the book.

The questions have been written in a form such that the answer is either "true" or "false".

TRUE OR FALSE QUESTIONS
Income Tax
A1

Taxable income is total income after relief for allowable loan interest but before personal allowance.

A2

Savings income is subject to income tax at rates higher than non-savings income.

A3

Dividend income may never be subject to income tax at 40%.

A4

Children under the age of sixteen are not entitled to a personal allowance.

A5

Students do not pay income tax on their earnings.

A6

All individuals are entitled to the full personal allowance.

A7

Savings income can be taxed at the basic rate of 20%.

A8

A landlord can always deduct the full finance costs when calculating taxable income from a property business.

A9

Part of a premium paid by a tenant to a landlord under a lease is subject to income tax on the part of the landlord.

A10

The rent a room allowance for 2019/20 is £6,000.

APPENDIX 2

A11

All income arising on an individual savings account is assessed as non-savings income.

A12

For individuals, property business income is taxed on an accruals basis.

A13

It is possible for an individual with a net income of £20,500 to have an income tax liability of £Nil.

A14

Client entertaining expenses are deductible in computing a sole trader's taxable trading profit.

A15

Capital allowances are available as a deduction in computing the rental profit from renting out of residential accommodation.

A16

Income tax at the basic rate of 20% is deducted by banks when crediting interest on an individual's deposit account.

A17

An individual paying charitable donations under gift aid of £1,000 during 2019/20 would increase their basic rate band from £37,500 to £38,500.

A18

If the tax deducted at source from earnings under PAYE exceeds the individual's income tax liability, the excess is repayable.

A19

Unused personal allowances for a tax year can be carried forward to be offset against an individual's taxable income in future tax years.

A20

The tax year starts on 1 April.

A21

Under self assessment, payments on account of an individual's income tax liability for a tax year are due on the 31 July in the tax year and on the 31 January after the tax year.

A22

Payments on account of an individual's income tax liability for a tax year are based on the individual's prior tax year's income tax liability.

A23

Losses arising from a property business can be carried forward against future property business profits.

A24

Personal pension contributions are deducted when calculating net income.

A25

The rent a room scheme does not apply where more than one room in an individual's main residence is let out.

A26

Company car benefits are reduced for high business mileage.

A27

There is no benefit in kind for the use of a company motorbike.

A28

The 40% rate of income tax can in certain cases apply to dividend income.

A29

Dividend income is treated as an individual's highest slice of taxable income.

A30

Income from letting an overseas property is never subject to UK income tax.

A31

The tax liability of a partnership is divided between the individual partners based on the partnership agreement.

A32

In calculating an individual's income tax liability for a tax year, earned income is included only after allowing for any income tax which has been deducted under PAYE.

A33

Expenses must be wholly, exclusively and necessarily incurred to be deductible when calculating assessable trading profits.

A34

Earned income from employment is treated as non-savings income when working out an individual's income tax liability.

A35

The basis of assessment for earned income from employment is the receipts basis.

A36

Dividend income from UK companies is taxable on a receipts basis.

A37

There is no benefit in kind in respect of the provision of a mobile phone to an employee.

A38

Rental income from UK property is treated as savings income when working out an individual's income tax liability.

A39

Any payment of interest on borrowings is a tax deductible expense when calculating an individual's income tax liability.

A40

An individual present in the UK for 183 days or more during a tax year is automatically treated as UK resident.

A41

Annual investment allowance can be claimed for all items of plant and machinery up to the annual limit.

A42

Capital allowances can reduce adjusted profits and create an overall trading loss.

A43

The accounts profit of a sole trader for a period of account is always equal to the taxable profit for the period of account.

A44

On a change of accounting date, a sole trader may obtain overlap profit relief.

A45

The taxable profit for a sole trader's first tax year of trading is based upon the period from the date of starting to trade to the end of the tax year in which the trade started.

A46

In the tax year of cessation of a sole trader's business the taxable profit is based upon the period from the start of the tax year of cessation to the date of the cessation.

A47

A sole trader's trading profit is treated as non-savings income when computing an individual's income tax liability.

A48

An enhanced capital allowance of 100% is available to a sole trader who acquires a second-hand motor car with CO_2 emissions of less than 50g/km.

A49

The payment of a personal pension contribution by a sole trader is eligible for tax relief at the individual's marginal rate of income tax.

A50

The level of tax relievable personal pension contributions which can be made in any tax year is determined by the age of the taxpayer at any time in the tax year.

Capital Gains Tax

B1

In working out an individual's capital gains tax liability any capital gains are treated as the top slice of an individual's income.

B2

Capital gains are subject to capital gains tax at the rates of 10%, 20% and 40%.

B3

Capital losses brought forward are deducted from current year capital gains before current year capital losses.

B4

Capital losses can be carried back and offset against the prior tax year's capital gains.

B5

Residential property gains are taxed at a higher rate for individuals than other gains.

B6

Making a charitable donation under gift aid can reduce the liability to capital gains tax.

B7

The annual exempt amount is deducted before in year losses.

B8

Enhancement expenditure on a chargeable asset is always deductible in computing the capital gain on a disposal.

B9

The gift of an asset is not a disposal for capital gains tax purposes.

B10

The gift of an asset is treated as if it had been sold for market value when computing any capital gain.

B11

The transfer of a chargeable asset from one spouse to the other can give rise to a capital gain or loss.

B12

A married couple are entitled to one annual exemption only.

B13

A couple who cohabit are entitled to one annual exemption only.

B14

The inter-spouse exemption applies only to a married couple who are living together.

B15

The sale of a chargeable asset by a parent to his/her child is a disposal at arm's length.

B16

A gain on the disposal of a motor car is exempt from capital gains tax.

B17

The most tax efficient manner in which a capital loss may be used by an individual is to offset it first against gains arising on the disposal of residential property.

B18

Any capital losses arising in the tax year of death can be carried back for offset against capital gains of the previous four tax years.

B19

Capital losses can be carried forward indefinitely.

B20

A child, aged under sixteen years old, at the start of the tax year is not entitled to the annual capital gains exemption.

B21

In computing an individual's capital gains tax liability for a tax year the last deductible item is the annual exemption.

B22

An individual's personal allowance for income tax purposes can be used to reduce an individual's capital gains tax liability.

B23

The amount of any annual exemption which is unused in a tax year can be carried forward for future use.

B24

Capital gains tax is included when calculating Self assessment payments on account for a tax year.

B25

Any capital gains tax liability for a tax year is payable on the 31 January after the end of the tax year.

B26

On the sale of shares in any company by an individual, the matching rules require that the shares be matched first with purchases of shares in the company in the 30 days before the date of disposal.

B27

One of the conditions for the capital gain on the sale of a business asset by a sole trader to be rolled over against the purchase of a business asset by the sole trader is that the new business asset must be purchased within two years before and three years after the disposal of the first asset.

B28

Movable plant and machinery qualify as business assets for rollover relief.

B29

To qualify for rollover relief the replacement asset must be of a similar nature to the asset disposed of.

B30

To obtain full rollover relief on the sale of a business asset it is only necessary to reinvest the amount of the capital gain on the sale of the old business asset.

B31

Gift relief can apply to the capital gain arising on the gift of any type of chargeable asset.

B32

On the disposal of part of a set or area of land, any reasonable apportionment of cost between the part disposed of and part retained is acceptable by HMRC.

B33

Gift relief can apply to a sale at an under-value.

B34

A loss on the disposal of a wasting chattel is not allowable against other gains.

B35

An issue of bonus shares is deemed to have occurred at the date of acquisition of the original shares in respect of which the bonus issue has occurred.

B36

The rate of business asset disposal relief is determined according to the length of ownership of the relevant asset.

B37

The transfer of a sole trader's business to a limited company in exchange for an issue of shares enables the sole trader to rollover any capital gains arising on any chargeable assets transferred.

B38

Capital losses of a tax year can be offset against a sole trader's trading profit for that tax year.

B39

A personal pension contribution can reduce an individual's capital gains tax liability.

B40

Capital gains of one spouse for a tax year can be offset against the capital losses of the other spouse for the same tax year.

B41

Gains on the sale of unquoted shares are exempt from capital gains tax.

B42

No chargeable gain arises on a "paper for paper" takeover (i.e. where shares in one company are exchanged for shares in another company which is taking over the first company).

B43

In calculating a capital gain on the sale of a chargeable asset any incidental costs of disposal may be deducted from the gross sale proceeds.

B44

For Business asset disposal relief purposes an asset which has been held for 23 months and 20 days is treated as having been owned for two complete years.

B45

Gains on the disposal of non-wasting chattels are always exempt from capital gains tax.

Corporation Tax

C1

Companies pay income tax on their taxable trading profits.

C2

An accounting period of a company cannot be longer than 12 months.

C3

Corporation tax is charged at various rates determined by the level of the TTP.

C4

Companies are not liable to corporation tax on dividends received from other UK companies.

C5

A company with TTP below the annual exemption has a corporation tax liability of £Nil

C6

A company is exempt from corporation tax on income from an ISA.

C7

All companies pay corporation tax at the same rate regardless of the level of their taxable profits.

C8

In calculating a company's taxable rental income interest on borrowings used to buy and/or improve the property is a deductible expense.

C9

Augmented profits of a company for an accounting period equal profits chargeable to corporation tax plus dividends received.

C10

Augmented profits are required to determine the rate of corporation tax applying.

C11

A single rate of corporation tax will always apply to a company's accounting period.

C12

Interest paid on non-trade related loans is included as non-trade related loan relationship debits.

C13

The write off of a loan to a current employee is included as non-trade related loan relationship debit.

C14

Companies are liable to capital gains tax on any capital gains.

C15

Companies are not entitled to an annual exemption when computing the tax liability on any capital gains.

C16

Trading losses of a company for an accounting period can be carried back to the 36 months prior to the accounting period of loss.

C17

Trading losses of a company for an accounting period can be carried forward indefinitely for offset against future trading profits only.

C18

Trading losses of a company for an accounting period can be offset against other profits chargeable to corporation tax of the same accounting period.

C19

Writing down allowances for main pool plant and machinery of a company for a 15 month period of account would be [18% x 15/12] x tax written down value at beginning of the period of account.

C20

All purchases of plant and machinery qualify for annual investment allowance up to the annual maximum.

C21

The rate of corporation tax is fixed for a tax year of assessment.

C22

Group relief refers to the offsetting by one company in a group of another group company's capital losses.

C23

A group for chargeable gains purposes is not the same as a group for group relief purposes.

C24

When calculating adjusted trading profits, any gifts to customers costing less than £50 are allowable.

C25

Company residence is based on where the company was incorporated.

C26

The number of group companies does not affect the rate of corporation tax which will apply to each company's profits chargeable to corporation tax.

C27

Corporation tax for an accounting period is always payable nine months after the end of the accounting period.

C28

Companies receive bank interest on deposits after the deduction of tax at source.

C29

Companies are entitled to a personal allowance.

C30

Relief for qualifying charitable donations is deducted after loss relief.

C31

Trading losses carried forward arising after 1 April 2017 can be carried forward and deducted from TTP of a future accounting period without limit.

C32

When computing the corporation tax on a chargeable gain arising from a sale of shares the matching rules require that the shares sold be matched first to shares acquired on the same day; then shares acquired in the previous nine days; and then shares in the pool.

C33

Companies are entitled to indexation allowance when computing chargeable gains.

C34

The indexation allowance can increase the amount of a capital loss.

C35

The indexation factor is normally restricted to two decimal places.

C36

The loan relationship rules apply to interest income and interest expenses.

C37

An excess of non-trading loan relationship debts over credits under the loan relationship rules can be group relieved.

C38

Where a chargeable gains group exists chargeable assets can be transferred between companies at no loss and no gain.

C39

Trading losses of the last 12 months in which the company's trade ceases can be carried back and offset against the company's TTP for the previous three years.

C40

A company can surrender brought forward trading losses as group relief in preference to offset against its own TTP.

C41

Rollover relief can apply where the company selling the qualifying asset and the company investing in the new qualifying asset are in the same chargeable gains group.

C42

Where a motor car is made available to an employee that is used for both business and private purposes, in computing the capital allowances available to the business an adjustment must be made to take into account the private use of the car.

C43

Capital allowances are not available on the purchase of second-hand plant and machinery.

C44

Enhanced capital allowances of 100% are available for new electric goods vehicles and vans.

VAT

D1

All limited companies are required to register for VAT

D2

A VAT registered business does not pay VAT on purchases.

D3

Late submission of a VAT return results in an initial surcharge of £100.

D4

Under the VAT cash accounting scheme, a business cannot claim relief for impaired debts.

D5

The VAT tax point for the supply of goods can never be earlier than the delivery date.

D6

50% of the VAT input tax can be recovered on the purchase of a car with private use.

D7

VAT is not payable if the registered business is making a trading loss.

D8

The first late filing of a VAT return will not give rise to any financial penalty.

D9

There are two possible tests to apply against the VAT registration limits.

D10

VAT on a bad debt can be reclaimed after three months have elapsed from the due date.

Inheritance tax

E1

IHT is only payable when someone dies.

E2

Any gifts to another individual are exempt from IHT after six years.

E3

Gifts of pocket money to grandchildren are always exempt from IHT.

E4

Taper relief reduces the amount of gift chargeable to IHT.

E5

Reasonable funeral expenses are deducted when calculating IHT on death.

E6

If a gift is subject to capital gains tax, then it is exempt from IHT.

TRUE OR FALSE ANSWERS

Income Tax

A1

False

Taxable income is total income of an individual after the deduction qualifying loan interest and personal allowance.

Taxable income is net income less personal allowances.

A2

False

Savings income and non-savings income are generally taxed at the same rates. However, the savings starting rate and savings allowance may also be due, reducing the rate of tax on some savings income to 0%.

A3

True

Dividend income is taxed at 0%, 7.5%, 32.5% or 38.1%.

A4

False

All individuals of whatever age are entitled to the same personal allowance, subject to the restriction for high income.

A5

False

Students are no different from other taxpayers and are liable to income tax on their taxable income.

A6

False

Individuals with adjusted net income above £100,000 are not entitled to the full personal allowance. The personal allowance is reduced by £1 for every £2 of adjusted net income in excess of £100,000.

A7

True

Savings income can be taxed at the rates of 0%, 20%, 40% or 45%.

A8

False

Finance costs in respect of residential property are not deductible for 2020/21. The finance costs are a 20% tax reducer.

A9

True

The taxable element of the premium is given by the formula:

[Premium – Premium x 2% x (n – 1)] where n is the duration of the lease in complete years.

A10

False

It is £7,500.

A11

False

Income arising from an individual savings account (ISA) is exempt from income tax.

A12

False

Where receipts are less than £150,000 a receipts basis applies to rental income.

A13

True

An individual could have non-savings income of £12,500, fully covered by their personal allowance, savings income of £6,000, £5,000 would be taxed at 0% due to the savings starting rate and £1,000 taxed at 0% due to the savings allowance, and dividends of £2,000, covered by their Dividend nil rate band. In these circumstances, the individual's income tax liability would be £nil.

A14

False

Under no circumstances is client entertaining ever deductible in computing a sole trader's trading profit.

A15

False

No capital allowances are available for residential accommodation; instead, an allowance is available on the replacement cost of domestic items.

A16

False

Income tax is not deducted at source from bank interest.

A17

False

The rate bands would be increased by the gross gift aid donation of £1,250 (£1,000 x 100/80).

A18

True

A19

False

Any unused element of the personal allowance available for a tax year cannot be carried forward or back to future or previous tax years; it is simply lost.

A20

False

The tax year or income tax year or year of assessment is the period 6 April to the following 5 April.

A21

False

Payments on account of an income tax liability for a tax year are payable in equal instalments on 31 January within the tax year and on 31 July after the end of the tax year.

A22

True

Generally, the payments on account are based on the prior tax year's relevant amount which is the prior tax year's income tax liability less any tax deducted at source.

A23

True

A24

False

Personal pension contributions are grossed up and extend the tax rate bands. In addition, gross personal pension contributions are deducted when calculating adjusted net income when calculating entitlement to the personal allowance.

A25

False

The number of rooms let out is not the test for application of the rent a room scheme; the key element is that the gross rents from the relevant rooms in total do not exceed £7,500.

A26

False

Business mileage has no impact on the calculation of car benefit.

A27

False

The benefit in kind would be based on 20% of the value of the motorbike when first made available.

A28

False

Dividend income is taxed at 0%, 7.5%, 32.5% or 38.1%; never 40%.

A29

True

Dividend income is taxed after non-savings and savings income have been taxed.

A30

False

A UK resident is taxable on their worldwide income subject to any double taxation agreement.

A31

False

A partnership is not subject to income tax. The partnership profits are divided between the partners and any tax liability is calculated on each individual partner.

A32

False

The gross amount of earned income from employment is included when working out an individual's income tax liability; any PAYE reduces the final income tax liability in arriving at income tax payable.

A33

False

Allowable expenses must be wholly and exclusively incurred. Necessarily applies to employment expenses.

A34

True

A35

True

A36

True

A37

True

The provision of *one* mobile phone will not give rise to a benefit in kind.

A38

False

Rental income is treated as non-savings income and is thus taxed at rates of 10%, 40% and 45%.

A39

False

Only interest payable on a qualifying loan is a deductible expense in working out an individual's taxable income; such a loan would include for example interest payable on a loan to purchase shares in a close company or an interest in a partnership.

A40

True

A41

False

AIA is not available for expenditure on cars.

A42

True

A43

False

Very rarely will the accounts profit equal the taxable trading profits; this is because of the need invariably to add back non-tax deductible expenses etc.

A44

True

Overlap profit relief may be available on a change of accounting date. Whether this is so will depend upon whether the length of the period of time from the "old" date to the "new" date exceeds 12 months.

A45

True

A46

False

On a sole trader's cessation, the basis period for the final tax year of cessation is the period from the end of the basis period for the previous tax year to the date of cessation.

A47

True

A48

False

The enhanced capital allowances for low emission cars only applies to new cars.

A49

True

On the making of a personal pension payment, a sole trader deducts income tax at source of 20% and if he is a higher rate taxpayer (i.e. is liable to tax at 40%) then his basic rate band is extended and extra tax relief of 20% (making 20% + 20% in total) is obtainable.

A50

False

Capital Gains Tax

B1

True

Capital gains are taxed after (i.e. on top of) non-savings, savings and dividend income.

B2

False

Capital gains are taxed at 10%, 18%, 20% or 28%.

B3

False

Current year capital losses are deducted from current year capital gains before capital losses brought forward are considered.

B4

False

Capital losses cannot generally be carried back; only in the case of capital losses arising in the tax year of death may such losses be carried back but then only to the three tax years prior to the tax year of death.

B5

True

Capital gains tax rates for residential property are 18% and 28%. The rates for other assets are 10% and 20%.

B6

True

As a charitable donation under gift aid extends the basic rate band, in some cases a larger part of the gain can be taxed at the lower rate of capital gains tax as a result of the donation.

B7

False

APPENDIX 2

B8

False

To be deductible enhancement expenditure on an asset must be reflected in the value of the asset at the date of sale.

B9

False

Disposal for capital gains tax purposes includes a gift or a sale at undervalue as well as a normal arm's length sale.

B10

True

As there are no actual sale disposal proceeds the assumption is that a gift has been sold for its then market value.

B11

False

Transfers between spouses and civil partners are made at no gain/no loss.

B12

False

Each individual, whether husband and wife or not, are each entitled to an annual exemption.

B13

False

B14

True

A married couple not living together are not entitled to the inter-spouse exemption.

B15

False

Transfers amongst family members (e.g. father to son; mother to son; brother to sister) are between connected persons and therefore by definition are not at arm's length; thus, market values are used not actual sale proceeds to calculate any capital gain.

B16

True

B17

True

This obtains tax relief at 18% or 28% rather than 10% or 20% against other gains.

B18

False

Capital losses arising in the tax year of death may be carried back but only to the previous three tax years, not four.

B19

True

B20

False

Every individual is entitled to an annual exemption.

B21

True

B22

False

The personal allowance is an allowance for income tax purposes not capital gains tax purposes and cannot, therefore, reduce an individual's capital gains tax liability.

B23

False

Any unused part of the annual exemption cannot be carried either forward or back and is simply lost.

B24

False

Payments on account are calculated based on income tax and Class 4 NICs of the previous tax year only.

B25

False

This is generally true. However, on residential property sales on or after 6 April 2020, the CGT is payable within 30 days of completion of the sale.

B26

False

The matching of shares sold requires matching with purchases on the same day first.

B27

False

The time limits for the purchase of the replacement asset are one year before (i.e. not two) and three years after the date of sale of the "old" asset.

B28

False

The plant and machinery must be fixed to qualify not moveable.

B29

False

Both assets must be on the list of qualifying assets but do not need to be similar.

B30

False

For rollover of the whole of the gain to apply the whole of the asset sale proceeds must be reinvested not just the gain amount itself.

B31

False

Gift relief only applies to gifts of business assets and certain shareholdings, not any chargeable asset.

B32

False

This would be a part disposal requiring apportionment of the cost using A/A+B

B33

True

However, on a sale at undervalue rather than an outright gift although gift relief may apply some part of the gain on the gift will be immediately subject to capital gains tax.

B34

True

B35

True

B36

False

B37

True

Assuming the various conditions are satisfied incorporation relief applies and a rollover of any gains arising on the chargeable assets transferred is available; if the consideration for the transfer is an issue of shares in the acquiring company 100% rollover applies; if any part of the consideration is cash, not just shares, then less than 100% rollover applies.

B38

False

However, ITA 2007 section 71 enables a trading loss of a tax year to be potentially off-set against capital gains for the same tax year.

B39

True

This will extend the basic rate band and as a result, in some cases, a larger part of the gain can be taxed at the lower rate of capital gains tax.

B40

False

The capital losses of one spouse belong to that spouse and cannot be used by the other spouse.

B41

False

B42

True

A take-over simply results in the new shares replacing the original shares with no capital gains tax liability arising at the date of the swap.

B43

True

B44

False

A minimum of 24 months of ownership is required.

B45

False

Only where cost and proceeds are both less than £6,000.

Corporation Tax

C1

False

Companies pay corporation tax on their profits.

C2

True

An accounting period for corporation tax purposes cannot be longer than 12 months; where a company prepares its accounts for, say, a 15 month period for tax purposes this must be split into two accounting periods of 12 and three months respectively.

C3

False

APPENDIX 2

Corporation tax is charged at a single rate as specified for each financial year.

C4

True

Dividends received from other UK resident companies are not subject to corporation tax but are used in determining if a company is required to pay CT by instalments.

C5

False

There is no annual exemption for corporation tax.

C6

False

A company cannot hold investments in an ISA.

C7

True

C8

False

For companies, any interest payable concerning the purchase or improvement of property for letting is treated as a deduction in computing the company's net interest income (or loss) under the loan relationship rules.

C9

True

C10

False

Augmented profits are used to determine if a company is "Large" and therefore needs to pay CT by instalments.

C11

False

Corporation tax rates can change from 1 April. TTP may need to be apportioned between FY to determine the tax rates applying.

C12

True

C13

False

This is trade related and allowed when calculating adjusted trading profits.

C14

False

Capital gains tax only applies to individuals; companies do, however, pay corporation tax on any chargeable gains.

C15
True

The annual exemption only applies to individuals.

C16
False

Trading losses of an accounting period may be carried back only 12 months; however, if a company ceases to trade then any trading loss of the last 12 months of trading (referred to as a terminal loss) may be carried back for offset in the 36 immediately preceding months.

C17
False

Losses can be set against future profits of any type.

C18
True

C19
False

Where a company's period of account exceeds 12 months it must be split into two separate accounting periods and capital allowances must be computed separately for each accounting period.

C20
False

AIA is not available on the purchase of cars.

C21
False

Corporation tax rates are fixed for financial years (i.e. 1 April to following 31 March) not tax years or years of assessment.

C22
False

Group relief refers to the offsetting of one company's trading losses against the TTP of another group company.

C23
True

The definitions of a group for chargeable gains purposes is different from that for group relief purposes; thus, companies may, for example, form a group for chargeable gains purposes but not for group relief.

C24

False

Only if the gifts carry the company's name or logo and are not drink, food or tobacco.

C25

False

It can also be based on where a company is controlled from.

C26

True

The number of group companies causes may, however, impact whether a company is required to pay CT by instalments.

C27

False

Corporation tax is payable nine months after the end of an accounting period unless the company is large; in this case corporation tax is payable by instalments in months 7, 10, 13 and 16.

C28

False

Banks do not deduct tax at source when making interest payments to companies.

C29

False

Only individuals are entitled to a personal allowance.

C30

True

Losses are deducted before QCD. If there is insufficient TTP remaining, relief for QCD may be wasted.

C31

False

Although losses can be set against TTP of a future accounting period, there is a cap on the limit.

C32

True

The matching rules for companies are not the same as those for individuals.

C33

True

However, indexation allowance is frozen from December 2017.

C34

False

Indexation allowance can reduce a capital gain to nil but cannot turn the gain into a capital loss nor can it increase a capital loss.

C35

False

It is rounded to three decimal places.

C36

True

Note, however, that loan relationships are divided into trade and non-trade relationships.

C37

True

Although group relief mainly applies to trading losses it also applies to deficits on non-trading loan relationships.

C38

True

C39

True

C40

False

Brought forward trading losses must be utilised as far as possible before surrendering as group relief.

C41

True

Assuming the relevant conditions are satisfied rollover relief is available to companies on qualifying business asset replacement.

C42

False

An employee's private use of an asset will not impact the calculation of capital allowances. However, private use of an asset by a sole trader or the members of a partnership will require an adjustment to the capital allowances claim.

C43

False

C44

True

VAT

D1

False

The registration limits apply to limited companies as they do for other business entities.

D2

False

However, a VAT registered business will be able to recover input tax paid.

D3

False.

If either a VAT return is not submitted by the due date or the tax due with the return is paid late, it will initially trigger a surcharge liability notice. Further failures may trigger a surcharge.

D4

True

Under the VAT cash accounting scheme, a business will not need to claim for impaired debts, as VAT will only be paid on receipts.

D5

False

The actual tax point may be the date of issue of the invoice or date payment is received if before the basic tax point.

D6

False

No input tax can be recovered on the purchase of a car with private use.

D7

False

D8

True

But the business will receive a surcharge liability notice and may incur a surcharge for any further late filing or payments during the next 12 months.

D9

True

There is a historic test and a future test.

D10

False

VAT on a bad debt can be recovered once at least six months have elapsed since the debt was due and payable, *and* the VAT charged on the supply has been paid to HMRC.

Inheritance tax

E1

False

A liability can also arise on transfers into trusts during lifetime.

E2

False

Seven years must elapse for the potentially exempt transfer to fall out of potential charge.

E3

False

They may be exempt if covered by the annual exemption, if less than £250 to any individual in a tax year or can be shown to be regular gifts out of income but otherwise can be chargeable.

E4

False

Taper relief reduces the amount IHT on the gift. IHT is calculated on the full value of the gift and the taper relief is applied to the IHT.

E5

True

E6

False

Index

The UK Tax System: an introduction (Third edition)

By Malcolm James

Paperback   ISBN 9781907444999   144 pages   Price: £29.95

The UK Tax System: an introduction provides a guide to the structure of the UK tax system, the interaction between UK and EU law, and its application to various classes of taxpayer, as well as explaining the roles of the government departments who administer it and the full range of taxpayers' rights and obligations. For the third edition, there is expanded treatment of tax anti-avoidance. The book is for anyone studying the UK tax system, or advising on UK tax, from the experienced practitioner to the newly-qualified professional coming to tax advice for the first time, as well as being an ideal starting point for any students of the legal system or government.

Introduction to European Tax Law: Direct Taxation (sixth edition)

Edited by: Michael Lang, Pasquale Pistone, Josef Schuch and Claus Staringer

Paperback   ISBN 9781913507213   392 pages   Price: £45.00

This handbook is a concise guide for all those who aim at obtaining a basic knowledge of European tax law. Designed for students, it should be useful as well for experienced international tax specialists with little knowledge of European law, European law specialists who are reluctant to approach the technicalities of direct taxation and non-Europeans who deal with Europe for business or academic reasons and need to understand the foundations of European tax law.

Significant tax developments have unfolded in recent years in the areas of both primary and secondary EU law. Besides the significant advances in the interpretation of the fundamental freedoms and State aid, we have witnessed an increase in the relevance of case law on EU fundamental rights and the issuance of directives in the fields of mutual assistance, anti-tax avoidance and dispute settlement. This fifth edition considers all such changes, without losing its traditional concise approach to the analysis of the relevant issues.